DIVERSITY
AND
UNITY

THE ROLE OF HIGHER EDUCATION IN BUILDING DEMOCRACY

2nd Tri-nation Campus Diversity Seminar
(March 1998)

Edited by
**M Cross, N Cloete, E Beckham, A Harper,
J Indiresan and C Musil**

MASKEW MILLER
LONGMAN

Maskew Miller Longman (Pty) Ltd
Howard Drive, Pinelands, Cape Town

Offices in Johannesburg, Durban, Bloemfontein,
King William's Town and Pietersburg,
and companies throughout southern and central Africa

© Maskew Miller Longman (Pty) Ltd 1999

First published 1999

ISBN 0 636 04184 0

Project management by Julie-Anne Justus
Typesetting by Daphne Visser
Cover design by Beverley Taylor
from an original design by Marc Edwards
Imagesetting by Castle Graphics
Printed by Creda Communications (Pty) Ltd,
Eliot Avenue, Epping Industria II, Cape Town

COVER ILLUSTRATION
'Voodooism' (Detail)
by GEORGE RAMAGAGA
Mahogany 1976
84 x 44 cm
Collection of the University of Fort Hare

The complexity of aesthetic experience and creative production in Africa
is evident in this carving by George Ramagaga, who produces a timeless
icon, borrowing from modernist Europe, and reconstructing meaning
much like Picasso did when he borrowed from Africa at the turn of the
century. This work illustrates the complex interaction between the
diverse (local) and the universal (global).

—Marc Edwards, 1998

Contents

SECTION III: CONTEXTUAL ISSUES 107

SECTION IV: CONCLUDING ISSUES 191

Foreword

Albie Sachs
*Justice of the Constitutional
Court of South Africa*

Non-racism and diversity are not in opposition to each other. It is not a choice: common citizenship, fundamental rights and non-racism versus diversity, uniqueness and difference. On the contrary, the trick is to find the connections between the two and it is through dignity, dialogue, association and respect for difference that these connections are found. To me what is frequently lacking in these debates is an acknowledgement that non-racism is the bedrock of diversity; that shared citizenship, far from being the enemy of difference, is the bedrock for the recognition of difference. It is only when culture, background, language and appearance become used as a means of controlling resources and political power – ethnic mobilisation for the purpose of advantage – that culture in that sense becomes politicised and is precarious and antagonistic to the culture of others. Where common citizenship is profound and strong, then the expression of one's culture in no way requires the disrespect of another's.

Preface

Nico Cloete
Centre for Higher Education Transformation

Michael Cross
Department of Education, University of the Witwatersrand

Edgar F Beckham
Education and Culture Programme, Ford Foundation

In March 1998, South Africa's Centre for Higher Education Transformation (CHET), with support from the Ford Foundation, sponsored an international seminar on diversity in higher education. For ten days, groups of eight delegates each from India, South Africa, and the United States, and two observers from Brazil, met in three South African venues to discuss the topic 'Diversity and Unity: The Role of Higher Education in Building Democracy'.

In addition to formal sessions attended by delegates, observers and staff from CHET and the Ford Foundation, the seminar included public discussion forums attended by more than 300 educators from the three regions. Visits to sites of historical significance in South Africa's encounter with diversity and democracy formed an integral part of the seminar. The seminar began in Durban, in the province of KwaZulu-Natal, where the University of Natal served as host institution. It moved to the University of Fort Hare, located in the town of Alice in the Eastern Cape, and concluded in Cape Town with meetings organised by the Peninsula Technikon. Details of the programme can be found in Appendix A; a list of the participants and their contact details can be found in Appendix B.

The seminar quite consciously tried to balance three distinguishable but inter-related components: the personal-social, the socio-political and the professional-intellectual. To some extent the seminar itself leaned towards the personal-social and the socio-political; this volume cannot reflect the richness of the event and focuses mainly on the papers presented.

The volume is divided into four sections. Section One outlines some of the issues raised at both the India and South Africa seminars. Section Two comprises conceptual papers outlining international perspectives on the question of unity, diversity and the building of democracy. Alison Bernstein, Ford Foundation Vice President, reflects on the historical background of the seminar, its purposes, and her hopes and fears for its success. Her paper calls for 'de-privileging or questioning the American campus diversity paradigm', a process which she believes started with the India Seminar. For Bernstein, arguments on diversity that do not address 'deep-seated inequities of power and privilege throughout our institutions' and which are not informed by an analysis of disadvantage, fail to challenge relations of dominance and subordination. Linking diversity to disadvantage allows for important social-justice values: the reaffirmation of identity; and the redistribution of power, privileges and opportunities.

Cloete, Cross, Muller and Pillay suggest a shift from cultural diversity to identity diversity, where difference pertains to identity, not to culture. Such an approach is more suited to the dynamics of identity formation within the context of cosmopolitan cultural convergence and globalisation. This re-conceptualisation of diversity contains the possibility of thinking communally. For this to happen, higher education has a central role to play through a curriculum for common citizenship and by providing sites for democratic practice in South Africa's fledging democratic project.

Visvanathan's paper is an attempt to reflect simultaneously on the university and Indian society, and the complex interactions between them. The university faces an unresolved dilemma: on the one hand, it is charged with the ambitious task of re-thinking the tensions between monoculturalism and difference in society; on the other hand, its own role is to perpetrate foreign and oppressive discourses.

Hassim and Gouws contextualise certain feminist debates around issues of representation and citizenship through a critical look at the National Women's Coalition and higher education institutions in South Africa. They conclude by arguing for a more permeable form of politics that is open to the diversity of women and women's networks and organisations.

Section Three of this volume deals with contextual and practical concerns. Brown and Kirwan provide an overview of the struggles and battles around affirmative action in the United States as part of the extension of citizenship and rights in the American society. For them, excellence cannot be achieved unless it draws upon the rich experience of an environment of diversity. To create such an environment, it is essential for institutions to make diversity part of their planning, build connections with historically black institutions through inter-campus co-operation, set common standards of learning with a core curriculum, and include class as a component of diversity programmes.

Indiresan describes campus and community interactions within the context of India's struggles with inequality, discrimination, and corrective/preferential policies. In a different way, Indiresan shares Visvanathan's argument for campuses to provide space for dialogue and new democracy and diversity practices. Nayak's concern is with the relationship between campus community and curricula. She outlines a number of programmes which deal with this issue and comments on some of the lessons emerging from the campus diversity initiative. Smith responds to the current demand in the United States for providing evidence about the benefits of diversity. She does so by proposing a strategic evaluation approach that simultaneously assesses issues such as representation, the dynamics of institutional change, and the use of evaluation as part of the development of an institution's capacity to learn and address the challenges of diversity.

Section Four concludes with commentaries and reflections on key thematic highlights of the seminar that we hope will illuminate some of the complexities of the topic and point toward some actions.

Participants' acknowledgements

As Alison Bernstein said in her remarks, the seminar would not have taken place, if it were not for the vision, creativity, humour and sheer persistence of Nico Cloete, Director of the Centre for Higher Education Transformation (CHET), seminar co-ordinator Judith Hawarden, as well as Bridget Shatkovsky, Jane Kabaki and the entire CHET staff. On the Ford Foundation side, gratitude must be expressed to Edgar Beckham (New York office) and Richard Fehnel (South African office), who as the Foundation's 'front men' made sure that the seminar happened, while Alison Bernstein and Janice Petrovich provided moral and material support.

The local co-ordinators of the seminar, Ann Harper in Durban, Zin Jiya at the University of Fort Hare, and Shirley Levendal in Cape Town, played crucial leadership roles in organising the public forums, which projected the voice of the seminar into the larger academic community, and the social history tours, which illuminated the social context of South Africa's encounter with diversity and democracy. We also owe a debt of gratitude to our institutional hosts, Brenda Gourley, Vice-Chancellor of the University of Natal, Mbulelo Mzamane, Vice-Chancellor of the University of Fort Hare, and Brian Figaji, Rector of the Peninsula Technikon. And every participant in the seminar offers deep personal thanks to Linda Benwell and her staff, who managed the logistics of the peripatetic seminar effectively and with aplomb.

Section I

Introductory issues

Introduction

Edgar F Beckham

Education and Culture Program, The Ford Foundation

The India Seminar (January 1997)

The first tri-national seminar on diversity issues in higher education took place in Manesar, in the State of Haryana, India, in January 1997. It was sponsored by the Educational Resources Centre, which oversees the Ford Foundation's Campus Diversity Initiative in that country. Over a period of three days, delegates from India, South Africa, and the United States looked at each country's history and sought to appreciate the contrasting ways in which human diversity is construed and confronted in each country's respective higher education systems.

In the words of a metaphor, the delegates were initially like 'the frog in the well'. Having no awareness of worlds beyond its own, the frog is unable to communicate effectively with the frog from the river, which has been swept into the well by a storm. The metaphor, of course, overstates the case. These educators were all reasonably knowledgeable about each other, and superbly trained in methodologies for engaging human difference. But most of them understood diversity primarily in terms of their respective national histories and the paradigms these histories have produced.

The seminar became an exercise in thinking. To be sure, the Americans continued to think as Americans, the Indians as Indians, and the South Africans as South Africans. But as the seminar progressed, it became increasingly clear that that was not the only way to think.

Meetings like the seminars in India and South Africa are very likely to produce questions about what was learned. Often the questions rest on the assumption that learning from each other involves a direct transfer of lessons, lessons that have been contrived by a self-conscious teacher for delivery to a receptive student. But the assumption is itself a contrivance, and pedagogically not very useful. For frogs in a well, learning is reflexive. We are looking at ourselves and learning about ourselves through a newly refracted medium with which we were hitherto unfamiliar. We of course learn about the new medium too, and our appreciation of difference grows. But the learning that is most likely to have practical impact is what we learn about ourselves through a contrastive prism.

Six formal papers were presented in India. One paper from each country described the historical context out of which the current engagement of diversity issues had emerged. The Indian paper illuminated two historical perspectives, one in which Indian diversity was seen as a centuries-old legacy of distinctions based on caste, class, religion, region, language, and culture. The second perspective gave a close-up of current pressures – economic, political, social, and global – that challenge the traditional ways of managing the age-old diversity. The paper focused particularly on how the higher education community was intervening to manage diversity in a manner that would have a greater educational impact and prepare students better for effective participation in Indian society.

The South African paper was written in two parts by two authors, which in itself called attention to the challenge of achieving sufficient consensus in the South African context. While the paper located its understandings of diversity issues emphatically in terms of the historical distortions created by apartheid, it focused primarily on current concerns such as access, organisational structure, enrolment patterns, staffing, campus climate, and the way discourse on diversity is currently shaped and influenced. It was clear from the paper that, at that moment, higher education in South Africa was in a state of high anticipation. The National Commission on Higher Education had recently issued a major report on higher education and recommended its transformation. The Government's initial response (Green Paper) had been issued a month before the seminar. It indicated that the Government's final response (White Paper issued in July 1997) would be less ambitious than the Commission's report. There was concern that the Government's plan might not be thoughtful or aggressive enough to facilitate the complete transformation that would be needed to achieve South Africa's educational aspirations.

The American paper looked back upon more than 350 years of American higher education and traced its engagement of diversity through several phases. The paper emphasised the private and sectarian character of the early American colleges. It highlighted the massive intervention of the state through the land-grant movement, described the creation of historically black institutions after the Civil War, and cited the widespread discrimination against Jews in the early twentieth century as illustrative of higher education's approach to minorities. The paper concluded with an analysis of social and demographic factors that have influenced institutional change in the United States during recent decades.

affirmative action is still a work in progress

Delegates also produced three papers about issues prominent in their respective countries. The Indian paper traced the complex and controversial history of affirmative action in that country. It made it clear that affirmative action in India, a system of reserving places in higher education and the civil service for members of scheduled or target groups, is still a work in progress. In the view of the author, it will continue to require close judicial scrutiny and deliberate adjustment if it is to create and sustain fairer patterns of access to opportunity for members of so-called 'backward' groups.

The South African paper focused on the then current deliberations of governance issues in South African higher education. As in the other South African paper, the origin of these issues was located in the apartheid past and in the impulse to make post-apartheid higher education responsive and more accountable to stakeholders whose inalienable interest in higher education was democratically determined rather than resting on traditional privilege. The paper on governance also reflected concerns over the discussion of the Commission Report and the Green Paper, and worry over the eventual content of the White Paper. Section I of the paper described the 'apartheid legacy' and traced its history from 1948. Section II described the strategies outlined in the Commission Report for transforming South African higher education, installing a 'co-operative governance' structure within a 'single co-ordinated system', and providing adequate funding.

The American paper was entitled 'Faculty Development and Democratic Spaces of Possibility: Building Communities of Knowledge, Inclusion, and Commitment'. The paper identified faculty development as a critical strategy in making American higher education more responsive to the needs of a still-struggling democracy. It traced the evolution of faculty development since the 1970s, argued that diversity issues make faculty development intellectually more compelling, and used examples from the American experience to lay out broad strategies for creating successful faculty development initiatives. The discussion of this paper illuminated a point of high contrast between the United States, where institutions are relatively autonomous, and India and South Africa, where there is considerably more central control.

The final session in India was devoted to the identification of policy issues that had emerged from the previous discussions and the articulation of suggestions for future action. The seminar identified access to opportunities in higher education, for both students and staff (including faculty), as the most compelling issue. Related issues included the articulation between sectors of the higher education system, affirmative action, single-sex education, recruiting and retaining faculty, faculty and curriculum development, distance learning, and lifelong learning opportunities. The seminar viewed access for students comprehensively, as involving more than initial admission and entrance, but also retention in an environment conducive to learning and with resources appropriate to the student's needs. It advocated a system of multiple pathways to education, co-ordinated so as to encourage students to ascend the 'ladder of learning' flexibly and efficiently.

Issues of governance, its structures, and the relationship between the institutions of higher education and other sectors of society including government were also mentioned prominently. The role of government was linked to the urgent problems of financing higher education, especially in India and South Africa, where the lack of financial resources is a formidable barrier to extending educational opportunity to historically disadvantaged groups. In addition, the group admonished individual institutions to develop an institutional ethos that impels positive change.

The seminar also grappled with the meaning of 'diversity'. One delegate asked despairingly if we would ever achieve a stable definition. For others, definition was less important than evaluation. They wanted to promulgate the positive connection between diversity and educational excellence, between diversity and the well being of society. They argued that more research is needed into the benefits of diversity and better communication about the benefits to the public. The construction of diversity, they argued, should be a major public policy concern.

The group continued to focus on making the case for diversity when it was asked to suggest activities that should be undertaken to promote action on the issues identified. The activities included research on diversity outcomes, workshops on diversity, faculty development seminars, public information campaigns, collaboration with the business sector, and training programmes for diversity advocates.

Some suggestions were specific to South Africa, including a call for institutional performance criteria tied to funding, the development of a national qualifications framework that would permit uniform accreditation of study programmes and institutions, and a central agency (Higher Education Quality Council) to evaluate curricula.

Other suggestions reflected the value attached to the tri-national seminar itself. Participants advocated the development of a diversity fellowship and/or exchange programme, cross-national research on diversity issues, cross-national workshops on curriculum and faculty development, and the development of international electronic linkages among diversity practitioners.

Following the formal seminar, a public symposium was convened in New Delhi where delegates described the seminar's deliberations to an audience of educators, policy makers and concerned citizens. Former Supreme Court Justice P. W. Bhagwati, Chair of the Indian Committee on Campus Diversity, moderated the symposium.

Before the seminar began, and after the public symposium, delegates had an opportunity to visit several higher education institutions that have participated in the Campus Diversity Initiative. They included single-sex institutions for women, a Muslim college, and an institution in which courses are taught in three different languages.

The papers presented at the India seminar are available from the Association of American Colleges and Universities in Washington DC, the Centre for Higher Education Transformation in Pretoria, and the Educational Resources Centre in New Delhi.

The South Africa Seminar (March 1998)

The planners of the South Africa Seminar reached several conclusions early in their deliberations that had a significant impact on the meeting. First, they decided that the seminar should travel as a group to several venues where the foreign visitors could be exposed to different types of institutions located in diverse settings. Second, in each venue they created two structures, a public forum and a session for special interest groups that would open the conversation to more participants while maintaining the formal seminar at a manageable size. Third, they planned social history tours in each venue that would permit participants to engage the social context of South African diversity experientially. Fourth, they called for two kinds of papers, one conceptual dealing with the seminar's title theme, the other practical, dealing with more specific strategies for engaging diversity issues.

The effects of these decisions were stunning. The last ensured that the South Africa Seminar would offer a response, albeit a frustrating one, to the despairing calls from the India Seminar for a stable definition of diversity. The South Africa seminar looked at the concept of diversity from every angle, poked it mercilessly, and at one point threatened to put it out of its misery by abandoning it forthwith. The inquiry was serious and provocative, and not surprisingly so, given the South African context. As had been explained in India, and reinforced by Alison Bernstein in her welcoming remarks, the concept of diversity had been used by the apartheid regime to support separate development along racial/ethnic lines. It had propped up apartheid, and was therefore immediately suspect whenever it was invoked. That rendered it at best inefficient, since it had to be hedged about with explanatory disclaimers and boosted with amplifications in order for it to be understood as a positive value for a democratic society. So there will be no stable definition, and everyone who attended the seminar came away with heightened appreciation of how problematic the term diversity can be.

For the authors of the South African conceptual paper, part of the problem with 'diversity' was the propensity to use it in conjunction with 'culture'. They pointed to the old-fashioned, static connotations of culture, the cultures of our forbears that identified them in a compelling and permanent way, and insulated them from everything that was different. They suggested that the notion of cultural diversity is too suggestive of old 'divergent' cultures and less receptive to the contemporary convergent cultural forces that permit and indeed encourage individuals to construct their cultures dynamically and strategically. They suggested that 'identity' would be a better term for denoting these new dynamic configurations of cultural elements.

'identity' would be a better term for denoting these new dynamic configurations of cultural elements

But that suggestion too led to confusion. At least one delegate misconstrued the suggestion to mean that identity attached solely to individuals, while culture was characteristic of groups. The authors quickly corrected the misconstruction, noting that identities were multiple and collective, as well as strategic. But they also acknowledged that identity, as a concept, required its own set of explanations and clarifications.

The discussion of the South African conceptual paper was one of the liveliest of the seminar. Fortunately, it was first, and it succeeded in setting a high standard for the subsequent discourse. And it accomplished something else. In India, access to higher education had been identified as a top priority. In South Africa, the mandate was broadened and deepened to include access to all the cultural pathways that empower people to make strategic choices about who they are, what they aspire to, and how they will manifest their choices to the worlds in which they live. The corollary to this argument, which was emphasised again and again during the seminar, was that democratic nations have an obligation to use their higher education systems to advance this empowerment and to extend it to all people, especially to those who have been historically denied. Discerning who they are, in terms of their multiple identities and cultural affinities, their strategically chosen self-definitions and the historical associations with power and oppression that inflect their definitions, is imperative.

None of these terms – diversity, identity, culture – is likely to disappear from the language. And they will all remain problematic. We will continue to be annoyed by the fact that diversity gets invoked when we have some intimation of unity, or at least connectedness. What's within my purview is diverse. What falls outside is different. Identity will continue to conjure up notions of permanence, stasis, and isolation of the supreme individual, even though it takes only modest discernment to appreciate the dynamic character of today's identities. And culture will abide with us a bit longer, sometimes meaning the commodified cultural adornments of our festivals and flea markets, sometimes the crude intrusions of a global marketplace, and on occasion the apprehension and internalisation of something downright good, true and beautiful. We'll have to keep reminding ourselves that diversity can be perverse, identity stultifying, and that culture includes detritus. No definition. Just perseverance.

The seminar's movement from place to place had the effect of adding dramatically to the amount of information the participants were asked to absorb. The social history tours, which were led by experts, helped to organise the information. Since the seminar was about diversity, the travel and the tours reinforced the central theme.

On each campus, participants in the public forums were invited to join a special interest group for discussion of such topics as curriculum, technology, gender issues, and student affairs. These informal discussions, facilitated by staff of the host institution, extended the seminar's outreach and permitted small groups to deal with more specific questions about the planning and implementation of specific projects.

The public forums turned the seminar into genuine two-way conversations, in which the higher education institutions from each of the three regions had an opportunity to present their reflections on the issues and to engage the seminar participants in more direct dialogue. The presentations at the public forums varied from place to place. They included soliloquies and sermons, song and dance, confessions, exhortations, trenchant analyses, and several case descriptions of specific projects. They provided the seminar with an opportunity to see first hand how the challenges and promise of diversity play out in practice in South Africa.

The exchange at the public forum at the University of Fort Hare was particularly illuminating. It was there that the sponsors of the seminar, and particularly the Ford Foundation, which provided the funds, were asked what happens next, after the seminar visitors leave. How, it was asked, will the momentum be sustained?

In one sense, the question suggested its own answer. Clearly, the participants in the forum had benefited from being together and exchanging information and experiences with colleagues from other institutions. It gave them the feeling that they were not isolated, but rather part of a shared movement. That observation led quite naturally to the suggestion that such regional gatherings be repeated. The Ford Foundation has already signalled its interest in supporting efforts to deal more effectively with issues of diversity in South African higher education. We left the public forum at Fort Hare with a sense of enthusiasm over the prospect that the South African higher education community would soon achieve sufficient consensus to produce plans for a partnership with the Ford Foundation on these issues.

At the conclusion of the forum at the Peninsula Technikon, some delegates from India and the United States commented that the panel discussion featured in the forum should have come first. There were four speakers on the panel. The first was Naledi Pandor, Deputy Chief ANC Whip in the National Assembly and Chairperson of the Tertiary Education Fund of South Africa. She offered blunt commentary on the need for affirmative action in order to overcome the legacy of exclusion that had for so long denied equal opportunity to blacks, women, and the disabled. She pointed out that South Africa's failure to nurture its talent diminished its global competitiveness. She rejected the contention of affirmative action's opponents that it would lower standards and discard merit. Apartheid, she observed, did not meet a high standard and was notorious for ignoring merit. She challenged her own government and party to proceed with less caution and more deliberate speed toward the enactment of legislation that would require employers in the private sector to establish target affirmative action outcomes and be accountable for achieving them. She deplored the failure of South African higher education to achieve satisfactory levels of black enrolment and expressed concern over the depressed scores of black students on the standardised university entrance examination.

Pandor called for greater attention to the imbalance in access among academic disciplines, especially the low levels of enrolment among blacks and women in fields such as science and technology. She maintained that institutions of higher education must balance their desire for autonomy with attention to the economic and social needs of the nation. Meeting this challenge will require not only attention to the recruitment of students and academic and administrative staff, but also a change in the dominant male ethos of institutions, and modification of a curriculum that makes it easier to learn about Europe and the United States than about Africa. In conclusion, she praised the universities and technikons that are pursuing transformation vigorously, and chided those that still seem unaware of their location in post-apartheid South Africa.

she praised the universities and technikons that are pursuing transformation vigorously, and chided those that still seem unaware of their location in post-apartheid South Africa

Arjun Dangle, delegate from India, poet, militant, political activist, and a Dalit (the former untouchable caste), spoke with equal bluntness about the socioeconomic situation of Dalits in India, the affirmative action policy of reservations designed to relieve their oppression, and the shortcomings in the implementation of public policies. Dangle described the situation of India's lowest caste in stark and unrelenting terms that called attention to their abject poverty and other environmental disadvantages that reservations alone cannot overcome. He observed, for example, that many faculty and students were unwilling to accept Dalit students as full participants in the academic community, that the Dalit students often had no place to study, no books, and little encouragement. The universities, after all, are still run by members of the upper castes.

In his concluding remarks Dangle suggested that while Dalits are achieving political power, they still have seriously diminished access to economic power, and he predicted that the growth of globalisation and privatisation of the economy would impede progress in this area.

Yolanda Moses, a member of the Ford Foundation's Board of Directors and President of the City College of New York, described the evolution of affirmative action in the United States. She characterised affirmative action as at a crossroads and under threat from opponents who had succeeded in co-opting the language of civil rights for their assault on affirmative action. She cited two other factors that contribute to the current challenge: the massive expansion of post-secondary enrolments during the past fifty years, and the prospect of diminishing financial resources available to higher education. The prospect of less money has prompted some institutions to rethink their commitment to equal opportunity, while others are developing strategies for doing more with less. She advocated a closer alliance between higher education and the business community, which she views as being ahead of higher education in its appreciation of the value of diversity. In closing, she praised the leaders of the seminar for modelling a more democratic approach through the kinds of exchanges characterised by the public forums.

The fourth speaker was Barney Pityana, lawyer, activist, and Chairperson of the South African Human Rights Commission. He asked the audience at the outset to reflect on some current images of education in South Africa, including a picture of white parents attacking black school children with whips, and the picture of black university students occupying buildings on campus in protest over the raising of fees. Both incidents were in the news. These pictures, he said, are important to an understanding of what is happening today in South Africa. He identified the legacy of inequality as the major challenge in South Africa today. He offered stark statistical evidence of imbalances in educational attainment and employment, and called upon

She characterised affirmative action as at a crossroads and under threat from opponents who had succeeded in co-opting the language of civil rights for their assault on affirmative action.

the nation to question the autonomy of higher education institutions and their reliance on standardised entrance examinations for determining who has access to education. He suggested that standardised tests reflect past achievements rather than future potential, and that better means of assessing potential were needed.

In the course of his remarks, Pityana cited the core values contained in the South African Constitution – human dignity, the achievement of equality, and the advancement of human rights and freedoms. These values, he asserted, define South African identity and confer upon it its essential unity.

Did the last speaker in the seminar thus re-sound the theme advanced in the first seminar session? A more satisfactory answer to the call from India for stable definitions? Perhaps, but probably not. The differences between the first and last sessions of the seminar were differences of tone, emphasis, style, and mode of inquiry, not differences of substance. Some seminar participants were more comfortable with the analytical rigour of the first session, others with the blunt talk of the last. For some the analysis was too abstract, too far removed from the stark and humbling realities described so poignantly by members of the last panel. Those who wished to have heard the last panel first felt that it informed them concretely and equipped them to grapple with issues that affected people's lives directly. Those who were grateful for the provocative first paper were likely to suggest that these difficult and contentious issues need tough and relentless analysis, that the grand pronouncements of the Constitution provide the enduring foundation for continuing inquiry, that they are thus a starting point, not a final conclusion.

It is as unlikely that these two groups would agree as it is that 'diversity', 'identity', and 'culture' would fall out of the language and leave us alone. The debates, the contestations, the deep analytical probes will continue, and a satisfactory balance between conceptualisation and practical action will remain elusive. The Ford Foundation accepts that as a given for the next seminar.

As you read these essays and commentaries, we urge you to remember that they were addressed to a diverse audience, inlanders and outlanders, academicians and social actors, the powerful and the weak, those at the centre and those at the margin of a host of cultural clusters. If you read them generously and with keen attention, you may learn, reflexively, much more than did the frog in the well.

Section II

Section II

Unity and diversity

De-centring conceptions of campus diversity

Alison Bernstein

Education, Media, Arts and Culture Program, The Ford Foundation

The Ford Foundation began to focus explicitly on issues of Campus Diversity in 1989 in the United States, nearly a decade ago. We had been working on issues of access and equity in higher education for the previous two decades, but we began this specific work at the urging of our Trustees, who were concerned about a dramatic rise in campus incidents of racial tension and inter-group conflict.

In the first stage of our Campus Diversity Initiative, the Ford Foundation supported dozens of campus-based projects. This was later expanded to regional consortia, studies of how diversity affects student learning, and the identification of a national educational group, the Association of American Colleges and Universities, to serve as the Foundationís key partner in seeding projects that saw the diversity of student bodies as an educational asset.

The second stage of the Campus Diversity Initiative in the United States commenced when staff and grantees began focusing on telling positive stories to the public about practices that are working. During the early 1990s most United States campuses were becoming more racially and ethnically diverse, as well as diverse in terms of gender, sexual orientation, and religion. Telling positive stories served as a counterweight to the steady drumbeat of negative press about this new diverse student body and the growing attention in the curriculum to such topics as Women's Studies and Afro-American Studies. Telling stories meant sharing best practices and re-framing the discourse nationally.

To a very large extent, in the United States at least, we can claim some modest gains – though I would not call them victories, given the backlash over affirmative action. Indeed, the success of telling positive stories sometimes has made the diversity pitch seem almost bland, and as uncontroversial as home, mother, and apple pie! The good news is that only a few in the academy are now bashing affirmative action and diversity efforts. The bad news is that this might mean they do not see this effort as a fundamental challenge to the ways the academy has been operating.

Now, let me turn to the third stage of the Initiative. I call it 'De-centring the American conception of campus diversity', or 'De-privileging or questioning the American campus diversity paradigm'. This stage really began in India when colleagues, again at the urging of a Ford Foundation trustee, began an exploration of how campus diversity issues were conceived across colleges and universities in that extraordinary nation. More recently, we discovered that South African reformers intent on the total transformation of an apartheid-driven higher education system were trying to address many similar issues, including staff diversity and affirmative action. We eventually realised that even the word 'diversity' had to be contextualised because in South Africa it was largely tainted by its appropriation by the apartheid state as a way to inscribe and institutionalise social, economic, political, and cultural disadvantage. The fact that innovative individuals and institutions in three countries in which the Ford Foundation worked were grappling with similar, though not the same, issues led us to conceive of this tripartite seminar. The first seminar was held last year in India. This is the start of the second. It's our intention to support a third next year in the United States.

This seminar fills me with hope that our dialogues, though difficult, can result in the production of new knowledge and a reaffirmation to put that knowledge to use. If I am hopeful, that hope is also tinged with anxiety,

even the word 'diversity' had to be contextualised

17

because so much is at stake in all of our respective societies – the very notion of higher education's responsibility for producing democracy-loving, human rights-affirming citizens. So, let me end with two hopes/fears I have about the seminar.

1. While the Campus Diversity Initiative has had its share of success in the United States in creating an incipient movement of diversity practitioners committed to this work – and has told its share of positive stories – I want to caution my United States colleagues to join me in listening as intently as possible to our colleagues from South Africa, India, and now, Brazil. We cannot be too complacent about our progress – the Hopwood decision and Proposition 209 are having a chilling effect. So, we cannot see progress as inevitable. But, more than that, we need to be alert to the real danger of assuming that if people appear to be more tolerant, knowledgeable, or civil towards one another, the problem is on its way to solution. After all, our trip here reminds us that apartheid's leaders celebrated diversity in their own venal, perverse way, and this led to greater injustices and a denial of rights to the majority. If our focus on diversity in the United States fails to address long-standing, deep-seated inequities of power and privilege throughout our institutions, we provide a convenient feel-good excuse for the status quo. Unless discussions of diversity are informed by, and focus on, an analysis of disadvantage, we are not likely to fulfil our best aspirations. We cannot argue simply for diversity, because these arguments fail to challenge relations of dominance and subordination. On the other hand, linking diversity to disadvantage implies two important social-justice values: the reaffirmation of identity; and the redistribution of power, privileges and opportunities.

2. I hope that coming together face-to-face constitutes a useful step forward. As my community college students often reminded me when I taught history. 'Talk is cheap!' Unless we couple what we are learning from each other, with constructive, bold, innovative action when we return to our respective locales, then this will

apartheid's leaders celebrated diversity in their own venal, perverse way, and this led to greater injustices and a denial of rights to the majority

great

18

be nothing more than a great academic exercise in which participants flex their intellectual, ideological muscles. I would consider that a missed opportunity at best, and a terrible waste of the privilege we have all been given.

So, let me end with a few lines from a poet who for me best captures this hopefulness-and-worry dualism in all of us who are committed to transforming higher education. The poet is the American, Adrienne Rich. It's a poem from her aptly titled volume, *Dream of a Common Language*. The name of the poem is also appropriate. It is called 'Natural Resources', and these last lines sum up, better than I could, my hopes for the world in which we are all engaged in remaking:

> my heart is moved by all I cannot save:
> So much has been destroyed
> I have to cast my lot with those
> who, age after age, perversely
> with no extraordinary power
> reconstitute the world.

Culture, identity and the role of higher education in building democracy in South Africa

Nico Cloete
Centre for Higher Education Transformation

Michael Cross
Department of Education, University of the Witwatersrand

Johan Muller
School of Education, University of Cape Town

Surykumarie Pillay
Legal consultant

'Citizenship and ethnicity are contradictory principles of democratic political legitimacy.'

—Castells 1998: 110

Colonialism (and apartheid) had two contradictory consequences. On the one hand, through rigid legislation, colonialism fragmented people into racial, 'tribal' and 'national' groups defined around fossilised or reified notions of 'cultural diversity' and difference. In this sense, the birth of 'cultural diversity' in Africa must be understood with reference to the colonial project. On the other hand, colonialism brought together different ethno-linguistic groups who increasingly developed a sense of togetherness around the experience of colonial oppression. As such, colonialism can be conceptualised as having had both integrative and dissipative effects.

Against this background, if difference and diversity remain important and to some extent central to South African democracy, a critical question arises as to whether notions of difference and diversity should lead to strategies which reinforce centripetal rather than centrifugal, or converging rather than diverging tendencies. If, given the peculiarity of our history, this is the case, how do we best understand the nature, place, and role of difference or diversity in building democracy in South Africa at large and in higher education in particular? Further, how do we draw on difference and diversity to build unity within a democratic framework? These questions point to the need for a re-conceptualisation of diversity in South Africa. In this paper, we attempt to address these questions by engaging critically with prevailing theorisation of 'cultural diversity' and identity construction. This may shed light on the possibilities and limits of diversity in the context of transformation and democracy building in South Africa.

Colonialism and diversity

While the media attributes Africa's plight to inter-ethnic hostility, it fails to mention that these ethnic differences are almost always politically constructed, acting as agents of accumulation, both of wealth and political power. Mamdani's analysis of state formation in Africa is revealing in this regard. For him, the colonial process produced, on the one hand, the legal state as a racialised entity under the control of Europeans and, on the other hand, the customary native power structures in a form of institutionalised ethnicity, an ethnic/tribal identity (Mamdani 1996). The unity of the former and the fragmentation of the latter were essential mechanisms of control. Membership of the tribes was decided administratively, and this determined access to resources like land, protection, and even marriage.

After independence, the new nationalist elite de-racialised the legal state, but kept in place the fragmented, ethnicised customary state, reproducing a 'bifurcated state', which inhibits the formation of effective democratic constituencies and limits processes of democratisation. Ethnicity remained the main avenue to access the state control over resources (Castells 1998: 107). While the state remained ethnicised, it did not become nationalised. The short history of African nation-states, built on historically shaky ground, shows the undermining of nations and nationalism as a basis for legitimacy, and as a relevant unit for development (Castells 1998: 112). This is in sharp contrast to the Asian Pacific countries which, though consisting of a multitude of tribes and languages, were able to mobilise themselves into nation-states, under authoritarian rulers, around developmental goals, on the basis of a strong national identity.

For Mamdani (1996), South Africa is not an exception to the rule in Africa. Colonial conquest in South Africa had two contradictory consequences. It brought together

The state did not become Nationalised)

true

21

different racial and ethnic communities into a nation-state while simultaneously putting in place strategies and laws to prevent the unity of these communities into a nation. Racial, ethnic, cultural, gender, and numerous other kinds of divides were enforced during Dutch colonisation and magnified under British rule. It was, however, the Afrikaner nationalists with their white supremacy who established the system of apartheid, which consolidated and perpetuated the legacy of inequality, disparity, and poverty. These disparities were reinforced by policies, practices, and an enormous body of legislation that governed the way in which people led their lives. Legislation regulated fundamental rights of people 'from the cradle to the grave'. It defined how children were identified, where they were born, what type of education they received. When they became adults, it similarly regulated whom they married, where they lived, where they worked, whether or not they could own property, whom they could associate with, and whether or not they could join political parties.

Regulation of rights was accompanied by a cultural discourse emphasising cultural difference through which dominant groups identified themselves in relation to all other identity groups and portrayed the social and cultural life of subordinate groups. Norval (1993: 8) explains this in terms of what she calls the logic of difference and the logic of equivalence. In terms of the logic of difference, each group or social identity was portrayed as being culturally different from the other and as occupying a specified place in the social hierarchy (e.g. Afrikaner, English and Zulu identities). Identity frontiers were defined in purely relational and non-conflicting terms, as a consequence of natural 'cultural diversity' between social groups, while the relations of power and inequalities which underpinned this diversity were systematically played down. The fact that some groups were not only different from others but were constituted as different as a mechanism of exclusion and domination was concealed. The logic of difference justified the politics of separation, differential treatment in human rights and citizenship. In terms of the logic of equivalence, the other was portrayed as a threat (e.g. the notion of 'swart gevaar' – black danger – introduced by Malan in the 1948 election; the idea of 'total onslaught'; the notion of opposition as equivalent to communism or revolution). The distinctiveness of South African 'cultural diversity' in the minds of apartheid officials was captured by WW Eiselen (1969: 18), an important apartheid ideologue, in the following metaphor:

> It is in fact a reiteration of what Aggrey expressed so forcefully in his well-known comparison of multi-racial America with a piano on which you could produce music of sorts by playing either on the white keys only or on the black keys only but that to produce worthwhile music you had to make use of both. Now the piano is construed as an entity and whether you touch a white key or a black key you always strike a chord properly aligned to fit into one and the same scale of musical values, the colour and the level of the keys are there to aid the performer and are no indication of a significant difference. This may be perfectly true of the American people also where, if you pick a black or a white man, you find basically the same American language, culture and way of life underneath the different colour of skin. In South Africa conditions are entirely different. There your piano simile falls flat because in this instance you would have to demonstrate that good music cannot be produced unless you strike the keys of a piano and those of a marimba simultaneously, and that, I think, would not be a success.

How do we address the legacy of 'cultural diversity' under the new dispensation? At the 1997 conference of the African National Congress, Pallo Jordan (1997: 10) asked: 'Is there a national question in post- apartheid South Africa?' An easy answer for Jordan could have been no, because racism is no longer institutionalised, all South Africans have the franchise and we have a constitution that protects human rights. In the same document, Jordan provides a more nuanced response:

> … no one can pretend that South Africans share a common patriotism and a common vision of the future. Ours is still a highly racialised society and since the 1970s racism has been amplified with a sharpening of ethnic attitudes. [The] driving force behind this ethnic consciousness is competition with fellow blacks over scarce resources.

The unifying view that Jordan (1997: 11) proposes is one 'rooted in the universalist, liberatory outlook of modernity

white racist power structure (handwritten margin note)

and the realities and imperatives of South Africans of all races sharing a common territory'. The basis for this common nationhood is non-racialism, non-ethnicism, and the radical restructuring of the economy so as to destroy the material basis of the white racist power structure. The radical economics aside, this proposal must come as something of a surprise to advocates of a multicultural society in a globalising world. Could it be that South Africans like Jordan are simply ignorant of the dominant multicultural temper of the global debate? We suggest an answer to this question below.

The new legislative framework

The negotiated settlement that led to South Africa's first democratic election in 1994 ushered in a new vision, as well as a multitude of new legislation and policy aimed at bringing about social and economic transformation and laying the foundations for democratisation. The new vision was outlined by President Nelson Mandela in September 1997 as follows:

Madiba (handwritten margin note)

> As peace and security are established we will embark upon nation building. We are a single country, with a single economy functioning within a constitutional framework that establishes provincial and local powers, respect and protection for minorities, and a process to accommodate those wishing to retain their cultural identity. It is on this basis of our unity and diversity that we will consolidate our National Sovereignty.

Can you legislate non racism — sexism — free speech? (handwritten margin note)

The centrepieces of the new legislative framework are the New Constitution, the Labour Relations Act, and the Bill on Employment Equity. The broad aim of the Constitution is to create and nurture a non-racial, non-sexist, non-discriminatory country where all in the land can recognise each other's differences while at the same time live in peace and harmony. More specifically, the principles and values entrenched in the new Constitution are: (i) to recognise that South Africa belongs to all who live in it; (ii) to heal the divisions of the past and establish a society based on democratic values, social justice, and fundamental human rights; (iii) to lay the foundations for a democratic and open society in which government is based on the will of the people and every citizen is equally protected by the law; (iv) to improve the quality of life of all citizens and free the potential of each person; and (v) to build a united and democratic South Africa able to take its rightful place as a sovereign state in the family of nations.

In contrast to the past racially differentiated rights, the Constitution recognises the right to equality between all human beings regardless of any distinction or difference: 'Everyone is equal before the law and has the right to equal protection and benefit of the law' (Section 9.1). Departing from most other bills of rights in the world, redress policies or affirmative action are afforded constitutional protection as mechanisms for promoting equality defined as 'the full and equal enjoyment of all rights and freedoms' (Section 9.2).

The Constitution gives no room to any form of discrimination, which by implication promotes a full recognition of diversity: 'The State may not unfairly discriminate directly or indirectly against anyone on one or more grounds, including race, gender, sex, pregnancy, marital status, ethnic or social origin, colour, sexual orientation, age, disability, religion, conscience, belief, culture, language, and birth' (Section 9.3). For this purpose, national legislation must be enacted to promote the achievement of equality and prevent or prohibit unfair discrimination. The Constitution as an instrument of law does not however have an *a priori* definition of diversity or difference. This is dealt with through interpretation and practice of law.

The Labour Relations Act (1995) specifies the main types of disputes that could be considered unfair discrimination, namely: (i) unfair discrimination against an employee on any arbitrary ground, including but not limited to race, gender, sex, ethnic or social origin, colour, sexual orientation, age, disability, religion, conscience, belief, political opinion, culture, language, marital status or family responsibility; (ii) unfair conduct of the employer relating to the promotion, demotion or training of an employee or relating to the provision of benefits to an employee; (iii) unfair suspension of an employee or any other disciplinary action short of dismissal in respect of an employee; and (iv) failure or refusal of an employer to reinstate or re-employ a former employee in terms of any agreement. The Bill on Employment Equity makes provision for eradication of unfair discrimination of any kind in hiring, promotion, training, pay, benefits, and retrenchment. It introduces measures to encourage employers to remove unjustified barriers to employment for all South Africans, and to accelerate training and promotion for individuals from historically disadvantaged groups. It makes provision for the establishment, by government, of institutions to support, monitor, and enforce planning requirements, resolve disputes, and introduce sanctions and incentives.

The State has also introduced various institutions to deal with, amongst others, issues of diversity and the enforcement of human rights. These include the Constitutional Court, the Human Rights Commission (HRC), and the Commission for Gender Equity. The Constitutional Court intervenes in all constitutional matters involving the interpretation, protection, and enforcement of the Constitution. The HRC investigates human rights violations and monitors how the government promotes and protects human rights. It ensures that the rights of cultural, religious and linguistic communities are respected, and promotes peace, friendship, tolerance, and national unity amongst these communities. The Commission for Gender Equity is intended to protect people (women in particular) who have been discriminated against on the ground of gender. How these institutions will interpret diversity will become critical to the way in which South Africa addresses the question of diversity, equity, and social justice.

How these institutions will interpret diversity will become critical to the way in which South Africa addresses the question of diversity, equity, and social justice.

In reviewing this body of legislation, we have considered of the utmost importance the fact that South Africa should not repeat history, and must not devise strategies that will reinforce social fragmentation. In this sense, the new legislative framework has gone a long way to set the principles and values for an enabling environment and represents an indispensable step for democratisation. More precisely, it marks the end or abolition of racially defined rights and ethnically defined areas of residence. Its effectiveness, however, must be judged on the one hand with reference to the politics of reconciliation with policies which have to contend with past legacies as well as competing interests in the present; and on the other hand, in the context of new forms of contestation. This explains the tension between the human rights foundations of the Constitution and the concessions made to the right-wing groupings, referred to by Alexander (1997: 2) as the 'constitutionalisation of ethnic politics in the post-apartheid dispensation'. For some analysts, there seems to be also a tension between the idealistic notion of a single humanity (everyone is equal before the law) vis-à-vis human distinctiveness and difference (to advance particular categories of persons). How should this tension be considered and dealt with?

The meaning of diversity

The received wisdom of our time has it that the homogenising forward rush of modernity has been partly halted, partly derailed, by a series of changes in technology, in production regimes, in politics, and in cultural and personal life; that these changes have uncoupled the accumulated hierarchies of modernity to let loose a joyous babel of cultural voices, some new, some released from the bondage of silence in the shadow of dominant culture. This new plenitude of diversity is overwhelmingly seen as a **cultural diversity**, and social analysts who grapple with the phenomenon conventionally set up the primary issue as follows: how do we deal with the issue of social or national solidarity or cohesion in a time of proliferating sub-national cultural solidarities, however liberating and exhilarating they may be?

From here on, the narrative is set in an ever-narrowing frame with diminishing alternatives. Most analysts try to avoid the position of those who celebrate unrestrained cultural diversity and who reject all traditional unifying narratives altogether. The opposite excess, namely trying to invent a new commodious cultural category, usually 'South Africanism', may be seductive, but is not a serious contender except for those who do not mind being seen as cultural engineers. Why is it not a serious contender? Because most analysts realise that the problem is caused by the weakening of national solidarities, and simply inventing new ones will not automatically avoid this difficulty unless 'South Africanism' is defined in such an all-inclusive and pan-tolerant way that all diversities are accommodated, which merely begs the question. A brief review of similar projects in South African history highlights the difficulties of an inclusive South Africanism.

Milner (1907–1912) hoped to to build an imagined white South African nation by uniting Afrikaners and the English into a 'white volk' while marginalising blacks from mainstream political, economic, and social life. This project came under fire from Afrikaner nationalists, let alone the African majority. Soon after the proclamation of Union (1910), Smuts showed commitment to a new and broader South Africanism, based on the holistic idea of a white South Africa to be achieved through the mechanism of 'conciliation' and common citizenship among whites. This meant 'to do away with sectional differences and divisions' and 'to combine the whole of the white population of the country in a common system' as illustrated by the cosmopolitan integration of the United States, 'to foster an indigenous native culture or system of cultures, and to cease to force the African into alien European moulds' (quoted in Cross 1997: 4). In response Hertzog, the leader of the Liberal Party during the 1930s, proposed what came to be known as 'two streams' South Africanism, which would unite the English and Afrikaner populations, while preserving their linguistic and cultural identities. He considered two separate and distinct wholes, Afrikaners and English, moving to a situation where the articulation between them would be more or less equal in status and stature, without demanding their disintegration. This is how he described himself: 'I am for Holism; indeed I am an adherent of Holism; in this matter I am a follower of Smuts; but you cannot have European "holism" until the separate units, now in conflict, are themselves "wholes", relative to other "wholes"' (quoted in Calpin 1946: 386). Some might mischievously wonder how different this kind of South Africanism is from that elaborated in our Constitution.

Later proposals for a multiracial model by the Progressive Party and Liberal Party were rejected, and the Afrikaner nationalist idea of a multinational South Africa prevailed until the 1980s, when the liberal wing of the National Party led by De Klerk attempted to reformulate Afrikaner nationalism within a New South Africanism, which would accommodate both blacks and whites and preserve Afrikaner cultural identity by affording recognition to 'cultural diversity'. This effort also failed, as we now know. In short, efforts to build 'South Africanism' have so far failed. What the implications are, however, are far from clear.

To return to our argument, we may all agree with Gayatri Spivak (1990) that what we have in common is that we are all different, but this names the problem, not the solution. The judicious analyst is left in a rather narrow middle passage, having to argue for some form of stronger or weaker – usually weaker – national solidarity to offset the flowering of cultural diversities, welcome or otherwise according to inclination. The educational equivalents are some or other form of multiculturalism, leavened to a greater or lesser extent by core or common values (like 'tolerance') which have a seemingly hopeless task to stitch together all the self-differentiating sensitivities in such a way that a minimal collective bond may result.

This picture of the received wisdom depicted above depends critically upon seeing the new visibility of diversity as an essentially cultural phenomenon. Diversity in this understanding is always cultural diversity, and given that, the solution must somehow ineluctably also be a cultural one. It is easy to see why this understanding presents itself as so 'obvious': the recognition of diversity brings to visibility the creative meaning-making activity of large sectors of the populace, and as a collective phenomenon, the term 'culture' comes easily to hand. But obvious solutions have their limits. A particularly crisp account of these has been given by Appiah.

'The multi-culturalist mis-understanding'

Appiah (1997) has recently cast an appraising gaze upon the 'multicultural debate' in the United States and has questioned whether the diversity presumed by the multiculturalist solution is really cultural. In his estimation, Americans are living in a time of marked cultural convergence, not divergence. Recalling a time when 'the idea of somebody's culture really [did] explain something' (Appiah 1997: 30), he conjures up the era of the new immigrant communities with their different languages, religions, cuisines, indeed entirely different ways of life. Nowadays, he says, it is not only the Italians who eat Italian, the Jews who go to shul, and the Irish who march in the St Patrick's Day parade. The encompassing cultural environment of an earlier time, that constructed, constituted, and reproduced persons as coherent cultural entities, has all but gone. Pockets of old-time ethnic culture are naturally still to be found, but for an increasing number of young Americans, cultural tastes, beliefs, and practices have become uncoupled from their enclosure in whole cultures and are now increasingly available to all Americans as cultural resources to be chosen and consciously adopted, not as attributes prescribed by cultural edict.

Appiah (1997: 32) concludes from this that we would be far better off talking about diversity of identities rather than of cultures, that as cultures 'thin out', nostalgia too often kicks in, and he speculates provocatively: 'You may wonder, in fact, whether there isn't a connection between the thinning of the cultural content of identities and the rising stridency of their claims.' And if it is a diversity of identities, not of cultures, that lies ahead, then the multicultural route in education, at least in its strong or 'illiberal' form is profoundly mistaken. Identity politics is about respect and recognition, not about cultural content:

whether there isn't a connection between the thinning of the cultural content of identities and the rising stridency of their claims

> ... surely we don't have to teach black literature to show African-American students that we respect them or to teach non-black students a proper respect for their African-American peers. For that purpose *The Tempest*, imaginatively taught, can do just as well as, if not better than, *The Colour Purple* (and a good deal better than *The Colour Purple* taught in the wrong way). (Appiah 1997: 33)

In short, if 'culture' is the wrong qualifier for contemporary diversity, then multiculturalism is the wrong answer to its challenge. As Wrong (1997) has indicated:

> The rise of multiculturalism as an ideology has largely occurred because of the decline of the American left and because multiculturalism's accompanying politics allows individuals to find an identity and community in smaller groups that are missing as a whole. Moreover, multiculturalism is unlikely to transform American society or even endure as a major ideological theme much longer, because society is becoming more uniform, due to increasing urbanisation and sub-urbanisation and the pervasive influence of the mass media.

An even more harsh position is taken by Zizek (1997: 44) who argues that:

> The ideal form of ideology of this global capitalism is multiculturalism, the attitude which, from a kind of empty global position, treats *each* local culture the way the coloniser treats colonised people as 'natives' whose mores are to be carefully studied and 'respected'. That is to say, the relationship between traditional imperialist colonialism and global capitalist self-colonisation is exactly the same as the relationship between Western cultural imperialism and multiculturalism: in the same way that global capitalism involves the paradox of colonisation without the colonising Nation-State metropolis, multiculturalism involves patronising Eurocentrist distance and/or respect for local cultures without roots in one's own particular culture. In other words, multiculturalism is a disavowed, inverted, self-referential form of racism, a 'racism with a distance' – it 'respects' the Other's identity, conceiving the Other as a self-enclosed 'authentic' community towards which he, the multiculturalist, maintains a distance rendered possible by his privileged universal position. Multiculturalism is a racism which empties its own position of all positive content (the multi-culturalist is not a direct racist, he doesn't oppose to the Other the *particular* values of his own culture), but nonetheless retains this position as the privileged *empty point of universality* from which one is able to appreciate (and depreciate) properly other particular cultures – the multiculturist respect for the Other's specificity is the very form of asserting one's own superiority.

Compared to Appiah and Wrong's descriptions of the United States, South Africa may be another kettle of fish. It could be argued that old-time cultures are still potent shapers of identity, at least in some parts of the country. Our rich indigenous linguistic diversity also marks us off from the United States. Still, we should not be blind to the convergences. A large majority of the South African population would call themselves Christian, for example: probably an even larger majority of parents want their children schooled in English. Styles there surely are, but distinctively cultural or ethnic ways of dress are hard to find (ritual occasions excepted).

Against this background, a direct correlation between

'culture' and identity formation or, in other words, the assumption that an individual's actions or subjectivity could be seen as directly shaped by, relative to, and determined by their previous acculturation, must be taken with caution. Identifying the subjectivities represented in discourse and/or cultural rituals and routines is not sufficient to account for actions and identities assumed by individuals or collectivities. As O'Meara (1997: 5) points out:

> The mere representation of subjectivity in discourse is taken as sufficient to explain identity. This form of analysis simply does not even pose the crucial questions of why and how such representations eventually triumphed over others, nor the equally significant question of the process through which ideas and representations promulgated by specific groups of people are eventually wholly or partially assimilated (or not) by much larger and highly differentiated groups of people.

Certainly, it is not the mere teaching about identities that will lead to the adoption of such identities by groups of people targeted by the discourse. This makes one kind of multiculturalist argument – that learning about other cultures will necessarily result in common identity and social harmony – shortsighted. It precludes a comparative evaluation of different cultures and as Wrong (1997) puts it, the conclusion that some may be more desirable than others. It also precludes the possibility that these cultures may have to be changed, particularly if they represent an obstacle to the process of democratisation or social justice, a dimension that is clearly explained by Alexander (1997: 10):

> ... it is obvious that in a country such as South Africa that the reification of concepts and phenomena which buttress the oppressive inequalities we have carried over from the remote and the immediate past is a mountainous impediment to the transformation of consciousness. If we look at the manner in which – all of sudden – newly invented, so-called 'cultures' are being unearthed by culture brokers and ethnic entrepreneurs whose sole interest is in fact ethnic mobilisation in order to get parliamentary votes ..., it ought to be obvious that a discourse of process is essential if we are to demystify such claims and expose (some of) them for the fraudulent enterprises which they are. The dead hand of the past can

easily strangle the promise of the new South Africa unless we begin to teach people that it is not 'cultures', or 'languages', or 'racial groups', etc., that are the basis of our social behaviour but the practices and the beliefs that are associated with these phenomena. In other words, it is more likely that people will become amenable to transformation if they realise that it is these customs and beliefs that have to change or that are changing, rather than that they have to jettison some imagined comfort zone which they call their 'culture'.

The conceptual shift in the consideration of diversity – from culture to identity – resonates in interesting and fruitful ways with an influential set of diagnoses of late modern society put forward by Beck, Giddens and Lasch (1994) and others. These similarly begin with the way that the traditional cultures that used to provide unambiguous and stable resources for identity construction have become weakened, and identities have become disembedded. The new stress on diversity then becomes the watchword for a far more conscious attempt to re-embed identity in a stable field by assembling and appropriating resources from wherever possible. There are many ways to discuss identity stabilisation in a field of weakened cultural solidity. In what follows, we shall principally draw on the analysis of Bernstein and Castells to explore the question of identity stabilisation in a time of identity proliferation and disembedding.

Strategies of identity stabilisation

Basil Bernstein (1997) provides a clarifying model for the three new types of identity strategies for appropriating resources which emerge under conditions of disembedding. They can best be distinguished by the temporal location of the resources:

- a decentred identity strategy constructed on the basis of local resources oriented to the present;
- a retrospective (centring) identity strategy, appropriating narratives of the past to provide belonging and coherence; and
- a prospective (re-centring) identity strategy which uses future-oriented narratives of becoming to construct a new basis for social belonging.

Bernstein sharpens the analysis by distinguishing two sub-types within each of the first two types. Decentred present-oriented identity can be either instrumental (projected into market signifiers) or therapeutic (introjected into the self who becomes the project and organising core of the identity). Although these sub-types are essentially different, even antagonistic, it is still true that for both, the past offers no necessary guide to the present or future. They are open strategies, and prone to instability under resource-poor conditions. Retrospective identity likewise can be either elitist (an exclusive focus on the past cultural resources of high culture) or fundamentalist (which, whether religious, nationalist or populist, all provide consuming, un-ambiguous stable collective bases). Here too, whilst these sub-types are similarly oriented, they are in fact opposed to each other as strategies in the identity field.

Prospective identities, using new collective bases like gender, environment, and region construct a future destiny for the collective as defined by the identity. Prospective identities are often launched and carried by social movements. They can be 'evangelist and confrontational' and they have strong schismatic tendencies (Bernstein 1997: 175). This is because, though the destiny may be consensual (e.g. a 'green globe'; a 'non-patriarchal family'), there is more than one path to the new future, and struggles always emerge to define the canon, with heresies and expulsions common, and a consequent refinement, and often narrowing, of the definition of authentic membership.

This is a critical point. In our anxiety to latch onto solutions, we may well be inclined to reject the decentred 'narcissists' and the retrospective 'nostalgics' and sum-marily put our money on the prospective strategy and seek to foster it in the curriculum. Indeed, as we shall see, Castells (1997) is of the view that social change will only emerge from these quarters. But that change, even in the name of a new purified and inclusive order, may not be without social schism, as an analysis of its processes will reveal. We intend for that reason to stay with the analysis for a while longer before looking at the curriculum.

So far, then, our discussion has confined itself to a model of forms of sociality and solidarity that emerge under particular conditions of disembedding and cultural 'thinning'. We will now broaden the analysis in one final theoretical refocusing, by following the historical sociological analysis of Castells (1997) as he tries to capture both the historical specificity of disembedding, and the global forms of resistance and re-embedding that seem to him to be emerging in response, an analysis that conforms quite closely to Bernstein's as we shall see.

Castells (1997: 358) in a far-reaching and on-going work, is concerned with understanding the social and material effects of globalisation. Its principal effect is to turn the semi-insulated world society of nation-states into an open network society, a society that exhibits a 'placeless logic of space of (information) flows', where power is exercised in and through the flows. It is not possible to do justice to the theoretical and empirical richness of Castell's project here. Suffice to say that he detects – like Appiah and Wrong, but extended globally – a kind of global cosmo-politan cultural convergence. This is because globalisation dissolves local autonomies, and networking and flexibility blurs membership categories.

every individual in the global world partakes of both the local and the global

As we established at an earlier CHET forum (Muller 1997), every individual in the global world partakes of both the local and the global, albeit highly unevenly. The network society, however, creates a disjuncture between the local and the global (Castells 1997: 11), so the only people able to be at home in a non-dominated way in convergent cosmopolitan culture are those whom Castells calls the 'elite' – the 1/5th society. These are people who have the material resources to pursue de-centred identities successfully and fruitfully in network flows. The remaining 4/5ths are increasingly dislocated by the network society. Their only recourse is a direct defensive resistance identity, and less often, a project identity, which he conceives in similar manner to Bernstein's retrospective and prospective identities. What Castells adds here is to conceive of the retrospective, and some of the prospective, strategies as reactive attempts to re-centre identity in a new local terri-tory, with new local icons and guarantees. For Castells, project identities grow out of resistance identities: both are conscious reactions and resistances against the delegi-timation by the network society of old culturally-grounded identity formations, with feminism and environmentalism at the proactive end of the resistance continuum that includes fundamentalists and anarchists of all stripes at the other end. Whether we like it or not, says Castells (1997: 361), this is our future: 'ecologists, feminists, religious fundamentalists, nationalists, and localists – are the potential subjects [of change] of the Information Age'.

States are caught in the following bind in the global economy: the more they struggle to win in the global system, the more they face away from their people; the more they attend to their people, the less well they do globally:

> The more states emphasise communalism, the less effective they become as co-agents of a global system of shared power. The more they triumph in the planetary scene, in close partnership with the agents of globalisation, the less they represent their national constituencies. End of millennium politics, almost everywhere in the world, is dominated by this fundamental contradiction. (Castells 1997: 308)

Two issues with serious implications for unity emerge starkly from this discussion. The first is the state's dilemma: a state choosing competitiveness must necessarily neglect communication and unity. This neglect is structural. For example, while South Africa pursues the Growth and Economic Reconstruction policy (correctly in our view), it may simultaneously wish or intend to announce a programme of nation-building, but this can only be rhetorical since the global competitiveness strategy must produce differentiations, and resistances, which will undermine any 'thick' notion of nation. Conversely, a state that is oriented directly towards unity will find itself without the wherewithal to pursue it. The poorer the country, the crueller this paradox, since no matter how humane a state may wish to be, its relative powerlessness in the global power structure and its lack of resources will severely limit its communitarian aspirations and efforts.

The second issue that emerges from the discussion is that 'the potential subjects of change of the Information Age', the prospective/project identities of the new social movements are, according to Bernstein (1997), subject to schism and to progressively attenuated definitions of authentic subjecthood. Seen from the perspective of a more generous notion of social solidarity, this represents a 'shrinking of the moral imagination' as Bernstein (1997: 176) says, which is hardly a base from which to build unity across diverse identities. But then neither is retro-spective/resistance identity, whose collective stereotyping, again seen from the point of view of unity and solidarity, represents an 'eroding' of the moral imagination (Bernstein 1997: 178). The prospects for unity from an analysis of identity diversity, then, can hardly be said to be good. But they are not impossible, as we shall see.

Common culture or common identity?

Let us return to the culturalist perspective on diversity for a moment. As we saw above, the cultural view of the new diversity by and large approves of multiplicity and opposes forms of cultural unity on moral and political grounds. Hence 'voice' as the self-representation of situated singularity is the favoured mode of public address: '... un-like the decontextualised subject of the enlightenment, the subject is now no longer anonymous but eloquent in a new contextualising' (Bernstein 1997: 176). Similarly, on the educational front, multiculturalism is a mode of curriculum presentation that espouses cultural autonomy (or sepa-rateness) as an intrinsic moral good. As Appiah remarks, multiculturalism is an anti-assimilationist pedagogy; it was constructed both to reflect and to fight for non-assimilation into a larger cultural collectivity – the 'melting pot', as the original American assimilationist ideal had it. As such, it is a particularly poor vehicle for ideals of unity, indeed, it may be said to be unity's antithesis. Any notion of citizenship built on a multicultural foundation can therefore be expected to be a 'thin' one, with very little in the way of organically shared values to stabilise the new flux of disembedded identities. Rather, in its weak form it seems to have an elective affinity with the de-centred identities that are the privileged nodes of network society, and in its strong or 'illiberal' form, with the neo-tribal (Maffesoli 1996) resistance and project identities that constitute its dark side. Perhaps multiculturalism is the legitimating ideology of the network society.

multiculturalism is the legitimating ideology of the network society

Citizenship under such circumstances can only be built upon a procedural, rights-based notion of the citizen: if our

37

cultural being is defined by difference, then what we have in common is our humanity, and the human rights that protect all occupants of the national territory. The pedagogical equivalent would be a curriculum that teaches what rights are, how they are protected, and contested. Unity is thus a contractual and rational affair, only.

Unity and diversity look quite different from an identity perspective. Since difference pertains here to identity, not to culture, we are suddenly free to consider, as Appiah does, that a good deal of the cultural sea we swim in, far from being parcelled off into zero sum separate but equal bits, is in fact common or at least convergent. The South African nation, like the American nation, may well be not something we have to construct but something that is already there, merely invisible because our perspective is disposed to see difference in all things cultural. Unity may be something that is already latent and near to our grasp, something we have simply to acknowledge, and make visible.

This is the spirit that lies behind Pallo Jordan's recent paper: there are certain values we share because we have striven for them for a long time. Certain sentiments are inalienably ours, because they have emerged in the course of a long and determined struggle. These values, as Jordan and in another way Alexander see, are rooted in a humanistic non-racial ethic. A humane conception of citizenship merely awaits the instrument of a curriculum for common citizenship to make these self-evident, and for an education for citizenship to hold up this mirror to the nation.

A humane conception of citizenship merely awaits the instrument of a curriculum for common citizenship

This strategy depends optimally, of course, upon there being, as part of this common citizenship, a notion of respect and recognition for identities different to ours. This is a feature that may be lacking not only in contemporary South Africa but, as the analysis of identity formation in the network society makes plain, it may be a constitutive lack of the network society itself. In which case, the resistance and project identities will remain in ferment for some time to come. But this does not mean that the identification and nurturance of the other aspects of our common heritage need wait while the epicures of cultural difference settle their differences.

We endorse the idea of unity through diversity in which difference figures prominently in bringing about togetherness among all South Africans; but unity which does not emphasise cultural sameness or uniformity. In this sense, commonality does not preclude difference. We also see unity and diversity in a dialectical relationship, as congruent and not contradictory. In other words, we propose a different way of dealing with diversity, an approach which emphasises identity rather than culture; certainly not the past reified notions of culture. We have suggested that people differ in different identities but have access to and actually share culture(s). Unity conceptualised with reference to this notion of diversity is certainly different from the cultural construction of nationhood as expressed in the slogan 'One Language, One Culture, One Nation', which draws on the ghosts of South Africa's conflicted history and reproduces past (cultural) narratives of divergence, particularly ethnic legacies, which may lead to schisms and conflict.

Higher education and democracy building

A number of politicians and academics have recently argued that higher education must promote democracy more expressly. At the African Regional Consultation held in Dakar in April 1997, the secretary general of Unesco, Fredrico Mayor, repeatedly stressed to the heads of state the importance of investing in higher education as part of promoting peace and democracy and as an essential factor in citizenship education. He emphasised that higher education is an investment for world democracy that will discourage ethnicity, racism, sexism, narrow nationalism, and fundamentalism.

Guarasci and Cornwell (1997) suggest that, by promoting critical skills and habits associated with liberal arts education, higher education could play a role in pursuing the objectives of democracy. Students could find their own voices in a multicentric education that appreciates ambiguity, contradiction, and nuance, one which prepares them to accept the coexistence of difference and sameness. They describe a number of practical democracy education programmes located in different kinds of learning communities. They call for new definitions of democracy, community and difference and suggest a 'wholly different ideal of the democratic community in which difference and connection can be held together yet understood to be at times necessarily separate, paradoxical, and in contradiction to one another' (Guarasci and Cornwell 1997: 3).

Carol Schneider, President of the American Association of Colleges and Universities, argues that the challenge that universities face today is to expand their previous intellectual pluralism to articulate an ethos of democratic pluralism – a pluralism that grasps the role of human connections across difference (Schneider 1997). She posits that in South Africa, higher education needs to foster the following types of learning:

- cultural knowledge – knowledge of diverse cultural encounters and cultural transformations;
- power – knowledge of human projects to dominate other humans, and the way oppressed groups responded;
- equality and justice – knowledge of democratic ideas and principles (including constitutional principles);
- self-knowledge – study of own cultural roots and sources of identity; and
- diversity and equality issues in the context of the chosen field of study – a series of general courses, or core curriculum, with awareness of diversity issues in prime field of study (in South Africa core curricula across institutions are not yet on the table as a curriculum debate).

Rather boldly, Schneider (1997: 130) proposes that the goal for the nation as a whole is 'to develop broad societal knowledge of both South African diversity and of world cultures so that the community collectively holds the cross-cultural insight and competence required of a diverse democracy and a world-based economy'.

While Frederico Mayor's plug for higher education is most laudable in a general climate of scepticism of higher education, he does not clarify why and how higher education promotes democracy and tolerance – one assumes that he regards those higher education institutions that enthusiastically embrace less progressive causes a minority. A problem with the demands for higher education to promote democracy through knowledge and tolerance for diversity is that they do not problematise diversity.

Consequently higher education often ends up promoting cultural differences, intentionally or unintentionally. It is often assumed that the road to democracy and national unity is through an acceptance of difference – any kind of difference. The role of the curriculum as promoter of democracy is overemphasised, which leaves out the socialisation of students through more, or less, democratic practices on campus.

Higher education and democracy building in the South African context

In contrast to many other countries where the focus for democracy education is on the curriculum, the new South African policy framework for higher education emphasises governance and institutional climate – in other words, democratic practice. Its central aim is, firstly, to democratise institutions as part of the broader democratisation of society and, secondly, to produce 'socialised democratic citizens', a process facilitated by structures such as Institutional Transformation Forums and Student Services Councils aimed at providing space for greater participation. The Education White Paper (1997: 26) gets close to the American sentiment that unity and democracy will somehow emerge from greater tolerance in suggesting that it is necessary to 'promote a campus environment that is sensitive to racial and cultural diversity, through extra-curricular activities that expose students to cultures and traditions other than their own, and scholarly activities that work towards this goal'. It recommends, among other things, that higher education must 'support a democratic ethos and a culture of human rights through educational programmes conducive to a critically constructive civil society, cultural tolerance, and a common commitment to a humane, non-racist, and non-sexist social order' (Education White Paper 1997: 4). It does not however (and should not) suggest curriculum form or content. Instead, it establishes a new framework for national qualifications to ensure quality and greater responsiveness to social context and needs.

In practice, there seem to be mainly two types of curriculum reform that offer possibilities for citizenship education. First, some departments have been introducing significant changes in the content and form of their courses to accommodate issues of democracy, rights, and citizenship. Second, at institutional level, efforts have also been made to reorganise traditional discipline-based courses into 'programmes' offering modules on issues relating to citizenship (e.g. at the University of Cape Town, University of the Witwatersrand, University of Natal, University of Stellenbosch and University of Port Elizabeth). What is not clear is how these institutions are dealing with issues of culture, unity, and diversity in their curriculum, and what their notions of citizenship are.

In a provocative article, Bernstein and Cock (1997) argue that in older democracies, such as the United States, higher education must help students overcome political apathy, because citizenship has developed into a bland kind of individual volunteerism. In younger democracies, such as South Africa, higher education institutions must teach students peaceful political and civic behaviour. The authors recommend that students be instructed in 'four traits of citizenship':

- learning about themselves and gaining self-esteem;
- engendering an empathy and respect for difference;
- acquiring conflict resolution skills;
- critical thinking and analysis of one's own position and those of others (Bernstein and Cock 1997: 6).

Muller (1997: 181) asserts that the debate about curriculum is at heart a debate about citizenship. The central question in this regard is what citizenship is for, what kind of citizenship would we ideally want, and what is historically most appropriate for us. Muller does not answer these questions. Instead, he highlights possible tensions in addressing the questions, namely between the following oppositions: cosmopolitan and local subjects; autonomy and relevance; generic and specific discipline knowledge. What is clear, however, is that 'curriculum transformation in the new global/local order is not simply about the insertion of some local or global content. It involves, on the one hand, rethinking citizenship and the identity of the learner, and, on the other, a careful understanding of the way that knowledge is produced, organised and distributed' (Muller 1997: 199). It is towards an answer to these questions that the suggestions by Schneider, and Bernstein and Cock cited above, should be seen.

curriculum transformation in the new global/local order is not simply about the insertion of some local or global content

Problematising democracy-building and diversity: why aren't we all democracy builders now?

In South Africa and internationally, many higher education institutions do not seem to be self-consciously and enthusiastically committed to promoting democracy and diversity. The reasons are complex but generally seem to be related to the following factors:

- loss of confidence in what counts as democracy;
- loss of confidence in what counts as knowledge; and
- loss of community (and by implication of citizenship) in higher education itself.

In South Africa, the 'democratic revolution' brought about a profound loss of certainty as to what democracy means in higher education. As in Europe and the United States in the late 1960s, the demand for participation by those previously excluded from the 'democratic collegiality' of senior professors set up a tension between the hierarchy of pedagogy (or knowledge) and the running of the institution. In many cases, both senior professors and the management used their knowledge authority to assert and defend their control over all other aspects of the institution. The challenge by students, workers, junior staff, and outside communities for a voice about fees, salaries, and services (and transformation itself) spilled over into contestations about the curriculum. Struggles have emerged around redress, who makes what decision, what knowledge for who and by whom.

Like other civil society spheres, higher education faces profound uncertainty. Internally, it faces an epistemological crisis in knowledge production associated with postmodernism; externally, it has to grapple with the increasing demands from the state and the market, and new accountability and performance criteria (Barnett 1997). The United States and Europe in the last decade have seen the retreat of student participation in governance, and the assertion of new managerialism as institutions respond to issues such as financial constraints and demands for accountability. In this situation, academics have conceded a lot of power to management and many feel that they are no longer part of a democratic institution. Rather, they seem to be battling to assert control over an increasingly limited sphere of knowledge of institutional life (Scott 1995).

The so-called Enlightenment project was based on an

emancipatory ideal that promised that reason would be the basis of individual autonomy within a democratic form of society. It was the task of education to develop and spread this rationality. Science became yoked to this ideal, producing 'scientific men' and meta-discourses – at its best seen as democracy that enshrines moral values such as freedom, a belief in the autonomy of the individual and the community, based on equality and justice. Within this framework, education for a democratic society included strong conceptions of truth and objectivity. Reality (not rationality) was of course not entirely so rosy; meta-discourses dominated other discourses, stereotypical rationality has come to be seen as male and European, and local knowledges were excluded.

Postmodernity deconstructed dominant grand narratives and rejected universal and transcendental foundations of knowledge, with the focus on discourse and social-cultural locatedness (Barnett and Griffin 1997). In the words of Lyotard (1984: 7), small narratives can challenge dominant forms of power and uncover oppressive practices hiding behind confident affirmations of progress. Postmodern theory claims to respect the diversity of cultures and identities of social actors, and resist the imposition of universalising values and conceptions. Postmodernism is thus, with relativism and multi-culturalism, the dominant ideology of the network society.

The crisis in knowledge in higher education is less about what texts to read, as right- and left-wing critics in the United States seem to think, but more about how to read. The consequence is that:

> within the academy, broadly constituted, truth has been reduced to mere discourses incommensurably jostling for academic attention. The idea of 'science', robust theoretical frameworks built on sustained empirical inquiry, has been remorselessly deconstructed. The very methodologies of truth-seeking have been called into question, as well as their revisable results. Rigorous critique has been replaced with lax reflexivity. (Scott 1997: 14)

A serious weakness of postmodernity is that if there are no universal truths, then many forms of bigotry, fanaticism, and intolerance can flourish, thus undermining the very liberalness to which appeal is made in legitimising some postmodernist stance. In a sobering analysis of the epoch we are entering, Gray (1996: 40) asserts that:

> there will be conflicts fuelled by militant religions, resurgent ethnicities, and – not least – by the pressures of expanding populations and scarce natural resources. In such a world, we could not expect liberal values to spread. A sufficiently demanding objective for liberal cultures will be their survival.

An emphasis on difference rules out any holistic and objective analysis that allows us to define it as capitalist, communist, patriarchal or indeed totalitarian, and undermines the transformative project such analyses encourage. This form of postmodernism has led to a reluctance to engage with any value questions. It is within this context that Blake (1997: 161) asks the question: 'So can the university still find values to bind it together and give it shape and purpose?' The challenge is clearly to get students and staff to engage cognitively with difference, complexity, and uncertainty, whilst developing judgements about what is acceptable and what is not. It is unlikely that celebration of difference can achieve this.

While the atomisation of academia has contributed to a sense of loss of community, the more serious reasons are that the community has become much more diffuse, both in terms of unity of values and knowledge. It is not surprising that within such a context, academics are not rushing forward to develop democracy-building programmes.

Whilst the above may seem like support for the multitudes who are declaring higher education in crisis, or the doom prophets proclaiming the 'End of Knowledge' (Barnett and Griffin 1997) and the 'Death of the University' (Barnett 1997), our position is quite the opposite. The expansion of higher education within the new knowledge society means that higher education is flourishing as never before. Higher education, once marginal, has become socially pervasive at the very time when traditional intellectual structures are being dismantled (Scott 1997: 15). This poses exciting new challenges to higher education about how it can create new forms of knowledge and citizenship communities, and new criteria for judging

higher education is flourishing as never before

45

knowledge and performance. Diversity, defined as culture, will continue effectively to block a sober appreciation of conditions for cultural convergence, on which the spiritual survival of South Africa in all probability depends.

In conclusion, we have suggested a shift from a conception of diversity as cultural, to diversity as rooted in identity, which is more suited to the dynamics of identity formation within the context of cosmopolitan cultural convergence and globalisation. This re-conceptualisation of diversity has the advantage of creating the possibility for thinking communality. We do not have to wait for 'the epicures of cultural difference to settle their differences' to acknowledge that history has already made us more South Africans than we may think. Respect and recognition of identities different to ours may certainly result in acknowledgement that unity is already a project in an advanced stage. However, for this to happen, a curriculum for common citizenship and sites for democratic practices could be a central role for higher education in South Africa's fledgling democratic project.

REFERENCES

Alexander, N (1997) 'Language and the national question'. Paper presented at the Harold Wolpe Memorial Trust Inaugural Conference, University of the Western Cape, 1-2 April.

Appiah, KA (1997) 'The multiculturalist misunderstanding.' New York Review of Books, XLIV, 15: 30-36.

Barnett, R & Griffin, A (1997) The End of Knowledge in Higher Education. London: Wellington House.

Barnett, R (1997) 'Realising the university'. Inaugural Lecture, London: Institute of Education.

Beck, U, Giddens, A & Lasch, S (1994) Reflexive Modernisation: Politics, Tradition and Aesthetics of the Modern Social Order. Cambridge: Cambridge University Press.

Bernstein, A & Cock, J (1997) 'Educating for democracies young and old', The Chronicle of Higher Education, November.

Bernstein, B (1997) 'Official knowledge and pedagogic identities : the politics of recontractualising'. In I Nilsson and L Lundahl (eds) Teachers, Curriculum and Policy: Critical Perspectives in Educational Research. Umea, Sweden: Umea University.

Blake, N (1997) in R Barnett & A Griffin (eds) The End of Knowledge in Higher Education. London: Wellington House.

Calpin, GH (1946) *There Are No South Africans.* London: Thomas Nelson and Sons.

Castells, M (1997) 'The power of identity: the Information Age'. *Economy, Society and Culture*, Vol. 2. Oxford: Blackwells.

Castells, M (1998) 'End of millennium: the Information Age'. *Economy, Society and Culture*, Vol. 3. Oxford: Blackwells.

Cross, M (1997) 'Inventing and re-inventing "South Africanism": education, power and identity in South Africa'. Unpublished paper.

Education White Paper (1997) *A Programme for the Transformation of Higher Education.* Pretoria: Department of Education.

Eiselen, WWM (1969) Opening address, Conference on Bantu Education. Johannesburg: South African Institute of Race Relations, 16-17 January.

Jordan, P (1997) 'The national question in post-1994 South Africa'. Paper presented at the African National Congress's 50th Conference in Mafikeng.

Gray, J (1996) 'If the Fer Fitz'. *Guardian*, 8 January.

Glazer, N (1997) *We are All Multiculturists Now.* Cambridge: Harvard Press.

Guarasci, R & Cornwell, G (1997) *Democratic Education in an Age of Difference: Redefining Citizenship in Higher Education.* San Francisco: Josey-Bass.

Lyotard, J-F (1984) *The Postmodern Condition.* Manchester: Manchester University Press.

Mamdani, M (1996) *Citizen and Subject: Contemporary Africa and the Legacy of Colonialism.* Kampala: Fountain Publishers.

Maffesoli, M (1996) *The Time of the Tribes: The Decline of Individualism in Mass Societies.* London: Sage.

Muller, J (1997) 'Curriculum and citizenship'. In N Cloete, J Muller, M Makgoba & D Ekong (eds) *Knowledge, Identity and Curriculum Transformation in Africa.* Cape Town: Maskew Miller Longman.

Norval, AJ (1993) 'Against a theory of ethnicity: thinking political identities in a post-apartheid context'. Paper presented to the conference on Ethnicity, Identity and Nationalism in South Africa. Grahamstown: Rhodes University, 20-24 April.

O'Meara, D (1997) 'Thinking theoretically? Afrikaner nationalism and the comparative theory of the politics of identity'. Paper to the Inaugural Conference of the Harold Wolpe Memorial Trust, University of the Western Cape, 1-2 April.

Schneider, CG (1997) 'From diversity to engaging difference: a framework for South Africa'. In N Cloete, J Muller, M Makgoba & D Ekong (eds) *Knowledge, Identity and Curriculum Transformation in Africa.* Cape Town: Maskew Miller Longman.

Scott, P (1995) *The Meanings of Mass Higher Education.* London: Open University Press.

Scott, P (1997) 'Crisis: what crisis?' In Barnett, R & Griffin, A. *The End of Knowledge in Higher Education.* London: Wellington House.

Spivak, Gayatri (1990) *The Post-colonial Critic: Interviews, Strategies, Dialogues*. New York: Routledge.

Wrong, Dennis (1997) 'Cultural relativism as ideology', *Critical Review*, 11:2.

Zizek, S (1997) 'Multiculturalism: a new racism', *New Left Review*, 225: 28-51.

Democracy, plurality and the Indian university

Shiv Visvanathan

Centre for the Study of Developing Societies, Delhi

The recent debates on multi-culturalism and ethnicity have acquired an almost epidemic quality. Wading through the undergrowth of these works, one tries to understand what culture actually means in these texts. Of the various aphorisms I collect, two in particular convey a sense of the problematic. The first is the best known and the most blatantly philistine reaction, that of Goebbels. The Nazi minister of propaganda claimed that when he heard the word culture, he reached for his gun. Goebbels obviously does not belong to the sorority of ideas. The best reaction to Goebbels comes from a university don: the economic historian, Alexander Gerschenkron. In a seminar at Princeton, Gerschenkron is supposed to have said, 'When I hear the guns, I reach for my culture' – a moving reaction from a man who must have loved the university. It is a pity Gerschenkron's statement lacks the visibility of Goebbels' reactions. It marks the world of a man still intellectually haunted by the ghosts of Hitler and Stalin.

when I hear discussions on culture, I reach for my dictionary

When one moves up to the post-modern period and plays *Homo Seminaricus*, one feels a certain lack of clarity about culture. Now when I hear discussions on culture, I reach for my dictionary. The politics of knowledge and the discourse of culture as politics is enclosed in a hypertextual

49

circle that I find alien. It lacks a sense of the suppleness of the embedded quarrels of the university of the sixties. It impels one to locate the debates on diversity, plurality and the university in a longer duration of time ranging across the colonial and post-colonial era, and framing a wide range of issues.

This paper is divided into six parts. The first deals with the concept of the university and its relationship to the liberal imagination. We create a quick frame to look at diversity within the triangular goals of the French Revolution, namely liberty, equality and fraternity. It also analyses the Radhakrishnan report on education in this context. The second section explores one fragment of the nationalist debate to describe how it conceived the modern university. It focuses on the writings of the Scottish biologist and the first professor of sociology in India, Patrick Geddes, and his conversations with the poet, Rabindranath Tagore. The third sections deals with the issue of language and examines the problem of unity and diversity in relation to educational policy. It focuses particularly around the battles triggered by the Mandal Report. The fourth section examines the issue of fraternity in relation to knowledge systems. The fifth part of the essay moves to the more immediate question of the nuclearisation of India and Pakistan, and examines the possible role of the university in this context. This sets the stage to ask, finally, whether the current paradigms of the nation-state and its pursuit of development homogenise the other. This section also outlines a critical role for the university in this context.

The Radhakrishnan report and the theory of the university

The university is an outrageous hypothesis, and its survival a miracle. Yet if it did not exist, it would have to be invented. It is the almost anthropological peculiarity of the university I want to emphasise. It is a perpetually liminal institution, continually in conflict with society. Yet the structure of this socio-drama is such that the tensions are never solved completely. The university becomes a miniaturised embodiment of the dualisms of a society, a creative machine for the playing out of its tensions. The gauntlet of oppositions ranges from excellence versus relevance, assimilation versus diversity, town versus country, elitism versus equality, individual versus community, freedom versus social responsibility. But such a model of the university cannot be cast in a standard problem-solving mode, where an issue is solved and a solution is tabled. There is a sense of Penelope's Web to many of these plots: a work never ending, never beginning, never done, but ever in hand.

The university is a futuristic institution that makes innovative uses of the past. It is one of the last surviving medieval institutions, the only one of the guilds to adapt and survive in modern society. It is a microcosm of the walled city. Today the wall may not exist but the separation between the university and society is real. It is a source of both tension and creativity. Paul Goodman in his *Community of Scholars* observes that 'the wall, the separateness is inevitable for the culture of scholars is inevitably foreign. The scholars come from all parts and do not easily abide by local prejudices. They cannot always fly the national flag.' A university thus has a cosmopolitanism that trade schools and parochial seminaries lack. 'It is this foreignness, this humanism, that makes the university' (Goodman 1996:170). And this quality is part of its institutional methodology, its unspoken social contract with society.

This community of scholars, despite intrusions of the State, constitutes one of the longest surviving democracies in the world. Goodman (1966: 184) adds that the university is also a meditation on the modern city and the best realisation of its corporate and architectural ideal. In fact, it is the universities of Oxford, Bologna, Sorbonne, Heidelberg or Cambridge which constitute the real city-states of modern times.

In this democracy of scholars, the citizen is a man of knowledge, not a buyer, seller or consumer. If the market was a collection of individuals committed to the idea of property and the rules of the money economy, the university is a corporate entity which sees knowledge primarily as a gift and which has resisted the commoditification of knowledge. It is this reciprocity and difference between the two entities that has given liberal democracy its creative power.

The university is both text and pretext for this book. One senses underneath it a deeper question of the future of democracy at the end of the twentieth century. There is a particular need to explore the relation between the university and liberal democracy. Our decade is an ambivalent time for it marks the victory of liberal democracy over 'people's democracies' and also its paradigmatic crisis.

The modern university along with the market has anchored the liberal imagination. Yet meditations on liberalism ignore the theoretical centrality of the university. Despite the nostalgia of the New Left or even the tragedy of Tiananmen Square, university politics is seen as adolescent, evanescent or merely disruptive. The work of master liberals from Mill and Hayek to Rawls and Walser ignores the university. But if the market enacts out the pecuniary vision of the bourgeois individual, the university dramatises the life of reason without which the myth of liberalism would become desiccated. More importantly it is the university which eventually reveals the paradigmatic inadequacy of the liberal theory of culture.

the university reveals the paradigmatic inadequacy of the liberal theory of culture

One of the best meditations on the Indian university is the Radhakrishnan Report on education, published in 1950. One must emphasise that Indian reports on education are never parochial documents. They are cosmopolitan to the core, both in time and space, and in that sense they mimic the university as an imagination. Here Shakespeare and Cervantes, Ghalib and Kalidasa, Newton and Panini, Lenin and Manu rub shoulders in easy ambience. The Radhakrishnan Report also avoids the colonial pathos of educational sociology. It does not begin with the usual cry that university education in India was a colonial creation. The Report handles this matter-of-factly by stating that '[the] universities of modern India owe little to our ancient and medieval centres of learning, but one must not forget the existence of such centres since early times' (Radhakrishnan 1950: 6). It also states, 'The universities as the makers of the future cannot persist in the old patterns, however valid they may have been in their own day' (Radhakrishnan 1950: 7). This matter of factness is important, I think, because we attribute all too quickly the ills of today to the colonial era. It was the economist Sukhamoy Chakravarty, who emphasised the importance of this:

The description of university education as an 'alien implantation' strikes me as very inadequate and even somewhat a misleading presentation of what is lacking in university education. The post-Galilean development of human thought is largely a product of the West, especially of Europe. That the typical post-Galilean epistemological position leaves out many areas of enquiry which have been considered relevant in India and the East cannot be doubted. But that it has represented a tremendous advance in our understanding especially of nature and society is beyond any question. Even if India were not a colony of the British, it should be absolutely relevant to introduce from outside the 'new sciences' in our curricula. Hence the important thing is not that higher education in the contemporary sense was first introduced in India by the colonising power, but that it has largely remained encrusted within the late 19th and early 20th century mould that was characteristically British. (Chakravarty 1973: 29)

The Radhakrishnan Report saw the university as an attempt to realise the goals of the Indian constitution that included, primarily, justice. The university was a hermeneutic institution that read and reread and reinvented justice through the three axes of liberty, equality and fraternity. The Indian university thus becomes an attempt to internalise and meditate upon the slogans of the French Revolution. The structure of the discourse can be seen as a triangle through which the range of oppositions mentioned above are read. It is in handling these oppositions that the report also goes beyond the standard notions of a liberal university.

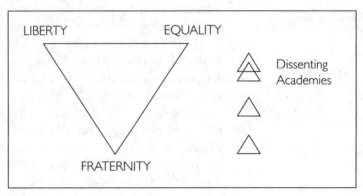

Figure 1

In terms of liberty, the Report reiterates the standard liberal view. Individual freedom becomes the 'idle curiosity' of the scholar and liberty, the autonomy of the university to pursue knowledge without external interference. 'We must resist, in the interest of our own democracy, the trend towards governmental domination of the educational process. Higher education is undoubtedly an obligation of the State but State aid should not be confused with State control' (Radhakrishnan 1950: 48). Standard liberal stuff. But it is in its handling of religion that the report goes beyond the conventional ideas of tolerance.

Tolerance as absolute neutrality is both necessary and inadequate.

Tolerance as absolute neutrality is both necessary and inadequate. Mere tolerance becomes the lazy man's pluralism where indifference replaces dialogue. It is in this context that the Report observes that while the absolute neutrality of the State should be maintained, the university need not maintain such a stance. It sees secularism as an enabling device but it is not 'an irreligious or anti-religious policy; it does not belittle the importance of religion as such' (Radhakrishnan 1950: 300). It holds, as does the later Kothari Report, that 'it is necessary for a multi-religious State to promote a tolerant study of religions so that citizens can understand each other better and live amicably together'. The Radhakrishnan Report advocated that 'it is in the detached atmosphere of an academic institution that we can study, analyse and eliminate the prejudices and misunderstanding which disfigure inter-religious relations' (Radhakrishnan 1950: 303). The Commission recommended firstly, that all educational institutions start with a few minutes of silent meditation (here the Commission is differentiating between religion and spirituality); secondly, that in the first year of the degree course the lives of great religious leaders be taught; and thirdly, that this should be followed by studies in the universalist character of all religious and discussions in the philosophy of religion (Radhakrishnan 1950: 303).

Here liberalism as tolerance moves towards a dialogic notion of plurality. Radhakrishnan (1950: 302) invokes as precedent the University of Nalanda 'which was the meeting ground of different sects and creeds with their possible and impossible doctrines'. It is the university as a life of dialogue that leads Radhakrishnan to insist that 'to be secular is not to be religiously illiterate' (Radhakrishnan 1950: 300). It is the slow but repeated encounter with culture and with the issues of culture as politics that the university reworks its notion of democracy.

The Indian theory of the university was not the standard monadic variant. Its encounter with diversity begins with its attempt to confront differences within and beyond itself. Unlike the liberal theory of the university which talks of autonomy in the abstract and unconsciously posits a homogeneous or potentially homogeneous community, the Indian variant argued against isolation or even the notion of assimilation.

The university as a formalised ecology of knowledges sees a tension, a dualism between the sciences and the humanities, and also a dialectic between itself and external other, the dissenting academy. Probably the finest exponent of the dissenting academy within the Indian tradition was our first professor of sociology, the Scottish polymath and university militant, Patrick Geddes (1854-1932).

The Geddesian construction of the Western university

Geddes was a town planner who saw the university as a microcosm of the city. In his innumerable town plans, especially in his vision of a new university at Indore, Geddes argued that no university was complete without its dissenting academies. He counterposes an ecological to a liberal view of the universities to argue that the career of the Western university as an organism reflected a frequent and often violent dialogue with the competing notions of knowledge and pedagogy residing in its environment. Its success lay in its ability to provide a working synthesis. 'The medieval university itself arose out of an attempt to reconcile the doctrines of the Christian church with the recovery of Aristotle.' Paralleling this tussle was the dialogue of the medical systems, where physicians of many faiths were comparing not only their drugs but also their doctrines. This medieval university became the Renaissance university by imbibing 'the new learning from the fugitive Greeks, the new astronomy from the persecuted heretics and the results of the new art of printing from wandering scholars and craftsmen.'

The Renaissance university grew into the contemporary German university system. Geddes claimed that like many

German innovations, it was basically French. The Germans translated, with great originality, the culture of the French *philosophes*. 'The Grand Encyclopedia of Diderot and Voltaire was broken up, so to speak, into its constituent articles, e.g., algebra, anthropology, architecture and so on right down, and chairs were created for the exposition and elaboration of each.' The ideas of liberty, equality and fraternity were displaced from the political to the intellectual sphere and acclaimed as the new freedom of teaching and learning. 'This modern revival of independent specialised research with its increasingly minute division of labour was the glory of the Berlin and German universities.' Its danger lay in the loss of intellectual unity and also a moral purpose, especially *vis-a-vis* the State. Geddes added that whereas the Germans innovated upon Napoleon's ideas with great originality, the latter had a devastating impact on England. After the Napoleonic Wars, the ideas of the French Revolution functioned as a leaven on English liberalism, serving as a model for the new University of London. However what London borrowed from France was not the enlightened research of the *philosophes*, but the Napoleonic idea of the encyclopedia as a well-digested summary and the possibility of constructing an examination system around it. Thus what India inherited was basically a sub-Germanic university (Visvanathan 1998).

For Geddes, then, the Indian university was already a decultured entity. During the nationalist movement Geddes and the poet Tagore (1864-1941) discussed the possibilities of a post-Germanic university. Tagore believed that the modern university as a collective representation embodied the essential world-view of Western civilisation. Thus a student from another land had no difficulty in obtaining a grasp of the Western mind because it was captured synoptically in the university. Tagore felt that the East had no equivalent institution. He sought at Santiniketan to build such a centre. Tagore was not content with a Swadeshism that settled for a voyeuristic variant of the Western university. He argued that before the dialogue between East and West could begin, there had to be an intellectual centre which embodied the spirit of knowledge in the East, reflecting each of its great civilisations. Only with the existence of such an institution could the

the Western mind was captured synoptically in the university

interaction of East and West be one of equality, of dialogic reciprocity exploring difference.

Tagore argued that each university was an embodiment of an archetypal set. The Western university as the microcosm of the *civitas* reflected the mind of the city. In India, however, civilisation was associated with the forest 'taking on its distinctive character from its origin and environment.' Its intellect sought spiritual harmony with nature, while the mind of the city sought its subjugation, extending its boundary walls around its acquisitions. The sage in the forest hermitage was not interested in acquiring and dominating, but in realising and enlarging his consciousness by growing with and into his surroundings. Even when the primeval forest gave way to the farm and the city, 'the heart of India looked back with adoration upon the great ideal of strenuous self-realisation and the simple dignity of the forest hermitage.' The West, on the contrary, took pride in subduing nature. As a result, the American wilderness, unlike the Indian forest, lacked a cosmic power. For the West, nature belonged to the category of the inanimate and Western thought posited a disjunction between nature and human nature. But the Indian mind freely acknowledged its kinship with nature, positing an unbroken relationship with all. Thus, while a city science sought to subdue nature, in India 'a whole people who were once meat-eaters gave up taking animal food to cultivate the sentiment of universal sympathy for life, an event unique in history.' For Tagore, the dialogue between the two universities would be between a city science and a forest science, between a mode of being that sought harmony with nature and a way of doing that sought possession of it.

Tagore did not deny the power of Western science or the dynamism of the Western university. He felt, however, that the dialogue of knowledges could only begin when differences were understood and recognised. Unfortunately, even Tagore's dreams of a new university were not fully realised at Santiniketan. For all practical purposes despite its attempts to propound an aesthetic view of the university, Santiniketan also remains a sub-Germanic university (Visvanathan 1987).

But I hope the importance and dialogicity of the

dissenting academy is clear. One must add that there has been a failure of dissenting academies in the West and in India recently.

The first sign of failure to adapt was the French and American student revolts of the sixties. David Caute remarks,

> In the vanguard of the rebellion were students scornful of representative democracy and distrustful of capitalist technocracy. They marched, demonstrated, occupied universities, courted police repression, driving university presidents, deans, vice-chancellors, rectors and directors to distraction and not infrequently to premature retirement. (Caute 1988: ix)

The institutiona-lised response of modern liberalism to these revolts was not creative.

But by the end of the seventies the universities had returned to normalcy. The institutionalised response of modern liberalism to these revolts was not creative. What it produced was an expanded version of the multiversity and its sibling multi-culturalism.

The multiversity was the standard university department with its epidemic of epicycles. It reflected an over-response of the Western university to the demands of society. The university became a collage of subjects. Allan Bloom observes that the word itself was coined by an administrator who had to provide for a mob of disciplines (Bloom 1990: 363). The sheer increase in the number of subjects did not add to the structure of the whole. The American university became a supermarket of subjects. One wonders whether the addition of gender studies, peace studies, Afro-American studies, et al. has added to the notion of the university. A mere multiplication of subjects adds little to the pluralisation of the university. Number by itself does not add to democracy or the ecolacy of the university. In fact to an outsider it appears to be an impoverishment of alternatives and their banalisation. If the multiversity, the gargantuan administrative monster of liberalism had a response to culture, it was the belated notion of multiculturalism.

Liberalism has no theory of cultural differences except in a negative sense. Liberalism is based on the axiometics of homogeneity. The liberal capitalist State sought a theory of citizenship which had no place or only a ghettoised place for the tribal, the Jew, the hobo, the gypsy. In terms of a theory of culture it offered only the options of ghettoisation, museumisation or assimilation. The unstated option was genocide.

But, when in the sixties, the liberal felt that liberalism itself was threatened by homogeneity, multiculturalism was born. Multiculturalism is a bad subalternism, a hegemonic culture's idea of how to treat the marginal and the defeated. As John Gray remarks 'the liberal enthusiasm for policies of positive discrimination [is] a belated recognition of the desolation which liberal policies of social engineering have wreaked on our societies.' Gray describes it as 'that fashionable form of paternalism which aims to embalm the dead and dying vestiges of submerged or occluded traditions and preserve their remains as public spectacles' (Gray 1993: 261). Yet there are tremendous possibilities in multiculturalism especially as it becomes a subaltern discourse. It can inject the dissenting academy into the heart of the university. However, it can also become a part of the segmentalised margin if it does not continually challenge the Western canon.

there are tremendous possibilities in multiculturalism

Coming to India, the years of independence failed to produce any dissenting academies in a real sense. The traditional educational institutions lacked the power, confidence and even the vitality to challenge the exploding juggernaut called the Indian university. The Gandhian notions of education failed to scratch even the epidermis of Nehruvian modernism. But by the seventies two kinds of critique of the university existed outside it. Both forms were in strange complementarity to it.

The university in its British incarnation was seen by many students as an alien thing. In a fundamental sense it was based on the Macaulayite axiom that a shelf of books in an Occidental library was worth more than all the culture of the Orient. The Indian response to such hegemony was not open resistance but subversion through mimicry. We understood Macaulay literally; we reduced Western civilisation to a shelf of books and proceeded to memorise it. Thus was born the tutorial college and the bowdlerised textbook – the 'guide'.

The tutorial college was unerring in its understanding of the modern Indian university. It was an examination machine. What it did was to abbreviate, miniaturise, the official syllabus of Western culture. It is Charles Lamb rather than William Shakespeare who is the real hero of the Indian university.

If the tutorial college propagated Western culture and science through mimicry, the science movements – whether the BGVS (Bharatiya-Gyan-Vigyan-Samiti) or the KSSP (Kerala-Shastra-Sahitya-Parishad) – became attempts to diffuse Western knowledge, particularly science. These were not movements that critiqued science but took science to the villages. Their radicalism consisted in the act of diffusion. Established and innovated by university teachers, these experiments eventually helped legitimise the system of higher education by diffusing its contents. But neither the tutorial college nor the science movement functioned as radical critiques of knowledge, its epistemology, its pedagogy or its use. In that sense the structure of higher education remained inviolate and intact.

The more interesting debate in India was the controversy particularly between the arts and the sciences. The most forceful polemicist of the dangers of this divide was the anthropologist of religion and science, JPS Uberoi (Uberoi 1985). For Uberoi, the University is structured around the difference and the reciprocity between the arts and the sciences. There might be frequent asymmetry between them but there is always exchange and reciprocity. The university departments were a *kula* ring[1] of such reciprocities, which bound them into a whole.

For Uberoi, the current attempt to disrupt the ecological balance of the university goes back to Ram Mohan Roy, one of India's leading modernists, and particularly to his advocacy of Western science. Uberoi sees in one sweep a repetition between Roy's move to privilege the Western sciences over the traditional forms of *Vyakaran* (grammar) and the current moves to emasculate the universities either by building scientific institutes outside or by creating science cities by fiat. Such a physical segregation of the sciences from the university is justified on grounds of economy and governance. There is a general view that science departments slave away like worker bees and arts departments play the drones. But to eliminate the possibility of exchange between the two disrupts the university as a knowledge system. In addition, to disrupt by fiat from outside also questions the universities system of self-rule. Uberoi emphasises the importance of reciprocal traffic for science. He remarks that people forget that 'mathematics, the queen of sciences is not itself a science but it is always either a branch of the faculty of arts or it may rightly be on its own'. Citing an example of negative reciprocity, Uberoi observes that 'every scientist may have to know mathematics but every mathematician need not and must not be a scientist.' Unlike science of science that is knowledge of the growth of science, 'creativity or innovation in science, like improvisation in technology, is an art; that literature of course is an art, but the teaching of language as an instrumentality can be a science; and that in fact pedagogy in the school and the university is both science and art i.e. a craft' (Uberoi 1985: 1782).

I am emphasising the inner debates of the university in detail because issues of democracy and diversity often ignore the intellectual anatomy of the university. As a result we often tend to get an externalist as opposed to an internalist theory of plurality. It is the complementarity of the two that provides an adequate framework.

Language, caste and the Indian university

We have so far concentrated on the question of liberty, difference and the university. We will now examine the axis of equality in relation to the university. The question of culture mediates the two as cultural politics is not only about access to education but the question of the language within which education takes place.

The history of the language question in India, like language itself, has to be seen in a diversity of frames. In fact as Radhakrishnan remarks, it is in language that the problem of reconciling 'the claims of diversity with those of unity' becomes perplexing. There is first the problem of number and the complexity of diversity. Take the simple question of percentages. As one leading educationist remarked, 'In terms of sheer numbers every language is a major language. To speak in terms of percentages is to shut out the truth.' English might be spoken by 1% of our people but in terms of numbers, the English-speaking population of India is equivalent of half the population of England. Secondly, one must differentiate between a 'search for a common language for India and the question of a medium of instruction.' There is also a question of political frames because many of the issues of language planning are resolved not as problems of pedagogy but as unravelling of wider democratic issues. Questions of language thus become not mere questions of instruction or identity but markers of interest group politics. 'Language promotional activities tend to become facades for the promotion of group interests.' In this context, one must quickly differentiate between the Nehruvian era of language management and the later era of regional politics embodied in the style of Mulayam Singh Yadav. Finally we must add that while language is a great source of angst and violence, it is no longer as threatening and as divisive as it once promised to be. India has bypassed the Selig Harrison Syndrome, which predicted its breakdown by the end of the first decade.

There is a final point that needs to be made. Sometimes politics whittles down the alternatives available in culture. As a result, in a battle to retain a pool of alternatives, one hegemony merely replaces another. I must emphasise that the ordinary Indian is a polyglot or at least a bilingual creature. Prabhod Pandit in his Dev Raj Chanana Lectures captures this:

in a battle to retain a pool of alternatives, one hegemony merely replaces another

> Consider the language routines of a Gujarati businessman, a spice merchant, fifty years ago, settled in Bombay, how many languages would he use in the course of the day and in what contexts? Our Gujarati businessman, who was more likely to have hailed from the Saurashtra coast, spoke his variety of Gujarati at home. He probably lived in Ghatkopar, a suburb of North Bombay; when he went out in the morning to buy vegetables, since the vegetable vendors spoke colloquial Marathi (spoken in the coastal district of Colaba), he spoke colloquial Marathi with them; he caught the 9:35 suburban train to the city. To buy his ticket or transact any business with the officers of the railway, who were more likely to be Anglo-Indians rather than speakers of Gujarati or Marathi, he spoke in colloquial Hindustani. As a spice merchant his sphere of activity was in the spice market around Masjid Bunder; because the merchants in the spice trade were mainly speakers of Gujarati, Kacchi and Konkani, our merchant spent his business hours

speaking and listening to these three languages. If he was educated in English, say up to matriculation, he might occasionally read an English newspaper; he might also see a Hindustani film with his family. The number of languages he used in a day's routine was about six; but note that he used them in limited and specific contexts only. (Pandit 1977: 4-5)

Pandit adds that one consequence of such contacts is a continuous convergence of diverse linguistic structures. His competence was restricted to maybe two languages but he extrudes its grammar on to the other languages so that his Marathi or his Kacchi has a Gujarati flavour. Pandit observes that 'these languages are not acquired through any formal channel of education, they are not a load on any curriculum nor are they a burden on the speaker' (Pandit 1977: 5). Such competence in fact is the norm in India but official discourses tend to be less playful.

Both the Kothari and the Radhakrishnan reports partake in what might be called a Nehruvian perspective. They belonged to an elite world which equated modernity with English and English as the language and value frame of modernity. They also celebrated English as language and it is the children educated in that era who dominate the English language novels that we are so proud of. And yet as pedagogues they realised they were creating a split-level world, a cultural schizophrenia. The Radhakrishnan report is sensitive to the fact that

> it is educationally unsound to make a foreign tongue the means of acquiring knowledge. [Children's] minds become split into two water-tight compartments, one for ordinary things and actions expressed in their mother tongue and another for school subjects and the world of ideas expressed in a foreign language. As a result they are unable to speak of their home affairs in the school language and about learned subjects in their mother tongue. (Radhakrishnan 1950: 317)

But the report also realises clearly 'to choose the language of the Indian federation is not tantamount to the solution of the problem of higher education.' Each solution opens its own Pandora's Box of problems. One can understand the fears of the Nehru era as a two-fold problem. The staggering cost of partition still lurked in every one's mind. Nehru was not easily going to allow language to be a source of divisiveness or secession. There was also ambivalence about Hindi. Nehru's openness to Urdu contrasts with his sharpness towards Hindi enthusiasts (King 1997). The Radhakrishnan report echoed this view. It claimed that 'Hindi does not enjoy in India such natural ascendancy over other provincial languages as to incline the inhabitants to accept a secondary position for their own language.' It claimed that

> Hindi is the language of the minority, although a large minority. Unfortunately it does not possess any advantages, literary or historical over other modern languages. Tamil, for instance, is hallowed with age and possesses a literature which vies with Sanskrit. Marathi goes back to the thirteenth century and Bengali claims continuous growth since the 9th [century]. (Radhakrishnan 1950: 321)

The Commission also felt that privileging Hindi immediately would give those whose mother tongue was Hindi an undue advantage. Both in terms of cosmopolitanism, regionalism and national stability, the Commission argued that a three-language formula, or minimally a bilingualism, was essential for the universities. The search for a common language was postponed in the Nehru era with the tacit understanding that it would eventually be Hindi.

While the three-language formula was an easy solution, as an exercise in pedagogy it was a failure. The classification of language types which the Education Commission of 1964-1966 proposed was three-fold. There was (1) the mother tongue regional language; (2) the official language of the Union; and (3) a modern Indian of foreign language not covered by 1 and 2. Pandit points out that the three-language formula was not a celebration of heteroglossia. It was more what he calls a 'handicap' model i.e. if students in one region learn three languages, formally, then the students in other regions must formally learn three languages even if they are dysfunctional (Pandit 1977: 36).

the three-language formula was not a celebration of heteroglossia

Pedagogically, one needs to differentiate between the role of different languages and the uses to which each of them are put. In fact Pandit talks of the crippling burden of language education, contending that a BA (Pass) student spends half his time in college in language studies and yet all he learns is a few embellishments (Pandit 1977: 32). It would have been better if the student had learnt the language as a subject course rather than as a language course. Interestingly the first Review of Education in 1866 had a linguistically more competent solution.

In the Punjab a pupil received instruction in the vernacular up to the middle standards and thereafter in English. The object was to enable those who had stopped their education with the middle school standard to gain some knowledge in the various subjects. Those who continued their education in the high school and prepared for the university entrance examination had to go over the same portions in English.

The Review reports: 'In Punjab no objection has been raised to this practice; nor is it alleged that a student suffers from being compelled to learn history, science, or Euclid first in the vernacular and then by means of English textbooks for the Entrance Examination. Indeed, if he has been well grounded in these subjects through the vernacular, his subsequent study of them in English textbooks would partake, partly in the character of an easy revision of matter already known and *partly of a new series of lessons in English.*'

It is such imaginative pedagogy that the Nehruvian approach to education lacked. Eventually it was failure both in a pedagogic and a political sense. The new regional elites that arose in the seventies and eighties altered the terms of discourse. For them there was none of the niceties of pedagogy. They had not even read about the elite equation between English and modernity. They attacked the problem not through the university but through wider politics. Archetypal of them was Mulayam Singh Yadav.

Mulayam, as DL Sheth notes, was not a hesitant liberal (Sheth 1995). He did not rest content with pious pronouncements about Hindi which secretly protected the role of English. He introduced Hindi across the board, insisting on Hindi both as a language of education and as a language of administration. He eliminated English even in interstate communication by insisting translations be done directly from one regional language to another. With this set of radical moves, Mulayam removed the question of Hindi as a problem of pedagogy (Sheth 1995: 188). It was no longer a question of how Hindi is taught or when it would become more official, but a more Laswellian politics 'of who gets what and how in politics'. It now becomes, as Sheth points out, a battle between the pan-Indian English educated elite and the new regional elites moving on the national scene. The latter, to state the obvious, lack the trappings of English education. If the Radhakrishnan and Kothari reports reflect the discourse of the English language elite, the Mulayam era probably does not bother about the trappings of a report. Unlike the former it is not interested in the veneer of a scientific temper, but is easily open to the new practices of scientific agriculture. What it did break was the easy equation between English, modernity, progress and Hindi as obscurantist, revivalist. The large frames of adult franchise and democracy solved instrumentally what the university had failed to do. It eliminates for one the invidiousness, the desperation of these groups making pathetic efforts to join English language classes or the derision they meet in charmed English elite circles (Sheth 1995: 196). While democracy has opened certain spaces in terms of entry, the nature of pedagogy still remains archaic. The mix between pedagogy and politics that plurality needs is still not there. One can recite this same story in a different way through the debates on the Mandal report.

The Mandal report was published over a decade ago. Its three detailed volumes gathered dust on government shelves till it was retrieved and dusted by the VP Singh government keen to consolidate the constituency of the Other Backward Castes (OBCs) for his National Front Government. The decision to enforce Mandal unleashed an orgy of violence in the universities which demands a response.

No report has united the elite as much as this one. Yet no report has unwittingly exposed it as much as this one. It has questioned our radical and academic pretensions, our models of social change, our involvement in social justice. It has shown us what we are, nervous, pretentious, deeply intolerant, mouthing radicalisms as long as they are gloriously abstract and romantic.

For years a whole generation of sociologists talked of caste as a fundamental reality. We talked of the vitality of the caste system and how it adapted to industry and the city. We boasted about the modernity of tradition. The literature of this generation provides the framework of many reports and many of those luminaries apparently served as consultants to commissions on reservation. One remembers some of them declaiming along with an informant, 'When I go to office I put on my shirt, when I come home I put on my caste.' Instead of condemning it as a parochial structure, they spent hours portraying it as a protean system quite at home in office and the city. They celebrated the grammar of purity and pollution, heralding the sheer geometry behind it. It was the basic stuff of the Indian Administrative Service (IAS) course and candidates forgot it at their peril.

radicalism and the idea of social justice was of an abstract kind

In all these perspectives, radicalism and the idea of social justice was of an abstract kind. And it is this abstractness we must understand. It is an abstractness based on models of social change like the plan and the revolution. Both operated not in terms of the humanely concrete and the particular, but the general, the historical and the universal.

What is also lost in the current controversy is any real defence of the autonomy and quality of the university. The fact is that our pedagogues have not asked once about the quality of education.

What the university OBCs and Scheduled Castes wanted to 'break and enter' into was the club, including the gymkhanas called Delhi University and Jawaharlal Nehru University. What worried the radicals, the yuppies on their way to the banks, the services, UN or World Bank, was this threatened invasion. So our radicals talked about the dangers of populism. What drawing-room radicalism feared most was populism, or even democracy by which they meant the entry of the more rustic or *mofussil*[2] brethren into the university. These new groups saw the university not as a seat of culture but as a ticket to a government job.

These new entrants, we feel, reduce the cosmopolitan character of the university, turning Delhi University into a mofussil akhada, or wrestler's amphitheatre. The backward as a servant, *subziwala*[3], *dhobi*[4] or cobbler is all right, but God forbid if his children were to rub shoulders with you. Teaching agricultural economics is relevant but heaven forbids if you have to teach it to the lesser Devi Lals of the

67

world. Populism is the fear that Delhi, cosmopolitan Delhi, might become another Haryana.

The sense of the club may not be enough to convey this fear. There is in fact a feeling of lifeboat India. The biologist Garret Hardin used the picture of the lifeboat to convey a basic idea in socio-biology (Hardin 1977). Picture an ocean where a lifeboat full of rich people is floating. Swimming around them are the poor. The question is, should one go to the aid of the poor and backward, or let them drown? Hardin argues that the poor are irredeemable and going to their aid may sink the boat. Only our elite does not use the language of socio-biology. We talk the language of merit, of justice, assuming that life is a race without handicaps. We feel that radicalism is only an extension of our privileges. Yet the bare fact remains that our hearts – instead of being larger than the Constitution – are smaller than it.

The post-Mandal years, rather than being a period of breast-beating at the wailing wall of excellence, can still be a creative phase. One should not deny the call to social justice. But social justice is not a quick ticket handed out by a machine. There is a possibility here for different kinds of creativity, especially for radical innovations in pedagogy.

But first the Mandal Commission should be seen within the overall context of the regime. If one thing characterises the present regime, it is an attack on higher education. Having burnt its 'Janata' fingers, it is not openly attacking science, but social sciences and humanities are being subject to benign neglect. Here the university should take a critical and creative role.

The university must recover some notion of the craft community, the guild from which it grew. Thus even if it admits students on the basis of a 'backwardness' index, there is no reason why they should leave as half-competent people. I think we must accept the responsibility and anticipate the human consequences of such a reform. The causal link often made in elite conversations between increasing recruitment of backward castes and rail accidents, or even a fall in production, is neither necessary nor inevitable.

We must be strong enough to contend that once a student enters the university, he must accept the disciplinary evaluation of the university. Done with compassion, allowing for flexibility and time, the university can insist on higher levels of competence on grounds of ethics, autonomy and justice, not merely from the arrogance of formal competence. No competence means no certification. The university should have the courage to say this to the government. To prevent the travesty of the university, pass percentages should be raised to at least 50%. If the government insists on recruiting students with less than 50%, let it be forced to justify it.

To respond creatively to Mandal, the university must insist on a series of innovative reforms. It must revive the old proposal of delinking jobs from university degrees. This should not sound like a clinical decoupling of two trains but an experiment in the true sense of the term. Proposed as early as the great debates around the Indian Industrial Commission of 1916, there is no reason why basic jobs in banks and the lower cadres of the various governmental services need degrees. Anyone with a school certificate should be able to study for it.

The paradigmatic subject of the Indian university is not law, economics, physics, biology or medicine. It is commerce, that everyman's MBA to the modern world. Here is the real subject of the Indian university, *that produces PhDs like confetti*. Commerce is not a subject in the classical sense of the term. It is a *mélange* of recipes drawn from other disciplines. There are a series of such vocational subjects in the university – home science, social work, business administration. Viewed critically, these are fabricated disciplines welded by political will rather than inner logic. Is it possible to first tell the government that these 'disciplines' may need a different form of ordering?

Once the university recovers its core of law, physical and natural sciences, medicine, social sciences and humanities, the next series of reforms could be introduced. The 'pass course' as a category should be abandoned. A diluted concoction of education just won't do. It can't be a niche for rich tribals, boys dreaming of plantation jobs, sportspeople and politicians' sons serving time for three years. It is a waste and a colossal subsidy on the part of the State that needs to be questioned. With this, the policy that subjects taught as subsidiaries need only a 40% pass grade should be abandoned. We should stop devaluing education

that produces PhDs like confetti

69

at every level of pedagogy. In fact, the pass course could be worked out as a good liberal arts course, parallel to but as challenging as the honours course. At least this way those who opt for this acquire a sensibility that might affect their later choices as consumers. The target is quality. Period.

In addition, the university needs a graded series of experiments, without unnecessarily hierarchising them. The model of honours course for Brahmins, 'pass' for football-playing Kshatriyas, polytechnics for Vaishyas, and correspondence courses for the outcastes should be abandoned. Instead we need a pluralised model of the educational system.

To the land grant agricultural universities and the revitalised polytechnics, we add a model of service through the community college. Here we have a college for workers, housewives, which operates in a less alien environment. The idea of dumping students in a standardised fashion down the university chute Mandal-style is crude. Community participation in these boards, not just of political goons, will help. This model is different from the model of extension lectures or the pretence about Socially Useful and Productive Work (SUPW). Here we embed the college in a community and take the excitement of education to the community.

The debate between the axis of liberty and equality has already vitiated the sense of fraternity within the university. That much Mandal has cost us. But there is a second kind of fraternity which needs to be emphasised and this is the fraternity between forms of knowledge. This becomes particularly important in this age of professional expertise when the craftsmen, the tribal, the working women are not seen as part of the citizenship of knowledge. One must not assume that the history of knowledge begins with one's entry into the university. It was the political scientist and Dalit activist Kancha Illaiah who captured this poignantly:

the working women are not seen as part of the citizenship of knowledge

> When I talk about our illiterate parents I am not even for a moment suggesting they are unskilled people ... For example, my mother was an expert wool thread maker, she was an expert seedler; she was an expert planter. My father was an expert sheep breeder. Each caste group acquired lot of skills in its own sphere ... Many of our farmers have scientific skills. They know when it will

rain. They can tell us what natural signals would bring forth certain climatic changes. They know where a bridge should be built ... (quoted from *Manusi* 1991: 25).

It is this sense of local knowledge that the university tends to ignore. I think this problem also receives an ironic twist with the new hysteria around patenting life forms. The Hindu recently reported that scientists were busy patenting bits of knowledge which have been a part of the life-world of the tribals for eons. It is the fraternal ecology of knowledges that I want to emphasise in this paper.

The plurality of knowledge systems

Modern development tends to privilege scientific knowledge over other forms of knowing. Science in its relation to other forms of knowledge has tended to hegemonise them either by museumising them into ghettoes or by treating them as occult or oriental superstition. Traditional forms of knowledge had helped in the survival of our people. One thinks in particular of the variety of medical systems in India. But the debate on medical systems reveals the hierarchisations of knowledge endemic to the structure of the university.

The finest case study of this was the debate around the fate of medical systems in India in the twenties embodied in the Usman Committee report. It was the minute of dissent by the secretary Captain Srinivasmurthi that made it a memorable document.

Srinivasmurthi was trained in Allopathy, but was also a great authority on Sanskrit. His was a biculturalism not only of languages but of medical systems. Srinivasmurthi wanted a dialogue of medical systems similar to the dialogue of religions. His was an invitation to grapple with systems and systemic differences, without strapping indigenous system to the procrustean bed of Western medicine. The Srinivasmurthi report emphasises the most important criteria of the fraternity of knowledge, cognitive justice, the right of different forms of knowledge to survive and survive creatively.

But Srinivasmurthi's appeal to create a plurality of medical systems for India did not work. It survived only as a hierarchical system. The official medicine in India is Western medicine. It is the medicine of the university system. Traditional medicine is taught separately and is seen as a lesser form of expertise. Folk medicine belongs to the desperate and the superstitious. An experiment in cognitive justice can turn this hierarchy into circle. But it is not only a search for equality but also a method of dialogue. Only with a methodology for exploring difference, and providing for reciprocity and an empathy is fraternity at the cognitive level born. It is not just respect for the knowledge system. It is understanding for the other as a life form, a livelihood and a way of life. It is fraternity at the epistemological and ontological level that the university needs.

A theory of the university must be theoretical. Fraternity cannot be reduced to community hostel programmes or summer visits. Without this mix of theory, the communities of knowledge one is searching for might be stillborn. It is in this search for cognitive justice as a fraternal act that the future of the university lies. Local knowledges, tribal knowledges, gendered knowledges, civilisational knowledges, dying knowledges all need a site, a theatre of encounter which is not patronising, not preservationist, not fundamentalist but open and playful. For me it is this that is the lifeblood of the future university. In the next section we discuss how the university encounters the other beyond national borders.

The Indian university and the Pakistani other

A theory of the university must encompass not merely dissent and diversity but the question of violence relating to the other beyond the border. If the nation-state constructs the other as an object of hate, extermination or violence, education must be the dialogue with the other. The Indian subcontinent is a neighbourhood of others – not just the immediate otherness of Pakistan, but the otherness of Bhutan, Nepal, Burma, Bangladesh and Sri Lanka. Some of them also constitute a part of the civilisational identity called India, and yet short of Pakistan, these are countries that exist by absence. There is nothing in the Indian educational system that provides an understanding of these countries. The great experiments in Nepalese democracy, the Burmese struggles against militarism or even the Sri Lanka attempt towards ethnic normalcy is ignored. India is a country born out of genocide and yet studies in partition are non-existent in syllabi.

I would like to argue that the university must embody a notion of 'Perpetual Peace' in the Kantian and Gandhian sense. Let me explain. The separation between politics and knowledge, or truth and power marks even the way one looks at the greatest philosopher of the Enlightenment – Kant. The Critique of Pure Reason is rarely juxtaposed to Kant's writing on politics. Yet in a deep and fundamental way an Indian approach would argue that Kant's politics was an extension of his notion of enlightenment. That is, politics is not merely relation between states but a relation between universities. Agencies of civil society must construct their own dialogues of peace.

Kant was explicit about the first aspects of such an exercise. Even if the legislature is the ultimate font of wisdom, it must ask the advice of its subjects, especially the philosopher. Kant saw the philosopher as an archetypal individual, above the noise of factions and cabals. And secondly he regarded the state as a vehicle of Machiavellian enterprise. The prince is only interested in the perpetuation of his own interests and those of the state. Given his obsession with the state, the Machiavellian is a parochial creature. One needs a universalism beyond it and I believe institutionally this is provided by the city-state called the university. It is the university that has to encapsulate the 'Pakistani' other into its structure. In this sense departments of Area Studies or Foreign Relations won't do. They fetishise the other and instrumentalise it. One needs a cultural encounter, not policy studies. Knowing the other in the Heideggarian sense of 'dwelling', which is the essence of a university, is different from 'foreign policy' that objectivises the other as a thing. The internationalism of the university must be widened to playfully engage the other. Kant's theory of the behaviour of states is actually a projection of the behaviour of scholars and yet Kant is clear that kings cannot be philosophers and philosophers kings because power corrupts reason (Reiss 1984: 115).

How then does one mellow the anti-Machiavellianism of the state? Kant proposed, unlike earlier theorists, a tripartite approach of relations at the level of the individual, the community and the state. I think we can adapt this to the possibilities of the university as institution. Kant himself suggests the first two steps regarding openness and ethics.

Kant eliminated the possibilities of secrecy; what he wanted was a strict pursuit of truth instead of power, even in the domain of power. The university must embody the knowledges of the other to increase the multiplicities of itself but not as an act of 'intelligence gathering'. The use of universities as instruments of foreign policy destroys the true sense of diversity. It turns every university academic into a potential spy. In this sense 'foreign relations' and 'the museum' are two forms of violence against the other.

For Kant, knowledge and power were different domains. One needs to go beyond 'Perpetual Peace' to a Gandhian understanding of the other to complete a theory of diversity. What happens if the other attacks one? What ethical-political positions does one take? And how can education, particularly university education, help under the present environment of an atomic war?

Pyarelal, Gandhi's biographer, aptly caught the links between the two problems. He remarked 'never before ... has the acceptance of the ideals of equality, brotherhood and world peace been so ubiquitous and yet never has humanity or human values stood nearer to the brink of total destruction than they do today under the menace of the bomb' (Desai 1981: 53). Let us follow Pyarelal's analysis of Gandhi and then link it up to a theory of the university.

Like Kant, Gandhi argues that 'to carry on a cold-war or a diplomatic war often bordering on the verge of actual war, and initiating talks on disarmament of the other side is contradictory' (Desai 1981: 54). Gandhi's notion of patriotism is crucial. 'For me patriotism is the same as humanity. I am patriotic because I am human and humane. It is not exclusive' (Desai 1981: 54). Patriotism thus was not a parochiality or a demonisation of the other. Gandhi's plan for a non-violent defence is crucial. He saw non-violence as an invention and in fact claimed that the inventor of non-violence was a great genius as Newton.

And it is in inventing further possibilities for non-violence that the university becomes central. Peace cannot be solved by a department of Peace Studies anymore than security is guaranteed by defence institutes. In fact they may have a vested interest in perpetuating the problem. It is the university as a form of knowledge that must seek new possibilities of peace. It must guarantee a free flow of

knowledge must travel in flows of reciprocity

scholars and students between these countries which will eventually anticipate a free flow of citizens. If knowledge is a gift, it must travel in flows of reciprocity across these countries. The Indian university must be responsible for the freedom of the intellectual in neighbouring countries and in fact must provide seats and fellowships to dissenting individuals. What the New School of Research in New York did for émigré intellectuals must be generalised more innovatively in India. Such institutions may not immediately produce a Claude Levi Strauss or harbour a Max Horkheimer but they may help create microclimates of understanding, which can help breach the wider environment of mistrust. The International Youth Hostels can be significant as a social movement if they are not ghettoised. It is a pity the Indian University Grants Commission or its Pakistani equivalents is so much an adjunct of its nation-state. At a personal level I would go much further.

Gandhi was once asked by an American journalist: 'How do you meet the atom bomb?' 'With non-violence,' his reply came a few hours before he died. It is a deep theory of the other breaking through the expert idiocy of escalation and mutual deterrence. Gandhi said,

> I will not go underground. I will not go into a shelter. I will come into the open and let the pilot see I have no trace of evil against him. The pilot will not see our faces from his great height, I know. But that longing in our hearts – that he will not come to harm – would reach up to him and his eyes would be opened. If those thousands who were done to death in Hiroshima, if they had died with that prayerful action – died openly with prayer in their hearts – their sacrifice would not have gone in vain and the war would not have ended so disgracefully as it has. (Desai 1981: 57)

This one statement captures something the universities of India should attempt to be: not just syllabi but forms of life which need to be sustained. It goes against the objectivisation of the other so dangerous both to theories of knowledge and to any construction of diversity. In this sense the university can provide the heuristics, the methodological discipline that *satyagraha* as a knowledge system requires. If the university is to combine the ethical and the political, a theory of the other as a thought experiment and as a form of life becomes central to it.

The forms of violence

The question we have raised about cognitive justice and nuclearism triggers fundamental doubts about the monoculturalism of the nation-state paradigm and of modernity itself. The modern nation-state is a hegemonistic regime that homogenises the other. The three anchoring points of this regime, the quest for security, the commitment to modern Western science and the pursuit of development, all tend to create a flatland of monoculturalism.

Modern western science has been contemptuous of traditional and folk knowledges, allowing them an existence mainly in the reservation and the museum. The museum, rather than signifying diversity, represents the dyingness of the other in modern cultures. Ananda Coomaraswamy stated it brilliantly when he said, 'We preserve folksongs at the very moment our way of life destroys the folksinger' (Coomaraswamy, 1947: 8). The idea of development has become genocidal today. One recollects Leo Kuper's anecdote about complaints made by human rights activists about the genocide of tribals in the Brazilian north-east. The Brazilian delegate in his reply admitted matter of factly that the tribals had been eliminated but added it was an inadvertent consequence of the pursuit of development.

Development projects in India have created more refugees than wars have done in the last five decades. Large dams in India in particular have displaced around 20 million refugees. Many of these victims are in fact subject to serial displacement. The question of development is particularly relevant to the university because development theories are first articulated and refined in the academe. What looks like antiseptic syllabi taught as 'objective scholarship' becomes a series of death warrants. Let us not forget that even Pol Pot's genocide in Cambodia was merely an attempt to apply a 'developmental model', a mirror inversion of the Western notions of development.

We finally come to the idea of the national security state and its final apogee in Nuclearism. The recent protests against the bomb in India showed that any dissent was seen as anti-scientific and anti-national. Giri Deshingkar observes that between the last Indo-Pak war and the futile encounters in Sri Lanka, all the awards for gallantry in the army have been for action against our own people. To this we can add the fact that India possesses over a million para-military troops for maintaining internal order. This triangular nexus between national security, development and science has created a nation-state with genocidal possibilities in the normal pursuit of its goals. The university then becomes a mere legitimiser and extension counter of these regimes. This sordid picture and the responses to it can be visualised in terms of the following diagram:

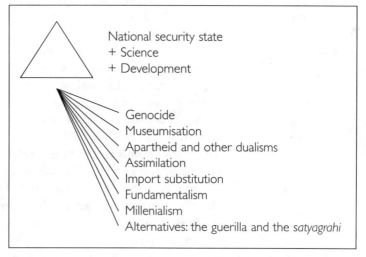

Figure 2

The picture is at one level simple. The state wants a monocultural ideal where all citizens inhabit a homogenous domain. The university is an embodiment of hegemonic knowledge forms and provides access to this domain. It is an enabling structure. Attitudes to such hegemony and its consequence can be elaborated across eight dimensions. The first is erasure or genocide. The victim as a collective other is systematically eliminated in Stalinist models or even in liberal variants in Asia, Africa and Latin America. Museumisation allows the other to live but as a lesser order of reality. The American Indian in the reservation is a classic example. He is an object of study for cultural anthropologists but not an agent of change, an actor with his own voice and theories. Apartheid represents a different form of segregation which is marked by participation in the system but under perpetual bondage and domestic disruption. In assimilation the victim imbibes the values of victor and erases and abandons his own values. He imitates the master. The school becomes fundamental to these acts of socialisation.

Import substitution, a policy term, is a more ambiguous category. It begins as an act of liberation where a colonial country overthrows the coloniser and then internalises his modes of production and his forms of knowledge. This is rule by technology transfer and the university becomes the new plantation. The system is the same but now the overseers are home grown.

This is rule by technology transfer and the university becomes the new plantation.

Millenialism and fundamentalism are reactions to modernity, which are captive to modernity in the very act of estrangement. Millenialism seeks Western goods from planes to refrigerators as acts of religious magic but under native leadership. Fundamentalism defies modernity but by imitating its violence. There is nothing Islamic about Khomeini's bomb and nothing about civil society in his idea of the nation-state. Fundamentalism accepts national security and the nation-state and destroys any notion of plurality, particularly within the university.

We come then to the quest for alternatives. Two in particular have stood out, making two ends of the spectrum. The guerilla in the Vietnam War and the Gandhian *satyagrahi* are two forms of resistance to the monocultures of modern state. But the theories of the university that must anchor these two have not been fully developed. The other still needs to articulate its conceptions of an alternative world and its vision of the university in it. It needs in particular a theory of the West within the ambit of an alternative vision of the world. This reminds one of an anecdote from Gandhi. When he was asked, 'What do you think of Western civilisation?', he replied, 'That would be a good idea'. If he were to return today and were asked, 'What do you think of Indian civilisation?', he might be tempted to reply, 'That would also be a good idea.' It will be the task of any future university to ensure that it becomes more than a mere idea.

NOTES

1 A kula ring is a gift exchange system among the Tobriand islanders immortalised by the Polish anthropologist, Bronislaw Malinowski.
2 Provincial town.
3 Vegetable seller.
4 Washerman.

REFERENCES

Bloom, A (1990) *Giants and Dwarfs.* New York: Simon & Schuster.

Caute, D (1988) *The Year of the Barricades.* London: Paladin Books.

Coomaraswamy, AK (1947) *The Bugbear of Literacy.* London: Dennis Dobson.

Chakravarty, S (1973) 'Inaugural Address'. In JN Kaul (ed.), *Higher Education, Social Change and National Development.* Shimla: Indian Institute of Advanced Studies, 25–33.

Desai, N (1981) 'Education for disarmament: A Gandhian perspective'. In M Haavelsrud (ed.), *Approaching Disarmament Education.* Surrey: IPC Business Press Limited.

Goodman, P (1996) *Community of Scholars.* New York: Vintage Books.

Gray, J (1993) *Post-Liberalism.* London: Routledge.

Hardin, G (1977) 'Life Boat Ethics'. In W Aiken and H La Follette (eds), *World Hunger and Moral Obligations.* New Jersey: Prentice Hall.

King, R (1997) *Nehru and The Language Politics of India.* Delhi: Oxford University Press.

Kothari, DS [Chairperson] (1966) *India Education Commission.* Delhi: Government Press.

'Marks, Merit and Competence' (1991) *Manusi* Nos. 63–64, 19–27.

Pandit, PB (1977) *Language in a Plural Society.* Delhi: Devraj Chanana Memorial Committee.

Radhakrishnan, S (1950) *Report on University Education.* Delhi: Manager of Publications.

Reiss, H (ed.) (1984) *Kant's Political Writings.* Cambridge: Cambridge University Press.

Sheth, DL (1995) 'The great language debate: politics of metropolitan versus vernacular India'. In U Baxi and B Parekh (eds), *Crisis and Change in Contemporary India.* Delhi: Sage Publications.

Uberoi, JPS (1985) 'The sciences and the arts in the university'. *Economic and Political Weekly.* XX(42), October 19, 1781–82.

Visvanathan, S (1998) 'Magus, Patrick Geddes and the Indian City'. *India Magazine,* January, 15–23.

Visvanathan, S (1987) 'Ancestors and epigones, environmentalism in India'. *Seminar,* February.

Gender, citizenship and diversity

Shireen Hassim
Human Sciences Research Council

Amanda Gouws
Department of Political Science, University of Stellenbosch

The concept of diversity is not a new one for feminists. In fact, feminist debates on difference introduced the concept of diversity into the citizenship literature long before many mainstream political scientists. In exposing the way in which citizenship is gendered, feminists have problematised the relationship between universal notions of citizenship and the practice of real democratic participation – including both entitlements and obligations – by everyone (the corollary of effective citizenship). Feminists have questioned whether in fact the ideal of citizenship – its universalist emancipatory potential – has symbolic resonance or real political force for women. Indeed, it has been a constant challenge to feminists to develop conceptions of citizenship that are open to difference without losing the emancipatory potential of citizenship's universal aspirations (Lister 1995: 32). In these debates, there appears to be an irreconcilable tension between the ideals of equality and universality of citizenship on the one hand and the post-modern emphasis on difference and diversity on the other (Lister 1995: 3). Soper (1994:14–15) captures this dilemma well:

> [Feminism] as theory has pulled the rug from under feminism as politics. For politics is essentially a group

affair, based on the idea of making 'common cause', and feminism, like any other politics, has always implied a banding together, a movement based on the solidarity and sisterhood of women, who are linked by perhaps very little else than their sameness and common cause as women. If this sameness itself is challenged on the grounds that there is no 'presence' of womanhood, nothing that the term 'woman' immediately expresses and nothing instantiated concretely except particular women in particular situations, then the idea of a political community built around women – the central aspiration of the early feminist movement – collapses.

The issue of diversity has also been central to the practice of women's politics in South Africa – explicitly so in the last decade. The struggle to find common political ground among women of diverse social, economic and cultural backgrounds has defined the possibility and bounds of a women's movement (and not only in South Africa). Although the discourse of women's organisations in South Africa has predominantly been one of liberation, citizenship as an ideal has animated political debate since the early 1990s, in the context of the construction of a post-apartheid democratic state. In formulating what were in effect a set of citizenship demands (The Charter of Women's Demands), the Women's National Coalition dealt with the issue of difference in a sophisticated and concrete way. In this paper, we look at both theoretical and practical efforts to deal with differences among women, and consider the implications of these for the sector of higher education.

The liberal ideal of citizenship

In mainstream political theory, difference has been contrasted with equality as though they are fixed and oppositional categories. For liberal feminists, difference meant that women were the other to men and all women had the same experience of oppression. Equality could be established through the negation of otherness. As a consequence, a false dichotomy was established between different and equal, and the analytical category 'women' was used in an essentialist way to mark off a biological distinction. The achievement of equality was regarded as a way of being 'the same as' men and entailed an inclusion into the public sphere of paid labour and formal politics.

81

Feminist critiques of liberal democracy go to the heart of the idea of abstract individualism which embodies a male citizen (Lister 1995: 3). According to the liberal theory of citizenship, human beings are atomistic, rational agents with needs and capacities independent of social and political conditions. Citizens are all ungendered beings whose pursuit of their own happiness is acceptable to the extent that they do not deprive others of theirs. Equality is based on equal access to the market and to opportunities constructed by the market place. The individual is the bearer of formal rights (Dietz 1987: 2-3). Liberalism's solution to the problem of multiple identities and hence interests is pluralism, translated in normative terms to the values of openness and political tolerance. The greater the extent of civil society, i.e. the larger the scope of society that is outside regulation by government, the more likely it is that identities will find expression.

Liberalism is the ultimate belief in the worth of the individual expressed in political egalitarianism. Liberty is constructed as negative liberty – freedom from interference by the state and other citizens. In this case, the divide between the public and the private sphere goes unchallenged as does women's subordinate relationship to the public sphere. While liberal feminists have argued that women's equal inclusion in the public sphere and provision for reproductive rights will eradicate the gender inequality constructed by liberal theory, most non-liberal feminists reject this as a solution for the creation of equal citizenship.

Maternalism as a feminist ideal of citizenship

Second wave radical feminism constructed otherness as women's different experience from men, especially with regard to reproduction and sexuality. One articulation of otherness as an essential attribute is maternal feminism. Maternal feminists reject the liberal notion of the individual citizen as competitive marketeers involved in the labour market in which civic activity can only take place through membership of an interest group (Dietz 1987: 10). Maternal feminists further reject contractual conception of citizenship, liberal rights based on the grounds that women's experiences are effectively excluded from this conception. Maternal feminists rely *inter alia* on the research of Carol Gilligan and Nancy Chodorow to put women's experience as mothers central to their conception of citizenship. The caring and nurturing of mothers, also called the ethic of care, is contrasted with the male ethic of justice. The ethic of care pits responsibility and relationship needs, which are contextual, against abstract principles of rights and justice (Dietz 1987: 11). Women's central roles as mothers and caretakers form the basis of this alternative view of citizenship. The public discourse on citizenship should be informed by the virtues of mothering such as love, attentiveness, compassion and care (Dietz 1987: 12).[1]

The most notable problem with this conception of citizenship is that it still accepts the public and the private divide and, while putting women as central, instructs us to choose between the world of the family and public sphere. Women's virtues become constructed as superior and for that very reason induce inequality into their notion of citizenship by constructing male virtues as inferior (Dietz 1987: 13). Women's activism in the public sphere – the realm in which social (and educational) policy is formulated and implemented – is thus under-valued by maternal feminists.

It is clear that citizenship has to be an involvement with more general concerns than the private world of the family.

A more fundamental problem with this construction of citizenship is the essentialist use of the analytical category of women, which ignores characteristics of identity construction such as race, ethnicity, class, religion, and disability. Post-colonial critiques of the concept of citizenship informed by post-modernism and post-structuralism challenge this essentialist tendency in feminism.

Postcolonial critique

The essentialist use of the category women has been most strongly challenged by feminists who are not white or middle class but have other markers of identity (Patricia Hill Collins 1990; Bell Hooks 1989). Post-colonial theory and post-modernism introduced a more nuanced understanding of difference, leading to a better understanding of fractured or multiple identities. This literature argues that there is no necessary incompatibility between equality and difference, nor are all differences necessarily equal. Black feminists have argued that within

83

each category of difference, 'some people might face a multiplicity of oppressions; others might experience both disadvantage and privilege' (Lister 1995:4). Multicultural politics is critiqued from this standpoint because it is aimed at 'simultaneously including and excluding the minorities, locating them in marginal spaces and secondary markets while reifying their boundaries' (Yuval-Davis 1997: 86).

Lister (1995: 16) argues that feminists cannot afford to discard the concepts of difference or equality, but need rather to unmask their misrepresentation as opposites and the problems it poses for the construction of choices. What is crucial to the way in which we understand the political implications of these differences is to consider whether the articulation and representation of differences are posed in ways which close off or open up political choices. An adequate response to this problematic would have to consider the histories behind the emergence of particular differences and 'the power relations that have represented or structured conflicts' (Grewal and Kaplan 1994: 16).

This understanding of multiple identities in the post-modern condition is more than merely a reliance on multi-culturalism where difference is submerged in a new homo-genising nationalism, or where an extreme relativism is accepted and the problem is reduced to one of 'manage-ment', so that diversity is rendered benign. The under-standing of differences based on multiple identities needs to take into account the social and historical construction of identities that are treated as different, other, inferior, subordinate and marginalised. Without locating differences in their historical and cultural locations, Felski (1997: 11) argues that that a focus on multiple voices (as in the case of multi-culturalism) reinforces hierarchies between women. The politics of diversity is an inadequate alternative because it ignores systematic inequalities in power relations, know-ledge production, and material resources. A systematic interrogation of difference will have a greater disruption of preconceived constructions of identity. In describing some of these distinctions, Ang (1995: 68) argues that there is a tension in debates between difference as benign diversity and difference as conflict, disruption, and dissension. This disruption cannot be accommodated in a harmonious way because it leads to struggle and the unmasking of power

a focus on multiple voices reinforces hierarchies between women

relations, unlike benign diversity which Ang (1995: 60) sees as empty pluralism. Ang (1995: 60) points out:

> the very desire to resolve [differences] in the first place could result in a premature glossing-over of the social irreducibility and inescapability of certain markers of difference and the way they affect women's lives. To focus on *resolving* differences between women as the ultimate aim of 'dealing with difference' would mean their containment in an inclusive, encompassing structure which itself remains uninterrogated; it would mean that 'these differences must comply with feminism's ... essentialising frame' ... In such a case, difference is 'dealt with' by absorbing it into an already existing feminist community without challenging the naturalised legitimacy and status of that community as a community. By dealing with difference in this way, feminism resembles the multi-cultural nation – the nation that, faced with cultural differences within its borders, simultaneously recognises and controls those differences amongst its population by containing them in a grid of pluralist diversity [emphasis in original text].

The fracturing of the category of women as structurally and historically entrenched cannot magically be eliminated by feminism through sheer political will or strategy (Ang 1995: 66). For Ang, the white/other divide is historically imposed, which means in terms of the politics of difference that a call for ambivalence, ambiguity, and multiplicity is not a celebration of difference but a description of the necessary condition of existence for those who are positioned as peripheral 'others' to white hegemony. No politics of dialogue or communication can transform what she sees as this binary divide but merely reinscribe otherness. In this case, difference is measured against white hegemony.

Ang (1995: 60) points out that solutions have relied on complex dialogue and communication. Yet, with such fragmentation of identities, communication is bound to fail, according to Ang's pessimistic view. She prescribes a politics of partiality rather than a politics of inclusion through which feminists place limits to their political interventions. A feminist identity cannot be the overriding identity because women have conflicting interests and identities that may be incompatible. For her, there are limits to feminism as a political project because of the importance of movements against other social oppressions.

With this fragmentation of identities in mind, Lister (1995: 4) argues that a conception of citizenship which could accommodate all social cleavages simultaneously has not yet been developed. What is missing is a praxis around which a politics could be constructed.

Radical democracy

Mouffe's (1992) concept of radical democracy offers us a theory of how to incorporate multiple differences into democracy but, as Kymlicka and Norman (1994: 369) point out, she offers no suggestions on how to compel this public-spirited participation. Radical democracy attempts to create a new conception of citizenship that would take into account all the constructed identities of women and would not single out some at the expense of others. It attempts to reconcile pluralism with the positive aspects of liberal-democracy without accepting the negative aspects of liberal individualism. Notions of the 'common good', 'civic virtue', and 'political community' must be reformulated to make them compatible with the recognition of conflict, division, antagonism, and contestation. This requires a radical reinterpretation of liberty and equality in a way that takes into account the different social relations and subject positions in which they are relevant: gender class, race, ethnicity, sexual orientation. As Mouffe (1992: 236) states:

> The creation of political identities as radical democratic citizens depends therefore on a collective form of identification among the democratic demands found in a variety of movements: women, workers, black, gay, ecological, as well as in several other 'new social movements'. This, as a radical democratic interpretation of the principles of liberty and equality, aims at constructing a 'we', a chain of equivalence among their demands so as to articulate them through the principle of democratic equivalence. For it is not a matter of establishing a mere alliance between given interests but of actually modifying the very identity of these forces.

The praxis is still lacking.

For feminist projects to be successful, they need to have a political praxis. When applying liberal theory the praxis was constructed around inclusion according to the constituted subject of woman. When that subject was fragmented due to the challenge of difference, the political project that relied on women's solidarity was shattered. The question now is how to construct a praxis that is empowering for women and still takes into consideration their multiple identities.

Difference and diversity: the political praxis

For Braidotti (1997: 26), sexual difference is a praxis through which a politics could be established. She argues that sexual difference is based on a theoretical and practical paradox which simultaneously produces and destabilises the category woman. For her, one can only speak as a woman – although the subject women is not a monolithic essence once and for all, but rather a site of multiple, complex, potentially contradictory experiences also known as signifying markers. These multiple differences need to be identified in terms of power relations which involve identity characteristics of class, race, ethnicity, religion, age, lifestyle, and sexual preference.

For her, the praxis is that one speaks as a woman in order to be empowered as a woman. But the praxis means working through difference toward greater understanding (Braidotti 1997: 28). Sexual difference is understood as multiple differences that structure the subject and which are neither harmonious nor homogeneous but could be potentially contradictory.

The political praxis is a move away from sameness (sisterly solidarity) toward coalition politics, where difference within and among is interrogated. The citizenship debate takes us back to a space where politics and political activity need to become central. Phillips (1993: 81) calls this the reinstatement of the political. It is a merging of a feminist consciousness with a democratic consciousness. Only through political activity that interrogates the universal pretensions of citizenship, but allows for difference, which does not override the generalities that citizenship needs, will a new form of praxis develop.

In the next section we want to look at difference and political praxis as applied to women in South Africa. To what extent is it possible to generate and sustain collective action with a transformative potential while at the same time avoiding a crippling framework of universalism?

The Women's National Coalition: mediating and managing difference

One relatively successful instance of the attempt to act collectively while recognising difference is the Women's National Coalition. In 1992, at the cusp of multiparty negotiations in South Africa, a unique coalition of women's organisations emerged at the initiative of the African National Congress (ANC) Women's League. The Women's National Coalition (WNC) drew together women's organisations as socially diverse as beauticians' unions and the Soroptimists, as economically diverse as the women hawkers' associations and the Business and Professional Women's Society, and as politically diverse as the Pan-Africanist Congress (PAC) and the National Party. The central aim of the Coalition was to draft a comprehensive Charter of Women's Demands, to be presented to negotiators for inclusion in the Bill of Rights. As Cock (1997: 310) argues, the driving force behind the Coalition was the shared sense of exclusion from the negotiation process rather than a recognition of common interests or a shared experience that transcended the divisions of race, ideology, ethnicity, and class. Inclusion, however, was the basis from which to launch a broader questioning of the assumptions of political transition, rather than an end in itself.

A detailed discussion of the WNC is outside the scope of this paper and may be found in several other sources. For our purposes, it is useful to consider the ways in which the Charter mediated a range of women's interests, and the implicit conceptions of citizenship embedded in the Charter. From the outset, the Coalition worked with a sophisticated organisational notion of the nature of a Coalition. Apartheid highlighted graphically the distinctions between women – the racial structuring of all social relations meant that the illusion of sisterhood never seriously took hold in South Africa as it did for a time in women's movements in other countries. Given the fractured history of women's politics in South Africa, and above all the powerful sense in women's organisations associated with the ANC and PAC that women's struggles could not be separated from other political struggles, the Coalition never assumed the existence of a 'sisterhood' (Meintjes 1996). Indeed, right at the beginning, the WNC argued that it was an organisation based on solidarity in pursuit of a narrow agenda. Political differences were acute: there was no common language in which to speak of women's needs, particularly as the 'common' discourse of feminism was itself highly contested. At various points, the political differences threatened to completely undermine the organisation. While the mandate of the Coalition slowly widened to include issues of violence against women, it was always understood that the terrain of common purpose was very narrow.

These limitations represented the wider dilemma of women's organisations in the age of destabilised and fragmented political identities, i.e. tension between the notion of 'women' as a common category underpinned by some distinct experience, and the lived experiences of women as diverse, multiple, shaped by non-gendered forces, and even competing in needs and interests. Without explicit reference to the extended postmodern debate in American and European feminism on the conceptual underpinning of feminism, the WNC refused to operate on the basis of essentialist categories or assumptions of political homogeneity among women. At the same time, there was a clear recognition of the need for a coherent strategy to ensure that gender was recognised as a socio-economic fracture by the party negotiators, and that women in each of the political parties were allowed to participate equally in decision-making within their different ideological frameworks.

The understanding of the common ground as that of political exclusion rather than of socio-economic interest was a way of shifting practice into a more manageable frame, but the Charter process threatened to pull the Coalition out of the comfort zone as it inevitably raised competing socio-economic interests overloaded with racial divisions. Cock (1997: 313) argues that nevertheless the Coalition succeeded in retaining a common ground and in building a collective identity:

> The coalition attempted to develop a political practice that incorporated and built supportive coalitions based on difference. This notion of 'coalition politics' avoided political fragmentation or the superimposition of a false universalism onto the women's movement. It allowed for both autonomous organisation and co-ordinated programmes.

Despite the driving strategy of inclusion, the WNC did not see inclusion in terms of 'becoming equal to men' – that is, there was no assumption on the part of the leadership (although there was on the part of some constituents) that the male 'political world' was unproblematic or even coherent in itself. The inclusionary task was to give women the space to articulate a broader notion of citizenship, and to define the content of citizenship in ways which recognised the plurality of interests in society, i.e. to broaden the substantive content of citizenship beyond the class and race interests initially represented at the multiparty negotiations. Nevertheless, Ang's pessimism about the politics of inclusion is not unfounded: the WNC accepted the current wisdom that a state-centred strategy of socio-economic transformation was not only acceptable but also desirable. The organisational implications for women's organisations have been disturbing, as they are depleted of senior leadership figures and the capacity to articulate demands in ways which go beyond calling for an expansionary fiscal policy are limited. At the same time, as we have argued elsewhere, there has been little questioning of the assumption that the state can be benevolent in the right hands (Hassim and Gouws 1997).

However, while recognising the plurality of interests, the Women's Charter was not pluralist in the sense of assuming all interests were equal. Rather, the Charter explicitly prioritised the needs of poor and economically vulnerable women for government attention. The Women's Charter demanded a consideration of the socio-economic needs of women: access to safe water, access to land, housing. In so doing, they put on the table the need to deal with so-called third generation rights in the initial framing of the Constitution. There was also a strong emphasis on the historical processes of exclusion and exploitation which produced differences among women, and this historical understanding formed the basis for a prioritisation of the needs of poor, especially rural, women.

The remarkable aspect of the whole WNC experience was the success of the organisation in the face of a range of difficulties. Whereas feminists in the West were despairing of the possibilities of political praxis as a result of the increasing dominance of disaggregated identity-based politics, the WNC showed how those disaggregated interests could be creatively woven into effective strategy. The victories were concrete and considerable: the Constitution guarantees gender equality, socio-economic rights are justifiable, the government has created an elaborate machinery for addressing women's concerns, and the Commission for Gender Equality has equal statutory status with the Human Rights Commission.

The extent to which the external impetus of transition played a part in sustaining the WNC cannot be under-estimated. Indeed, in the post-1994 election period, the WNC has declined significantly in its capacity to act as a representative umbrella for women's organisations. The dilemma of how to sustain organisational forms that respect diversity yet are able to achieve a degree of pro-grammatic coherence thus re-emerges in less tractable form. It could be argued, however, that the decline of the Coalition has less to do with the inability to manage diversity than with the weaknesses of the women's organi-sations that formed its base constituencies. This more hopeful interpretation would see the current weak status of the WNC as temporary rather than inherent in the nature of political practice in a post-structuralist era. The focus during the transition period was on high profile national level interventions, which left little room or energy for bottom-up organisational development. The strength of alliance-based political structures derives from the strength of its members, and in this regard women's organisations have some way to go.

Dealing with diversity in higher education: the implications of the gender and citizenship debate

The discussion thus far has focused on the theoretical shifts in the literature on citizenship and on the ways in which political practice can be built on the basis of different assumptions about social identities and interests. Of what relevance is this to higher education? In general, it has been argued that educational policies are tied to economic imperatives, albeit in a loose way. Kenway, in an examination of Australian educational policies, has argued that 'economics has triumphed over education' (Kenway 1997: 45). Increasingly, she argues, 'disadvantaged people cannot necessarily rely on education to help them to increase their autonomy, and their participation in an understanding of the power structures of working life'.

91

redress and equity are at the centre of South African educational policies

Although redress and equity are at the centre of South African educational policies (however imperfectly formulated), it is worth interrogating the extent to which the treatment of a range of differences in this sector will advance the position of marginalised interests by increasing their autonomy and their range of political choices.

The White Paper on Higher Education prioritises the development needs of society, in particular the role of education in providing for the labour market 'in a knowledge-driven and knowledge-dependent society' shaped by processes of globalisation. The failure to address gender in the conceptualisation of the White Paper on Higher Education leads to an assumption that globalisation, and the labour market itself, is not gendered. In fact, as feminist economists have shown, globalisation has exacerbated gender-based differentiations in the labour market, with international competitiveness in many Eastern countries being predicated on the hyper-exploitation of women and children (Bakker 1994). Samson argues that the exclusion of skills development strategies for the specifically female sectors of the economy (services, clothing and textiles, etc.) from the National Qualification Framework planning is 'not accidental, but central to [its[internal logic because these sectors will be the shock absorbers rather than the engines of South Africa's pursuit of international competitiveness' (Samson 1997: 148). Similarly, the Gender Equity Task Team (GETT) has called for a consideration of the gendered nature of development strategies, and their implications for educational policy (GETT 1997: 137).

Apart from these economic issues, the White Paper's aim that higher education should promote 'the socialisation of enlightened, responsible and constructively critical citizens' bears some consideration. As the discussion above shows, this task is by no means gender-neutral, and the absence of any detail on how diverse interests and cultural locations will be accommodated in the process makes us question whether the construct 'citizen' is adequately understood.

A second area of overlapping concerns between debates on citizenship and in educational policy is the extent to which nation-building as a political and educational project enables women's autonomy. In South Africa, strong arguments have been made for the education sector to act as a central medium for developing a sense of an overarching South African identity. This argument is a response to the 'systematic fragmentation pursued by the apartheid state', and posits that the idea of nation is a powerful unifying symbol that will promote reconciliation (Enslin 1993/4). Embedded in the dominant, progressive conception of nationalism in South Africa is a commitment to the principles of non-racism and non-sexism – indeed, these are the cornerstones of the Constitution. Progressive nationalism is a conception that has held together strong political organisations such as the ANC, provided the basis for a range of mass political struggles, and has constituted the moral glue of the opposition to apartheid.

However, as many scholars of nationalism have argued, it is by no means a benign concept. In South Africa, various critics have pointed to the tension between nationalism and women's interests (Walker 1990, Hassim 1991, Horn 1991, Enslin 1993/4). In brief, the argument made in general is that the articulation and practice of nationalism is profoundly male-centred, and based on a social and political separation between the public and private spheres of society. While in its progressive variant it explicitly includes women, inclusion primarily finds political expression in terms of women's roles as wives and mothers. Nationalism in South Africa, as elsewhere, has found it difficult to accommodate those demands of women which challenge the fundamental basis of gender inequalities.

The call for education to play a role in nation building therefore has to be carefully examined in terms of the likely impact for women. Some educational analysts, such as Enslin, have argued that nation building is not necessarily an 'appropriate goal of political and especially educational reconstruction in South Africa' (Enslin 1993/4: 14). She asks:

> Why do politics and education have to be constrained by the urge to found them on the assumed need for a common identity, defined as membership of the group, in this case the South African nation? If it is democracy we seek, why not propose that education should set out to persuade future citizens to embrace the central principles of democracy: freedom, equality, tolerance, and constitutionalism? (1993/4: 23)

Of course, while Enslin is correct in pointing out the dangers of making nation-building a core value in education, nation-building is more often animated by the need to create the conditions for social and political stability, rather than to promote democracy in the abstract. From this perspective, the problem remains somewhat intractable, as neither Mouffe-ian radical pluralism (which Enslin supports as an alternative) nor postmodern deconstructionism offer an actionable political praxis in the South African context.[2]

Identities, interests, and higher education

There are a number of parallels that can be drawn from a consideration of identities and interests writ large in society, and the microcosm of higher education. There are two aspects to the discussion. Firstly, we consider the implications of viewing the categories 'women', 'identities', and 'interests' as heterogeneous and multiple for the higher education sector. Associated with this discussion, we consider the linkages between education and citizenship from a gender perspective. Secondly, drawing on the discussion of the WNC, we consider whether it is possible to hold a balance within the institutions of higher learning between the diverse and gendered constituencies on campuses.

How can effective 'co-operative governance' take account of a variety of gender interests? The existing state of debate in higher education is highly inadequate from a feminist perspective. The conceptualisation of transformation addresses gender issues only peripherally. Thus far, the process has focused on shifts in both curriculum as well as in institutional structures of governance. A central concern has been the extent to which the tertiary sector has responded to concerns about racial representation, and to the demands for transformation in the direction of a democratic system of governance. In policy terms, this has led to a concentration on the issue of the racial structuring of higher education and, despite the creation of a Gender Equity Task Team, has hardly considered the gendered dimensions of higher education (Samson 1997: 146).

The prioritisation of racial exclusion as the dominant interest has led to a narrow perspective on equality in education as being defined by improving access to and redistributing resources within the education sector to redress racially based imbalances. As the report of the Gender Equity Task Team (1997: 25) points out, the most important political intervention in education was the National Education Policy Initiative (NEPI) which showed a remarkable failure to address seriously issues related to sexism. The problems of girls and women were absorbed into the bigger problem of equity in education (Truscott 1994). In 1994 the ANC's Education and Training Policy identified women as part of the most neglected and marginalised group. This policy also came under fire for not being more overtly gender sensitive (Wolpe 1994). Since 1994, the Department of Education has appointed a number of Task Teams of which the Gender Equity Task Team was the most significant for dealing with gender related inequality.

Women's representation in education

Women are a significant constituency in the higher education sector. Studies by Badsha and Kotecha (1994) and by the Foundation for Research Development (FRD)[3] have found that the proportion of women enrolled at tertiary institutions is relatively high, compared with female participation rates in other countries. In this respect, South Africa is exceptional in terms of developing countries in that girls are enrolled in relatively equal numbers from school through to undergraduate level in universities. This is confirmed by the most recent statistics for student enrolment at tertiary level in the table below.

Badsha and Kotecha's study of 1990 figures[4] found that women comprised 47% of students enrolled in universities. When these figures were disaggregated by race, however, 49,7% were white, 37,7% African, 5,9% coloured and 6,7% Indian (Badsha and Kotecha 1994: 47). African women are thus under-represented in tertiary education compared with their demographic density. Furthermore, women's distribution within the university follows the usual sex stereotyping of 'appropriate' professions.[5] Typically, Badsha and Kotecha found that women are concentrated in large numbers in the arts and caring professions (social sciences, languages and literature, education, business and public education). Similar trends are evident in 1997 statistics.[6]

ENROLMENT OF FEMALE STUDENTS IN TERTIARY EDUCATION: 1997

Institution	Technikons		Historically black universities		Historically white universities		UNISA		All Post-Secondary	
	% Female	Total	% Female	Total	% Female	Total	% Female	Total	% Female	Total
Whites	37	49 628	47	546	48	82 566	51	48 289	46	181 029
Coloureds	35	13 283	51	5 454	52	7 124	52	4 973	45	30 834
Indians	37	9 159	54	4 500	52	10 501	56	12 215	50	36 375
Blacks	45	121 209	58	87 639	53	41 890	59	60 867	53	311 605
TOTAL	42	193 700	58	100 004	50	141 984	56	126 344	50	562 032

Compiled from figures supplied by the Department of Education, January 1998.

Table 1

The National Commission on Higher Education Discussion Document (1996: 16) also points out that gender inequalities in higher education staff are most apparent when we look at the distribution of permanent research and teaching staff. In 1993, 68% of permanent research and teaching staff employed were men and 32% women. Women were also clearly absent from senior levels.

The prioritisation of racial exclusion as the dominant interest has led to a narrow perspective on equality in education as being defined by improving access to and redistributing resources within the education sector to redress racially based imbalances. As Samson (1997) has shown, gender is not integrated into policy documents; there is no consideration of the impact of multiple overlapping inclusions or exclusions when internal differences within race, class, and gender categories are taken together. As a result, women's interests and needs have been only tangentially incorporated into education policy documents and planning processes. However, focusing on numbers does not in any case address the underlying relations of power in society and within educational institutions which reproduce gendered patterns of inequality. Indeed, in terms of access, as the table above shows, women have not been seriously disadvantaged over men. Women's lack of educational opportunities in South Africa have been primarily shaped by the racial policies of apartheid and by class position, rather than by patriarchal bias.

women's interests and needs have been only tangentially incorporated into education policy documents and planning processes

However, while women may have relatively equal access to education, they lack access to employment and economic opportunities, and to positions of social and political power. It is this inequality in the distribution of power in society which constrains the achievement of equality. To address this would entail an examination of the relationship between the public world of paid work and formal political participation, and the private world of social stereotyping and unequal responsibility, and the institutions which structure and legitimise these relationships. As the Gender Equity Task Team points out, this relationship remains unexamined in South African educational policies (GETT 1998). The implication of this silence is that calls to locate greater control over education in communities do not problematise the unequal gender power relations within those communities, and within households, which constrain women's full participation in governance arrangements. As McLennan (1993/4: 66) argues, '[a] focus on gender relations therefore reveals that equal education cannot simply be seen in terms of distributive criteria such as access, provision and even opportunity, as schools and education are connected to the institutions, social relations and understandings which constitute our social roles.'

While statistics appear to reveal a promising picture of the position of women in higher education, they also obscure the difficulties experienced by women once they are within institutions. Research commissioned by the Centre for Higher Education Transformation in 1997 shows that women students as well as faculty experience high levels of dissatisfaction with conditions within the tertiary education sector.[7] Women are not present in proportionate numbers in leadership positions within student bodies, staff associations, or the governance structures of institutions. High levels of sexual harassment continue to exist despite the formal adoption of sexual harassment policies at several institutions. Comparative research relates high levels of sexual harassment to the prevalence of a sexist culture more generally, reflecting the differential distribution of power and status between men and women.[8] It is evident from a range of workshops involving university-based women's groups that women continue to experience discrimination at various levels within institutions, including assumptions about their levels of competence, resistance to the appointment of women to senior positions, and difficulties in accessing institutional resources for gender programmes (ACE/CHET 1997).

There have been some concerted attempts to address gender inequities faced by women. At several institutions, women have formed gender units or gender forums with the explicit intention of addressing curriculum transformation as well as problems of sexism (CHET 1997). The effectiveness of these structures has been seriously hampered by the absence of mechanisms for co-ordinated strategies across campuses. There is no association of women faculty that includes the majority of women across institutions. The Forum of African Women Educationalists (FAWE) has recently launched a South African chapter, although its membership and focus is limited to women at senior management level. The lack of an organised forum for women in higher education has impacted on women's ability to lobby for effective policies and legislation to address their specific needs. In addition, it has led to the ineffective replication of programmes, including their teething problems, across campuses

Implications of the citizenship debates

The White Paper of Higher Education's Programme for Transformation (Education White Paper 3 1997: 1.13) calls for increased and broadened participation which includes access for blacks, women, disabled and mature students, the generation of new curricula, and flexible models of learning and teaching. Greater responsiveness to societal interests and needs is also required. With regard to citizenship, this document calls for co-operation and partnerships in governance which would include a reconceptualisation of the relationship between higher education, the state, civil society and stakeholders. It argues that an enabling institutional environment and culture that is sensitive toward diversity needs to be created, in which the dignity of the individual would be protected. To give content to these requirements, a feminist analysis of what is wrong with the education system from a gender perspective is needed.

Truscott (1994: 11) argues that the most serious way in which the lack of a feminist analysis has weakened the education debate has been through the way in which the political economy has been conceptualised in a sex-blind way. In employing the sex-blind categories of workers, students, youth, and teachers, the working assumption is that men and women's experiences are the same. This assumption is evidently flawed. Some of the key areas of gender differentiation have been identified by Truscott (1994: 35) as the following:

- school organisation and curriculum structure tend to reflect the sexual division of labour and this differentiation is reflected in subject choice for boys and girls;
- science and technology are perceived by girls and boys as mainly a male terrain;
- patterns in teacher-pupil interaction are gender biased with teachers using sex-stereotyping and giving more

attention in class to boys than girls;

- school textbooks and other teaching materials are biased in terms of sex, race, and class; and
- the teaching hierarchy is male dominated with men concentrated in the top positions.

The challenge is therefore to conceptualise and devise programmes around transformation in ways that recognise gender as a difference as well as differences among women. There are two important levels at which change can be located: curriculum transformation and institutional transformation.

Curriculum transformation

One of the most difficult tasks facing feminists in the tertiary sector is to consider the ways in which it is possible to take account of multiple identities and interests in the structuring of curricula. In many disciplines in the social sciences, the minimal liberal feminist agenda of inclusion has been successful in ensuring that at least some consideration is given to issues such as the gendered dimensions of work, the influence of women writers, and to feminism in general. In some institutions women's studies courses have been introduced with varying degrees of success. In all cases, the paltry levels of funding and human resources have been a problem. In most cases, this has impacted on curriculum as it is easier with scarce resources to 'add-on' women to courses than it is to fundamentally re-think curricula from the standpoints of multiple groupings.[9] It seems also to be easier for developers to draw on Western constructed models rather than to include indigenous knowledge in the curricula.

In a consideration of the National Qualifications Framework from a gender perspective, Unterhalter shows the implications of the different feminist approaches discussed in the first part of this paper for curricular reform. She argues that the dominant liberal feminist approach has focused on 'how to turn absences into presences', i.e. how to include girls in areas from which they have been conventionally excluded. The underlying social and economic relations which shape access are left unexamined, and at best limited reforms are possible. On the other hand, curricular reform based on feminist standpoint theory (and maternalist thinking) is equally problematic in its essentialist assumption of a particular way of thinking common to all women. This has led to the development of pedagogies and curricular frameworks that are assumed to be universally applicable to women. The ability of this framework to deal with diversity among women is limited. However, she notes, this approach at least had the advantage of a 'perception of struggle, of a notion of what knowledge is for and what it is against' (Unterhalter 1997: 135). An alternative approach, rooted in the postcolonial work described above, links knowledge with power and 'draws attention to multiple readings of (learning) materials and complex ways in which position and processes of identification intersect with the process of giving voice' (Unterhalter 1997: 135.

Unterhalter's study concludes that 'as there is no single meaning for gender, there is no simple set of strategies for building gender equity' (Unterhalter 1997: 136). She argues for the need rather for a guiding gender policy that will consider both a range of meanings of gender, as well as a range of gender equity strategies. As Truscott (1994: 52) argues, designing a new curriculum according to the principles of non-racialism, non-sexism, equality, democracy, and redress, demands a profound reorganisation of the way the curriculum is designed.[10] It is not enough to merely have statements of non-sexism in the curriculum. Furthermore, more women should be involved in curriculum planning and development. Gender cannot only be added on but has to be an integrated part of the curriculum.

Institutional transformation

The macro demands of feminists for a redefinition of the boundaries of politics have similar micro-level implications within institutions. Campuses too operate as though there is a public space – Council, Senate, the lecture theatre, the mass meeting – in which participants are non-gendered (although not non-raced), and participants and relationships between constituents are governed by the principles of 'excellence' and democracy, and a 'private' space – residences, the alleyways between classrooms, women's groups – where relationships are structured by culture and 'traditions'. And yet, as feminist have made so clear, the boundaries between the public and private are fluid and the nature of the relationship between the two is at the heart of how societies – and their institutions – are constituted. Alexander and Mohanty (1997: xxviii) go even further to argue that 'sexual politics are central to the processes and practices of governance' – in other words, that the politics of excluding, of drawing away from public view is in itself a mechanism for establishing order.

women are often in the ironic position of being both 'invisible' and 'hypervisible' at the same time

Within institutions, women are often in the ironic position of being both 'invisible' and 'hypervisible' at the same time. Women, and women's concerns, are outside the core public agenda of Council and Senate decision-making, of student and union leadership, and women themselves are represented in extremely small numbers in these structures. Yet, the 'private' world of sexuality is brought into the glare of campus politics when rape is widespread; visibility is unwelcome. What counts for 'appropriate' representative structures and consultative forums rarely addresses the 'softer', 'private' areas of institutional concerns (except in an ad hoc way). The culture of gendered violence, the constraining forces of women's dual social responsibilities, the impact of assumptions of gender roles in society on women's equal participation are all treated as peripheral to the business of education management and delivery. As in the citizenship debates, these are seen as the 'third generation' of concerns and rights. And yet, as study after study shows, it is these factors which most directly impinge on women benefiting equally from education.[11]

Inequality of opportunity in education caused by gender-based violence was also one of the most important findings of the Gender Equity Task Team. The GETT Report (1997: 218) reflects that violence is not endemic to educational sites but reflects the gendered nature of violence that is so pervasive of many South African settings. Gendered and sex-based violence constrains the freedom of movement, choices, and activities of its victims, and contributes to poor levels of participation by women, forced isolation, low self-esteem, self-confidence, and drop out from education, as well as physical, sexual, and psychological damage. Appropriate measures need to be taken to prevent violence. The GETT recommended legislation that will include the concept of vicarious liability. This would mean that people with delegated responsibility may be liable for contraventions of legislation by their workers in the course of their work. Those with delegated responsibilities should take all reasonable steps to prevent harassment from occurring. It becomes the responsibility of all educational managers to ensure an environment free from harassment and violence.

Apart from the longer-term creation of a democratic institutional culture, it is also imperative that various constituencies in higher education develop stronger organisational forms which are granted formal recognition by educational managers. Social capital theorists are increasingly gaining purchase in their argument that effective public policy and healthy citizenship is grounded in the extent to which vibrant representative associations and networks are allowed to flourish. Excluding women's structures and networks from the mechanisms of institutional governance is similar to the exclusion of much of women's activities from conventional definitions of citizenship and its impact is the same: an impartial and excluding transformation process, and a potentially destabilised institution.

Although there is a growing recognition of the importance of gender issues on campuses (largely due to the crises associated with sexual harassment and violence against women), there is still an assumption that 'women's issues' can be lumped together. A less than cursory glance at tertiary institutions reveals a highly disaggregated female population: faculty (senior and junior), students, workers, administrators. Diversity within institutions is rarely taken to mean that women themselves are divided by a range of forces (not least their position within the institution itself) which may make it less than appropriate for women faculty to represent the issues of women students (or vice versa).

Nevertheless, representation is important. Ultimately, effective participation in both macro-level national politics as well as micro-level institutional politics is the true test of citizenship. This entails that women have to seek and occupy positions of power in institutions if they are to initiate and carry through changes. Studies of women in welfare states have shown that 'the more women there are in positions of power or close to positions of power, and the more women there are engaging the political system the

women have to seek and occupy positions of power in institutions

103

more likely it is that women's different interests will be articulated and acted upon' (Lister 1995: 12). Lister argues for a two-fold approach to politics that can be applied to institutions, i.e. a politics which validates at the same time informal kinds of political activity such as women's networks on campuses, as well as addresses processes which exclude women from effective participation in formal structures. This, she suggests, 'opens the potential for a more permeable form of politics' open both to individual women and to the influence of multiple women's networks (Lister 1995: 17).

NOTES

1 Interestingly, Kenway quotes Bob Connell as arguing that educational policies should be driven by an ethic of caring: 'an ethic of mutual care, not the search for competitive advantage, is central to policy making' (Kenway 1997: 54).

2 This is admittedly a sweeping statement to make without substantial discussion. However, we would argue that the emergence of a large plurality of political parties representing different interests is unlikely to happen in the foreseeable future.

3 South African Science and Technology Indicators 1996

4 More recent statistics are currently unavailable. However, the Women-In-Research Programme of the Centre for Science Development (CSD) has conducted a comprehensive survey of faculty in the humanities in all universities, and their findings will be available in 1998. Nasima Badsha and Piyushi Kotecha (1994).

5 See also Truscott 1994: 19–20.

6 Van Vuuren, A (1997).

7 Sacco, E (1996); Motshabi, EVN (1989).

8 Naidoo, R and D Rajab (1992).

9 A interesting discussion of the attempt to integrate feminist approaches into Social Work courses at the University of the Western Cape can be found in Bozalek and Sunde, 1993/4.

10 Curriculum 2005 is a far reaching reorganisation based on outcomes-based learning but is still quite gender blind.

11 An example of this is the inability of current mechanisms of evaluation of performance for

promotion purposes to take account of the effect on women's research output of periods of maternity leave.

REFERENCES

ACE/CHET (1997) 'Proposal on activities to support the development of women in higher education'. Internal document.

Alexander, MJ and CT Mohanty (eds) (1997) *Feminist Genealogies, Colonial Legacies, Democratic Futures.* London: Routledge.

Ang I (1995) 'I am a feminist but ...'Other' women and postnational feminism'. In B Caine and R Pringle, *Transitions – New Australian Feminisms.* Sydney: Allen and Unwin.

Badsha, N and P Kotecha (1994) 'University access: the gender factor'. *Agenda,* 21.

Bakker, Isabella (1994) *The Strategic Silence: Gender and Economic Policy.* London: Zed Books.

Bozalek, Vivienne and Jackie Sunde (1993/4) 'Shaking off the textbook paradigm – the value of feminist approaches in the research'. *Curriculum Perspectives in Education,* Vol. 15, No 1.

Braidotti R (1997) 'Comment on Felski's The Doxa of Difference: Working through sexual difference signs'. *Journal of Women in Culture and Society,* Vol. 23: 1.

Cock, Jacklyn (1997) 'Women in South Africa's transition to democracy'. In J. Scott, C. Kaplan and D. Keates (eds) *Transitions, Environments, Translations: Feminisms in International Politics.* New York: Routledge.

Collins, Patricia Hill (1990). *Black Feminist Thought: Knowledge, Consciousness and the Politics of Empowerment.* London: Routledge.

Dietz M (1987) 'Context is all: feminism and theories of citizenship', *Daedalus,* 116: 4.

Enslin, Penny (1993/4) 'Education for nation-building: a feminist critique', *Perspectives in Education,* Vol 15, No 1.

Felski R (1997) 'The doxa of difference signs', *Journal of Women in Culture and Society,* Vol. 23: 1.

Gender Equity Task Team (1997) *Gender Equity in Education. Report to the Department of Education.*

Grewal, I and C Kaplan (1994) *Scattered Hegemonies: Postmodernity and Transnational Feminist Practices.* Minneapolis: University of Minnesota Press.

Hassim, S & A Gouws (1997) 'Mediating women's interests: gender, law and state in South Africa'. Unpublished paper.

Hassim, Shireen (1991) 'Gender, social location and feminist politics in South Africa', *Transformation,* 15.

Hooks, Bell (1989) *Talking Back: Thinking Feminist, Thinking Black.* Boston: South End Press.

Horn, Patrica (1991) 'Post-apartheid South Africa: what about women's emancipation?' *Transformation,* 15.

105

Kenway, Jane. (1997) 'Change of address? Educating economics in vocational education and training'. In CEPD, *Reconstruction, Development and the National Qualifications Framework*.

Kymlicka W and W Norman (1994) 'Return of the citizen: a survey of recent work on citizenship theory', *Ethics*, 104, January.

Lister R (1995) 'Dilemmas in engendering citizenship', *Economy and Society*, Vol. 24: 1.

McLennan, Anne (1993/4) ' "And women, too, will play their part": the relevance of gender to equal education', *Perspectives in Education*, Vol. 15, No 1.

Meintjes, S (1996) 'The women's struggle for equality during South Africa's transition to democracy', *Transformation*, 30.

Motshabi, EVN (1989) 'The status and education of women', *Popagano*, June.

Mouffe C (1992) *Dimensions of Radical Democracy*. London: Verso.

Naidoo, R and D Rajab (1992) *A Survey of Sexual Harassment and Related Issues among Students at the University of Natal*. UND Student Counselling Centre.

National Council for Higher Education (NCHE) (1996) *Discussion Document: A Framework for Transformation*.

Phillips, Anne (1993) *Democracy and Difference*. Cambridge: Polity Press.

Sacco, Elaine (1997) *Study On Initiatives For Women In Higher Education*. CHET report.

Samson, Melanie (1997) 'Gender redress and the NQF: the terrain for feminist policy development'. In CEPD, *Reconstruction, Development and the National Qualifications Framework*.

Soper, Kate (1994) 'Feminism, humanism and postmodernism'. In M Evans (ed.) *The Woman Question*. London: Sage.

Truscott, Kate (1994) 'Gender in education'. Unpublished paper. Education Policy Unit: University of the Witwatersrand/NECC.

Unterhalter, Elaine (1997) 'Gendered spheres of education and training: a feminist perspective on one year of the NQF'. In CEPD, *Reconstruction, Development and the National Qualifications Framework*.

Van Vuuren, A (1997) 'A statistical overview of the position of women in science, engineering and technology'. *Scientech*.

Walker, Cherryl (1990) 'Book review: Women-Nation-State', *Agenda*, 13.

Wolpe, Ann Marie (1994) 'A framework for gender sensitivity', *Agenda*, 21.

Yuval-Davis, N (1977) *Gender and Nation*. London: Sage.

Section III

Contextual issues

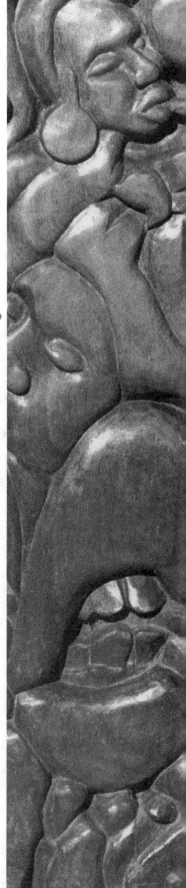

From exclusion toward inclusion: the struggle for diversity in American higher education

Richard H Brown

Department of Sociology, University of Maryland

William E Kirwan

President, University of Maryland

The struggle to overcome educational exclusion

A central theme in the history of the United States has been the expansion of citizenship and the extension of rights of participation to all members of American society. This theme has unfolded in a number of stages and illustrates the dynamic interdependency between civic inclusion on the one hand and the American political economy and access to higher education on the other hand. As a background to our current challenges, we can distinguish several major historical periods in terms of shifts in American political economy, higher education, and civic inclusion.

The first of these stages is the Federal period, from the time of the Revolution to about 1825. During this period a new nation was formed – democratic in principle but led by a small, propertied, male elite of northern European heritage. The franchise included only such persons, thereby excluding women, the poor and, of course, Native Americans and persons of African descent. The early Federal leaders, however, did set limits on the expansion of slavery in the North and West (for example, the Northeast Ordinance of 1787) and this enabled havens to be created by former slaves in which they established their own fraternities, mutual aid societies, and churches that became refuges for run-away slaves and resources for resistance.

The Revolutionary 'Spirit of '76' was reflected in and reproduced through the colleges of the period, which propagated Enlightenment values. Like the government itself, however, these schools were exclusively for prosperous white males. Less than two per cent of the population was able to go to college, although this included about half of the signers of the Declaration of Independence who were college graduates. The aim of a college education was to prepare sons of the leadership class for roles in the ministry, law, medicine, and public life. In terms of diversity, higher education in this period could be described as an exclusive club of wealthy white males largely of Anglo-Saxon Protestant descent.

A second period in the realisation of American pluralistic democracy is that between the Jacksonian Revolution and the Civil War, from about 1825 to 1865. Alexis de Tocqueville described the United States at the dawn of this period with a certain awe at the energy of its democratic culture and of its entrepreneurial farmers and middle class. He also noted that the institution of slavery, and the prospect of large scale industrial enterprises, were threats to democratic participation. The American frontier had crossed the Appalachian Mountains, opening up a vast terrain for colonisation by free-holding farmers who, in 1828, voted for the first populist (and non-patrician) American president, Andrew Jackson. This period also saw some growth in the popular, basic education – 'the little red schoolhouse on the prairie' – but it had little impact on higher education, which was still reserved for well-born white Protestant males mainly of the Eastern seaboard. Though democratic franchise expanded, for many higher education remained an almost exclusive club. There were, however, the first signs of a crack in the armor of exclusivity. In 1824, Dartmouth College opened admission to blacks. And Oberlin College, a private college founded in 1833 in Ohio, admitted blacks and women from its inception, despite the fact that at the time blacks were excluded from public education at all levels in Ohio. Wesleyan College in Georgia followed soon after in 1836, establishing the first degree-granting college for women with Mount Holyoke opening its doors in 1837, thus paving the way for the eventual development of the

109

prestigious seven sisters colleges in the Northeast. This period also saw the establishment of the first two predominantly black higher education institutions, Ashmun Institute (1854), which later became Lincoln University, in Philadelphia, Pennsylvania and Wilberforce University (1856) in Wilberforce, Ohio.

A third period of American history, and of the increased inclusiveness of democracy, runs from the Civil War through World War II. The Civil War began when eight, and then fifteen, southern states withdrew from the Union to defend the privileges of slavery. The Union victory and the defeat of the South had many consequences.

Although slavery had been abolished throughout northern states since shortly after the Revolutionary War at the end of the eighteenth century, slavery was formally abolished throughout the United States with the Emancipation Proclamation of 1863 and by the Civil War Amendments to the Constitution. With these new laws, people of African descent were declared citizens. The Supreme Court judged that the Civil Rights Acts of 1866 and 1870 were proper legislative actions in pursuit of the elimination of the 'badges and incidents of slavery'. These gains were rolled back within a generation, however, through an alliance between southern former slave-owning elites and northern capitalists eager to invest in the postbellum South (Lubbell 1964). By 1883, a the Supreme Court had severely restricted the applicable scope of the earlier anti-slavery laws.

The second consequence of the Civil War was the fact that the United States acquired a centralised governmental apparatus – a greatly expanded federal bureaucracy with the right and capacity to intervene much more deeply in the affairs of particular states. Third, the American Industrial Revolution, stimulated by the Civil War, created a new class of northern industrialists which largely controlled the new federal establishment. Moreover, with the growth of industry two other classes also expanded – the urban middle class and the industrial proletariat.

Industrialisation also brought great waves of immigrants from Ireland and southern and eastern Europe to provide labor for the factories of the North. The new immigrants – non-Protestants – were considered by many nativists to be non-white and were perceived as a threat to the earlier arrived north European Protestant groups. Asians also came during this period to drain swamps, build railroads, and work mines in the West. Indeed, in 1900 over half of the total population of the United States was either foreign born or children of foreign born.

The response of nativist groups was Protestant revivalism, on the one hand, and repressive assimilation on the other. These dual reform movements, often led by women but often financed by industrial magnates, included the anti-alcohol movement, the suffragette movement, the social welfare movement, and the good government movement. These movements were aimed in part at 'improving' society by controlling the new immigrants. For example, the temperance and prohibition movement was directed to some extent against supposedly hard-drinking Catholics; the movement for the women's vote was justified in part as a way of expanding the white Protestant voting bloc; and the good government movement was a way to limit the power of new urban ethnic and laborite political machines.

The consequences for education of these developments were twofold. First, there was a massive expansion of primary and then secondary public education that was both free and mandatory, although largely segregated. The schools were set up much on the model of factories – to mass produce large batches of similar persons, thereby turning children of immigrant peasants into functioning Americans ready for factory work, urban life, and democratic participation. Second, there was a transformation of American higher education with the establishment of universities dedicated to research and to the advanced training of professionals (other than the ministers, doctors, and lawyers produced by the earlier colleges). First came the so-called Land-Grant universities, one in each state, established in 1862 by the First Morrill Act of Congress. The mission of these colleges and universities was to provide training in agriculture and the mechanical arts to the sons and daughters of (white) middle and working class families, although the University of Iowa in 1855 set the pattern for co-education which others eventually followed after considerable pressure from women's groups. Many of the institutions founded by the Morrill Act have evolved into what today are some of the nation's largest and leading public research universities.

Another kind of university was established during this era, private research universities, modelled on the great centres of learning and scholarship in Europe. Johns Hopkins University, founded in 1876 in Baltimore, was the first of these. Its creation led to an expanded mission for many traditional colleges, such as Harvard (1636), Yale (1701), and Princeton (1746), and the establishment of several of what are today the nation's elite private research universities, including Stanford University in 1885 and the University of Chicago in 1891.

It was also during the period following the Civil War that predominantly black colleges began to spring up, largely in response to the segregation practised by the existing colleges and universities. Howard University (1866) established in Washington DC, Augusta Institute (1867; later renamed Morehouse College) in Augusta, Georgia, Hampton Institute (1868) in Hampton, Virginia, Clark College (1869) in Atlanta, Georgia, Centenary Biblical Institute (1869; later named Morgan State University) in Baltimore, Maryland, Alcorn State University (1871) in Alcorn Mississippi, and Straight University (1874; later named Dillard University) in New Orleans, Louisiana, are just a few examples of predominantly black colleges established in this era that continue to thrive to this day. Educational opportunities for blacks in the South were given a great boost when the Morrill Land Grant act was extended in 1892 to provide for a land grant institution to serve blacks in those states that operated segregated schools. This act led to the creation of many universities that continue to serve primarily blacks today, universities such as North Carolina A&T, Florida A&M, Jackson State (in Mississippi), South Carolina State University, and Maryland State University (now the University of Maryland, Eastern Shore).

In sum, this period saw a great pluralisation of education – with the inclusion of vast numbers of Catholic, Jewish, Eastern Orthodox, and other non-Protestant minorities and increased opportunities for blacks, though mostly at predominantly black institutions. The 'exclusive club' did begin to accept token minority members, however.

WEB DuBois, for example, learned Shakespeare in a Massachusetts schoolroom in which whites and blacks sat together. 'I sit with Shakespeare,' he wrote (1986: 438), 'and he winces not for having a Negro at his side.' DuBois went on to receive a PhD from Harvard University in 1895, the first black to get a PhD from that institution. Similarly, the great American actor Paul Robeson graduated from Rutgers University in New Jersey in 1919.

A fourth, and present, period began some 50 years ago, for it was only after World War II that American education began its journey toward a truly diverse student body, faculty and staff. World War II, fought in the name of democracy, also renewed the spirit of democracy at home. Moreover, by the end of the war, the United States had become the major global power with a mature, international industrial economy which, during the two postwar decades, accounted for nearly half of world trade. In 1950, for the first time, over 50 per cent of the American labor force worked in the service sector, more than in farming and manufacturing combined. Though most of this service sector was composed of sales clerks, typists, truck drivers and the like, much of it also was made up of technicians, managers, researchers, and others needing more advanced and specialised skills. Moreover, the old WASP ascendency (as Joseph Alsop called it, 1989) was not producing nearly enough men to fill all the new upper service sector positions. Added to this was the increased public demand for higher education, which was fast becoming a requirement of middle-class status, the growth of the welfare state with its increasing dependence on social science policy knowledge, and the Cold War military-industrial complex with its requirements of disciplinary knowledge from linguistics and anthropology to physics and computer science.

higher education was fast becoming a requirement of middle-class status

American colleges and universities expanded enormously in the post-War period in order to prepare workers for the post-industrial, Cold War, welfare political economy, and also in response to later status demands of minorities and women. In 1940 there were 1 700 institutions of higher education enrolling 1,5 million students and employing 147 929 faculty members in all ranks, including non-tenure track appointments. In 1994 there were 3 600 such institutions, 14,7 million students, and over 750 000

113

faculty members (Altbach 1995). The student population increased tenfold, and the numbers of institutions of advanced education and their faculties doubled.

During this same post-War period, largely through the GI Bill guaranteeing veterans admission and tuition support, the universities opened their doors to Jewish students and faculty, who before were largely excluded. Plant expansion and faculty shortage were important in this, but the fact that America's national enemy had been Jew-killing Nazis certainly played a role in the reduction of anti-Semitism. Perhaps most importantly for democratic pluralism, the GI Bill was instrumental in altering social class composition of the universities to include people from working class backgrounds. Indeed, the experience of such newly admitted working-class persons is eerily similar to that reported by minority students and professors today (Dews and Law 1995, Cuddihy 1987). In entering the mainstream of American life and gaining greater financial security and personal autonomy, they also knew that they had 'lost' certain connections – to their families or origin, to their bodies and physical labour, to spontaneity. Many talk about acting as 'double agents' who travel between the very different world of their families and that of middle-class academics. They write of their guilt about having 'made it'. They complain of the invisibility of working-class people in academe and the assumption on the part of faculty, even those originally from working-class families, that everyone is middle class. They describe the silence and sense of inferiority that come with this invisibility, and the triumph of finally speaking out and feeling pride in their class backgrounds (Gamson and Rice 1995: 744).

In addition to these great changes, there was also a massive migration of southern, mostly black farm workers to the northern cities. This was spurred earlier by the 'push' provided by the mechanisation of southern agriculture under President Roosevelt's New Deal policies of easy farm credit (but not for black farmers), and the 'pull' of work in northern war-time factories. Many African Americans also returned from the War having served with credit – in segregated units – in the victorious United States armed forces.

These events led to a greater political consciousness and

mobilisation of African Americans, which supported and was spurred by political and legal victories such as the Supreme Court's *Brown v. Board of Education* decision in 1954 that mandated the desegregation of schools, the civil rights movement, and the Civil Rights Act of Congress of 1964. Parallel to this, the magnates of a now advanced industrial economy needed social and labor stability and *not* the kind of racial and ethnic conflict that could help weaken unions and depress wages. Hence corporate financial backing was a major source of funds for moderate civil rights groups.

It was during this period that the concept of affirmative action emerged, first with regard to employment practices and then as a means of increasing the participation rates of blacks in majority colleges and universities. Shortly after his election in 1960, President Kennedy established the President's Commission on Equal Employment Opportunity (PCEEO) with the then Vice President, Lyndon Johnson, as its chair. The Commission documented shocking disparity in the employment of blacks in federal and federally supported white collar, skilled and trade positions. For example, in 1961 the Commission reported that 72 per cent of the black federal employees were employed in the lowest level government positions and only one per cent were employed in the top positions. The report

'affirmative' steps had to be taken to remedy past discrimination

concluded that 'affirmative' steps had to be taken to remedy past discrimination. A year after he signed the 1964 Civil Rights Bill, then President Johnson delivered a speech at Howard University in which he said, 'You do not wipe away the scars of centuries by saying: now you are free to do as you desire. You do not take a person who has for years been hobbled by chains and liberate him, bring him up to the starting line of a race and then say, "You're free to compete with all the others." On the contrary,' Johnson said, 'we need to make the playing field more level, we need not just freedom but opportunity ... not just equality as a right and theory but equality as a fact and as a result.'

It was President Richard Nixon, however, who in 1969 fully formulated the principles and practices of affirmative action in the workforce. This was done through the Philadelphia Plan, developed by the Secretary of Labor George Schultz and aimed at increasing the hiring of

115

minority workers in the construction industry. Under the Plan, companies doing federally sponsored construction work had to take *affirmative action*, that is, they had to develop specific hiring goals, with plans to achieve those goals, all aimed at increasing the number of black construction workers in trade and skilled positions.

In parallel with the use of affirmative action practices in employment, many traditionally white colleges and universities began to develop programmes and admissions policies aimed at increased participation of blacks, and eventually the admission of Latinos, Asians, and Native Americans as well. Large numbers of students from elite private and public universities in the North had served as foot soldiers in the civil rights movement, traveling to the South to stand side by side with blacks in demonstrations and acts of civil disobedience. When these students returned to their universities flush with the victory of the 1964 Civil Rights Act, they turned their activism on their own institutions, protesting the under-representation of blacks in all aspects of the collegiate life they experienced. Supported by progressive white students, black students took over the administration building at Cornell University in 1969, demanding greater numbers of black students and faculty. Similar demonstrations followed at other universities including Brandeis University, Ohio State University, the University of California at Berkeley. Affirmative action efforts were embraced by virtually every university in the land and the participation of blacks and other racial minorities in predominantly white institutions began to show a marked increase. In 1960, for example, there were 200 000 blacks enrolled in American higher education institutions, with 90 per cent of these students attending historically black institutions. By 1970, there were 470 000 blacks enrolled in colleges and universities, with over half attending predominantly white institutions.

Affirmative action efforts suffered a setback, however, in a 1978 landmark Supreme Court decision, *Regents of the University of California v. Bakke*. In this decision, the Court said that the University of California could not separate its pool of blacks applicants from the general pool of applicants, a means by which the university had ensured that blacks were admitted to the medical school. Ironically, the

Court based its decision in part on the 1964 Civil Rights Act which states, 'No person ... shall, on the ground of race, color or national origin be excluded from participation in, be denied the benefits of, or be subjected to discrimination under any program or activity receiving federal financial assistance.' Allan Bakke, a white applicant to the medical school who was denied admission, claimed that the separate pool for blacks had discriminated against him. The decision was not a complete loss for affirmation action, however. Justice Powell, writing the 5-4 majority opinion, acknowledged the value of diversity in an education setting and asserted the right of educational institutions to take the diversity of the overall student body into account in selecting its admitted pool of students from the general pool of qualified applicants. This so-called 'Bakke Principle' became the foundation upon which most higher education affirmative action programs have been built.

The Bakke Principle, however, is now under severe attack. In a recent decision, *Hopwood v. the University of Texas*, the Sixth Circuit Court of Appeals ruled that the University of Texas Law School could *not* use the diversity of its student body as a factor in determining admission. The university appealed this decision to the Supreme Court, which refused to hear the case. A similar suit has been filed against the University of Michigan for its use of diversity in making admissions decisions and the state of California recently passed a law denying the use of race as a factor in admissions decisions at state-supported institutions. The initial impact of these actions in Texas and California are alarming. For example, neither the University of Texas nor the University of California-Berkeley had any blacks in their first year law school classes.

A second principle upon which universities have based affirmative action programmes is the *elimination of continuing effects of past discrimination*. The argument buttressing this principle is that the effect of several centuries of pernicious discrimination and segregation cannot be eliminated in a few decades; the impact of the loss of educational and employment opportunities for generations cannot be undone in one generation. For many, the evidence for this view is overwhelming. One need only look at the plight of the residents of our inner cities, the vast majority

117

of whom are people of colour. For most of these citizens, the housing stock is poor, local schools are inadequate, and meaningful job opportunities are rare. In recent years, however, the courts have become increasingly less tolerant of affirmative action programmes based on eliminating the continuing effects of past discrimination.

A case involving the University of Maryland provides a good example of the courts' increasing rigidity. The state of Maryland, like the other states in the southeast quadrant of the United States, operated segregated school system until *Brown v. Board of Education.* Following *de jure* integration, most schools in the South, even colleges and universities, operated under *de facto* segregation. At the University of Maryland, for example, as recently as 1969, blacks represented less than 4 per cent of the student body, whereas blacks constituted more than 20 per cent of the total state population.

Alarmed by this phenomenon in Maryland and other southern states, the Office of Civil Rights placed these states under a mandate, which is in still in effect, to develop desegregation programs aimed at accelerating the pace of integration. Among the programs created at the University of Maryland was the Benjamin Banneker Scholarship, named for a talented African American mathematician who did much of the work laying out the shape and boundaries of Washington DC. The Banneker Scholarship was a merit-based scholarship for high achieving black students. The programme was established on the premise that if the best black students in a high school choose to come to the university, other qualified black students were more likely to join them. It was also felt that if high achieving black students populate the campus, they could help to break down unfortunate racial stereotypes.

The programme proved to be highly successful. African American participation rates at the university rose steadily. By 1992, blacks constituted about 15 per cent of the entering freshman class and 12 per cent of the total student body. This same year, however, a student, Daniel J Podberesky, filed suit claiming the Banneker programme discriminated against him since he was not allowed to compete for one of its scholarships. In a protracted court battle, finally settled when the Supreme Court refused to hear the University's appeal, the Fourth Circuit Court of Appeals ruled that the University had to abandon the race-exclusive nature of the scholarship. The University's case was based largely on eliminating the continuing effects of past discrimination. Its argument was buttressed by the fact that, even though the situation had improved since the inception of the scholarship, black participation at the university was still considerably below the representation of blacks among high school graduates. Moreover, the image of the university as a formerly segregated institution still had an impact on people who were most influential with prospective African-American students – high school guidance counsellors, parents, and grandparents. The impact of this decision has national significance. It suggests, in effect, that universities will no longer be able to base affirmative action programmes on the elimination of the continuing effects of past discrimination. This fact, coupled with the attack on the Bakke Principle, threatens to compromise significantly affirmative action efforts in higher education.

Thus, in the domain of pluralistic inclusion, the period from World War II to the present may be characterized by *compliance and affirmative action*. This model characterises most American institutions up to the present. Universities of this type are committed to remove the discrimination inherent in the earlier exclusionary club and, indeed, to actively recruit and encourage minority and women students and faculty where they are under-represented, although in recent years with increased opposition by the courts to race-based affirmative action programmes. Usually, however, compliance and affirmative action are undertaken in the spirit of assimilating the newcomers into the institution as it already is, with little re-examination of that university's existing character, culture, and distribution of power.

From affirmative action to excellence through diversity

One of a university's central purposes is to serve society and its students by preparing the latter for citizenship in an increasingly diverse national population and for the emerging intercultural and international world of work. In this regard, in America and in many other societies today, there are striking increases in the internationalisation of our economy, the global nature of many of our problems, and the more plural character of our labor force and citizenry.

119

Our economic position is challenged by many rivals and our military power and political wisdom are tested at this very moment in distant parts of the globe. At the same time, issues like imbalances of food and population, the environment, technology, and health, require cooperation across national boundaries in a diverse and multicultural world as never before. Is our nation preparing itself to face these challenges? Will we have adequate numbers of people with the skills and knowledge necessary to compete successfully in this emerging national and global environment? Can we make real the national motto, *e pluribus unum*, in a nation with a degree of diversity unimagined by the founding fathers and rapidly becoming more diverse?

Already more than one American in four defines himself or herself as Hispanic or non-white. Today, more than 80 per cent of the net new entrants into our labour force are women or minorities. Moreover, given differential rates of birth and immigration, the Hispanic and Asian populations are increasing ten times faster, and the African American population more than five times faster than that of whites. By 2020, the number of US residents who are Hispanic or non-white will have more than doubled, to nearly 115 million, while the white population will not be increasing at all. A recent study (reported in the October 15, 1996 issue of *USA Today*) estimates that between the years 1990 and 2050 the percentage of non-Hispanic whites living in the United States will decline from 76 per cent to 52 per cent. By 2056, when someone born today will be 58 years old, the 'average' US resident, as defined by Census statistics, will trace his or her ancestry to Africa, Asia, the Hispanic world, the Pacific Islands, the Islamic World – almost anywhere but Europe (Henry 1990: 28). In the years ahead, diversity in the American workplace will not be a goal, but a fact of life.

Our nation and its particular communities will be better served if we have women and minorities in a wider range of positions. Our cities would be better served had they more black police officers, not only on the streets but also in positions to bring their understanding of high crime communities to bear on policy decisions. Our foreign service would be enhanced if more of its officers had a bicultural awareness. By the year 2010, 50 per cent of all jobs will

diversity in the American workplace will be a fact of life

120

require a college education. In the coming decade and into the 21st century, we simply will not have enough technically trained and culturally adaptable people in our workforce to support a sophisticated internationally competitive economy, unless we dramatically increase the rates of participation of minorities and women in all fields and most especially where they have been traditionally excluded. The challenge faced by higher education is not just whether there will be sufficient numbers of minority students well-prepared for success in this new environment, however. The challenge is also whether students from all races and backgrounds will be prepared to work effectively in a decidedly more diverse workplace. In short, the moral imperative for diversity in higher education is now united with social and economic necessity in a nation that within a little more than one generation will be without a racial or ethnic majority.

Thus, the encouragement of cultural diversity and greater inclusiveness in higher education should be seen as enhancing the learning environment of the entire university community, and especially those students who have lived mainly within a single cultural orbit. We need to raise standards by subjecting everyone's provincialism to assessment from multiple perspectives. As Justice Powell wrote in the Bakke case, a university should be allowed to assemble a varied student body in order to create a more dynamic intellectual environment and a richer undergraduate experience. Quoting from an earlier ruling (*Keyishian v. Board of Regents*) Justice Powell also said, 'The nation's future depends upon leaders trained through wide exposure to that robust exchange of ideas which discovers truth "out of a multitude of tongues," [rather] than through any kind of authoritative selection.' In the same spirit, the President of Harvard University, Dr Neil Rudenstein (1996), insisted that '[we] need to insist upon the essential part that colleges and universities play in creating opportunities for students to live in association with peers who are, in many respects, different from themselves but who also have much in common. The process is not always smooth, but its complexity only highlights its importance.'

Such an environment of diversity can foster a plurality of perspectives and become a center of discourse and learning for talented people of all cultures, backgrounds, and generations, an environment where students come together, challenge each other's ideas, learn new perspectives, are enriched and grow as individuals and, ultimately, come to understand that our differences are our strength, that our deployment of diversity can be the essence of our excellence. As Eugene Hughes said,

> A culturally aware education is necessary for everyone who is going to participate intelligently and responsibly in the pluralistic society that surrounds us, rather than in a mythological and sheltered subculture not truly representative of our nation as a whole. With such participation comes the realisation that the university environment as it has traditionally been structured has not met the needs of either the minority population or the majority population that lives in a pluralistic society. (Hughes 1990: 25)

Indeed, such distinguished groups as the American Council on Education insist that 'an educational experience that does not reflect the pluralism of our country and the importance of minority individuals and cultures is simply deficient'.

Moreover, through study and comparison of other cultures and civilisations, students are better able, as Kjelberg writes (1996),

> to understand what is distinctive about the Western tradition. People trained only in that tradition, without any points of comparison, would perhaps think like Westerners. Ironically, with such training, they wouldn't know what that means. Our present position at the confluence of so many great traditions gives us an unprecedented opportunity to know who we are, as Westerners, as moderns, as human beings, and as unique individuals.

Hughes (1990: 24) makes the point even more sharply:

> For example, if professors elect to focus the coverage of American history on European-based cultures, they are not simply engaging academic freedom, they are failing their job responsibilities to teach an American history that goes beyond Anglo-American history. It is not the prerogative of a physics instructor to elect to exclude nonlinear physics from a curriculum that demands it. It is not the prerogative of a literature professor to exclude nonwhite literature in the teaching of American or world literature.

In sum, a university in pursuit of academic excellence will not succeed unless it draws upon the rich diversity of human experiences and expressions. The great river of knowledge loses its richness if diverse intellectual and cultural streams do not flow into it. An intellectually vibrant environment neither uncritically affirms positive values nor negatively deconstructs all values. Instead, it is in the very tension between affirmation of a centre and criticism from the peripheries that curiosity awakens and knowledge is born. Diversity is the way to keep the canon alive!

Moving toward an environment for diversity

Equity in education is a battle that will never be fully won because its meaning and goal will always be contested. Nonetheless, I believe that we can do far better than we have done both in responding to the principled critics of diversity and in improving our efforts to achieve it. These efforts include establishing programmes of diversity, meeting propaganda with information, creating links with minority institutions and scholars, establishing core standards, and expanding race-based criteria towards geography and class.

A basic element in the effort toward diversity is of course creating specific programmes that foster diversity. In doing so, the process of planning is as important as the resultant plan and programmes. That is, planning for diversity should itself be an exercise in creating an environment for diversity, a process of inclusion and debate among a wide range of voices both within and outside the university. This also will build consistency for the implementation of any resultant plan. Because an environment for diversity depends on voluntary, non-enforceable behavior, positive incentives (and not negative sanctions) must be primary in such programmes. Plans and programmes for diversity should include curricular changes to reflect the perspectives and contributions of minority groups, women, and other cultures; voluntary cultural awareness training for faculty, staff, and administrators, starting at the top; infusion into the administration and staff of women and minority leaders who are active in their communities; recruitment, support, retention, and advancement of women and minority students, faculty, and staff; and clear timetables for implementing the above with measures for assessment and accountability.

123

We also have to respond more effectively to the larger publics who have criticised diversity, in part by bringing them more fully into the conversation, in part by responding with arguments and information. For the first, leaders of diversity should welcome their critics, both as sources of improvements and also as a central component of the environment for diversity itself. The full freedom of speech of our critics is the clearest sign of our success. But we also need to do a better job of telling our story, especially to a skeptical public outside the academy. For example, few people know that two thirds of the people who live in poverty in America are white, or that affirmative action has been a major (perhaps the major) force in assimilating women into campuses and the work place. We need to show that diversity is about equality of opportunity and not special privileges for the unqualified or undeserving. 'If whites realise that the beneficiaries of affirmative action have made good use of their opportunities and have, for the most part, shown themselves to be competent, white opposition may diminish' (Fredrickson 1997: 75).

diversity is about equality of opportunity

We also need to establish deep and ongoing connections with historically black colleges and universities, tribal colleges, and Hispanic-serving institutions. Diversity thereby can become an inter-campus project much broader than what any single institution could accomplish. Such institutional links could include not only acceptance of each other's courses for credit, but also exchange of faculty and students, perhaps in a kind of 'junior year at another campus' type of programme. Historically white colleges also could offer graduate fellowships to students from such institutions which would be based on institutional affiliation rather than on race as such. Similarly, post-doctoral fellowships for minority students could be offered by appropriate departments, with a requirement to teach a seminar on their dissertation topic. This could serve especially to recruit minority junior faculty in schools or departments where they are severely under-represented.

It also is important to create clear common standards of learning. This would seem to be the opposite of diversity but in fact it is central to it, for it establishes a core of skills and learning that is vital to community and communication across different cultural perspectives, and it affirms an equality of access to a more general and less parochial intellectual culture. A core curriculum should be understood as basic to the common intellectual culture to which diverse perspectives may contribute, contest, and elaborate. It should not be a two year programme in Western Civilisation, but it might well be (for the United States) a series of required courses in Sources of American Civilisation, which perforce would focus, though not exclusively, on European traditions. The Association of American Colleges and Universities, for example, has recommended that preparation for meaningful citizenship in the United States include places in the college curriculum in which students can explore the following: a) experience, identity, and aspiration by studying one's own particular inherited and constructed traditions, identity communities, and significant questions that evolve in their complicated relationships; b) United States pluralism and the pursuits of justice which attends to the differing experiences of United States democracy as groups seek equal opportunity; and c) experiences in justice seeking in which students encounter directly through community-based learning the systemic constraints to social justice.

Of course there are many obstacles to core curricula, and efforts by many universities to establish them have failed. Among these obstacles is the criticism of elitism, which comes from the inability to conceive of the co-existence of general standards of excellence co-existing with and enriching equity and diversity. Another obstacle, which we discussed earlier, is the ethnocentric and territorial conceptions of knowledge which, in principle, exclude a larger common learning. A further obstacle is the intellectual hyper-specialization and even anti-intellectualism of many faculty members. General culture being no one's specialty, who would want or be able to teach it? Thus the clarification and advancement of a common learning requires new incentives and a major institutional effort. If we avoid this challenge, however, we may create a smorgasbord of contradictory knowledge claims, none of which can unite with others in the common search for truth that is the central mission of the modern university (see Gagnon 1995, Berger 1993: 522, 526).

Finally, we need to extend our conception of discrimination to include more fully the stigma and exclusions of class, while openly acknowledging that discrimination based on race still plagues American society almost a century and a half after the Emancipation Proclamation. Affirmative action and diversity might be more effective, and more broadly supported by the non-academic public, if it were less explicitly based on race. Indeed, if less emphasis is placed on race as well as on standardised tests, and more emphasis on high school grades and evidence of sustained effort to overcome initial disadvantages, we might have a method of determining qualifications more acceptable to the courts. For example, state universities could guarantee admission or fellowships to all students with the highest grade point average (GPA) of their class in the high schools of the poorest 20 per cent of the postal zip codes of the state, or of all the high schools in the inner cities, or of all top students neither of whose parents attended college. This of course would include more whites who have had to attend poor schools in poor environments, but it would tend to avoid legal constraints and challenges in court, de-stigmatise such fellowships as race-based, de-territorialise the diversity of environments, gain greater popular support and funds and, if carefully designed, ultimately provide more places for qualified minorities as well. This strategy appears to side-step the issue of racial discrimination, still so evident in our nation. Consequently, such a strategy might be seen as hypocritical by some and cowardly by others. These perceptions could be partly avoided if the sponsors of geographic or class-based policies were explicit that their intention is to pursue the goal of desegregation and to overcome discrimination based on race – but to do so in ways that both conform to the Supreme Court requirements and also avoid polarising race-based categories and discourse.

The challenges of creating a more just and democratic society are concentrated in microcosm in the university. To meet this challenge our universities must become places not only of academic scope but also of collective hope, not only of individual advancement but also of community enhancement, environments where peoples of different colours, cultures, and conditions can come together, challenge each other's ideas, learn new perspectives, be enriched and grow as individuals and, ultimately, come to understand that our differences are our strength, that our diversity can be the essence of our excellence. As the preamble of the 1966 constitution of South Africa says, we must be 'united in our diversity'. One university, many cultures. *Simunye!* We are one.

REFERENCES

Alsop, Joseph (1989) 'The WASP ascendency', *New York Review of Books*, November 9: 48-56.

Altbach, Philip (1995) Introduction to Logan Wilson's *The Academic Man: A Study in the Sociology of a Profession*. New Brunswick, NJ: Transaction.

Berger, Brigette (1993) 'The politics of political correctness', *Partisan Review*, 4.

Cuddihy, John Murray (1987) *The Ordeal of Civility: Freud, Marx, Levi Strauss, and the Jewish Struggle with Modernity*. Beacon Press.

Dews, CL, Barney and Carolyn Leste Law (1995) *This Fine Place So Far From Home: Voices of Academics from Work Class*. Philadelphia: Temple University Press.

DuBois, WEB (1986) 'The souls of black folks'. In Nathan Higgins (ed.) *Writings*. Library of America.

Frederickson, George M (1997) 'American's caste system: will it change?' *New York Review of Books*, October 23, 68-75.

Gagnon, Paul (1995) 'What should children learn?' *Atlantic Monthly*, December, 65-74.

Gamson, Zelda F and Eugene Rice (1995) 'The academy', *Contemporary Sociology*, 24:6, November, 742-744.

Henry, William A III (1990) 'Beyond the melting pot', *Time*, April 9, 28-35.

Hughes, Eugene M (1990) 'Commentary: taking responsibility for cultural diversity', *Black Issues in Higher Education*, 6: 21, January 18, 24-27.

Kjelberg (1996) 'Multicultural education and the virtue of comparative philosophy', *Report from the Institute of Philosophy and Public Policy*, Summer/Fall: University of Maryland, College Park.

Lubbell, Samuel (1964) *White and Black: Test of a Nation*. New York: Harper and Row.

Rudenstein, Neil (1996) 'Why a diverse student body?', *Chronicle of Higher Education*, April 19.

Campus-community linkages: a dialogue on diversity

Jaya Indiresan

Asian Centre for Organisational Research and Development

College and university campuses do not exist and operate in a vacuum. They are inextricably interlinked with the society of which they are a part. Education is a complex system with several subsystems. At the same time, education is a subsystem of the larger society. But society itself is composed of several subsystems that may be termed as communities. A community in general refers to a set of interlocking or integrated functional and social subsystems based on economic, political, caste, religious, ethical, educational, legal, social, and other dimensions. A community can also be conceptualised as a group of people living as a unit who consider themselves as a whole. They have informal social interaction, have common interests, and there is a condition of sharing. A community has a specific identity. A community in this sense can transcend physical proximity and still be inclusive of members spread all over spatially.

In India, however, the use of the term 'community' is complicated and has several connotations. Everyone belongs to a particular community based mainly on their religion or caste. This gives them a distinct identity. For example, an individual belongs to Brahman community (an identity based on caste) or Muslim community (an identity based on religion) and so on. Depending on the situation, the identity can be based on a broad categorisation that would include all persons belonging to that community. For example, when one wants to buy a house, an individual would feel comfortable in an area where people of the same community live. On the other hand, if the purpose is marriage, one might restrict one's choice to a very narrow range and look for an alliance in the sub-caste!

In a multicultural, multi-ethnic, multilingual, pluralistic society like India, belonging to a particular community is an intrinsic part of every individual's identity. It is also significant to note that individuals can have affiliation to several communities at the same time based on various permutations and combinations of caste, religion, region, language, etc. For example, Christians in India – though they have embraced Christianity generations ago – still cling to the customs and traditions of the original caste from which they were converted. There are clear and marked divisions among Christians who originally belonged to the upper caste from those who belonged to the lower castes. Christians in northern India are different from the Christians in the south. Similarly, the languages in which services are conducted in the churches, the dress code, and food habits also vary from region to region. Thus people have multiple identities as illustrated in Figure 1. These identities emanating from various communities guide the values and thus the behaviour of the individuals.

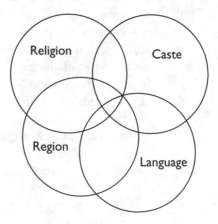

Figure 1: Diversity and multiple identity

The term 'community' does not only refer to identity based on caste and religion. It also refers to any group of people who live in a physical/geographical set-up outside the institution. So campus-community interaction generally refers to the mutual developmental efforts or contributions made by both the campus and the community outside for the betterment of the other on various dimensions including physical, social, economic, cultural, and other aspects. The campuses, endowed with people with knowledge and skills, are expected to contribute to the community around them.

Any discussion on campus and community interaction has to be seen in the multiple connotation of the term 'community'. For the sake of simplicity, the term 'community' is used here to refer to the social and psychological identity based on caste, religion, and language, while the term 'society' is used to refer to the conglomeration of communities in the surrounding physical context.

There are several communities present within the campuses and one can simultaneously be a member of several communities and have several identities. Similarly, there could be several communities outside the campus and individuals who constitute the campus could be members of these communities and have other identities by virtue of belonging to them.

The changing campus profiles

It is significant here to observe that Indian higher education has not only shown a tremendous change in its quantitative growth but there has been a perceptible qualitative change in terms of the demographic profile of the students entering the various campuses. While upper caste and upper class students dominated campuses a few decades ago, campuses now have students from diverse caste, religion, region, and language backgrounds. The gender composition has also changed with over one third of the students being women.

Similarly, the societies around the campuses have also undergone significant changes in their social composition. There was a time when particular streets were exclusively earmarked for the upper-caste people and people from lower castes could not even enter these streets. No longer do people of different communities live in total isolation. Of course, there are still pockets where such isolation does exist. By and large, there is greater diversity in the composition of the society, more so in urban settings.

As the campuses and the society around it have changed tremendously, their interactions have become very complex and have significant impact on each other. However, it must be noted that the interaction between the campuses and society are time, space, and situation specific. One campus may respond totally differently from another campus to the same event inside or outside the campus. For example, when Mujibur Rehman, the then prime minister of Bangladesh was assassinated in 1975, the highly politicised campus of the Jawaharlal Nehru University (JNU) was out in the streets demonstrating its concern. On the other hand, the Indian Institute of Technology (IIT), a highly prestigious professional institute just a stone's throw away from JNU campus, did not respond at all and the classes went on unperturbed. However, when students took to the streets protesting against the Mandal Commission[1] implementation in 1990, the students of IIT also joined the agitation. They perceived that this affected them as well. The IIT students were not concerned about a very sensitive event that was of no direct consequence to them. Thus, how the campus and society respond to each other depends on several factors or combination of factors.

Under these dynamic scenarios it would be interesting to examine how the changing composition of the campuses and the changing characteristics of the society around it affect each other and what needs to be done so that both can benefit from each other. In this paper, an attempt has been made to analyse, understand, and examine the implications of the campus and society linkages in the context of the diverse nature of the Indian society in a secular, democratic set-up. This paper also examines the role of higher education in preparing students to live effectively amidst diversity.

The dynamics of diversity context in India

A brief portrait of the current Indian society may help to illustrate the dynamics of its diversity in order to place higher education in a proper perspective. India is a country of fascinating contrasts in the various dimensions of social, cultural, political, economic, and technological aspects. India can be justifiably proud of her technological progress – she has been able to put an indigenously designed, most sophisticated satellite into orbit and is fully poised to enter the 21st century. At the same time, there are still bullock carts as the only means of transportation in several parts of the country. Economically, the five-star culture and affluence of some sections of the society is amazing while 50 per cent of the population live below the poverty line. Politically, there are all hues of affiliation from extreme left to right. Culturally, a section of the population is totally westernised and modern while another section is very traditional and conservative. An outstanding feature of secular India is its multi-ethnic pluralistic society with a heterogeneous population. The population of 970 million is composed of people belonging to different castes and religions, speaking different languages, following varied customs and traditions. They vary extensively in their food habits and dress codes. Eighty per cent of the population lives in rural India, minimally affected by modernisation.

One of the distinct and very powerful aspects that affects the entire country to a large extent is the caste factor. The caste system reaches deep back into prehistory of India. The closest Indian word is *jati*, which is common nearly in all the major languages. Galanter (1984) defines *jati* as:

> an endogenous group having a common name and claiming a common origin, membership of which is hereditary, linked to one or more traditional occupations, imposing on its members certain obligations and reactions on matters of social intercourse, and having a more or less determined position in a hierarchical scale of ranks.

The number of castes, including subcastes, in modern India has been estimated to be of the order of 2 000 to 3 000, ranging from a small group of a few hundred individuals to large groups numbering a few million.

The most significant aspect of the caste factor is its hierarchical nature with castes being classified as upper or forward castes and low or backward castes. This hierarchical dimension conditions the social interactions from inter-dining to inter-caste marriages. But Indian society has not been static. With changing economic activities and employment patterns, urbanisation and rural migration, and the impact of technology on the way of life, several caste barriers are breaking down. At the same time, caste factors are being re-enforced by vested interests, for political gains. The caste system continues to have a significant influence on social interactions.

As far as religion is concerned, India has been a traditionally Hindu society with a large majority belonging to this religion. The Moghul emperors conquered a large part of India and introduced Islam into the country. Now there are over 140 million Muslims constituting over 12 per cent of the total population. With the Christian missionaries coming in, a significant section of the population, especially the lower castes, were converted to Christianity. There are nearly 24 million Christians and they constitute nearly 3 per cent of the population. In addition, there are 22 million Sikhs, 10 million Buddhists, 5 million Jains and several adherents of other faiths.

minority religions enjoy certain privileges that even the majority religion does not have

In India there is a long tradition of religious tolerance. In 1947 the country opted for secularism as a state policy and the constitution secures certain rights and privileges for minority religions. In fact, minority religions enjoy certain privileges that even the majority religion does not have. For example, minority religions have special provisions under which they can set up their own educational institutions. Such special privileges provided to the minority religions have had an undesirable backlash effect. Some sections of the majority religion feel marginalised and this has triggered off extreme fundamentalism and resulted in the black event of the destruction of the Babri Masjid. The secular fabric of India is being torn in the name of religion, again by vested interests for political gains.

India is a multilingual society with eighteen officially recognised languages with different scripts. It is estimated that there are over 2 000 languages and dialects spoken in different parts of the country. Though people experienced problems of communication when they moved from one part of the country to another, there was no animosity against people who spoke a different language. When the states in India were reorganised on the basis of language, then language became a divisive factor. This led to a lot of conflict and confrontation. People became possessive, did not want to share, and wanted to grab as much territory as they could. People in the south were voluntarily learning

Hindi (spoken by a large percentage in the north), but when it was thrust on them as the national language, there was rebellion. Again, language became a contentious issue dividing the nation.

Developmental efforts after independence were somewhat lopsided, with a large share going to the mega-cities. Those who had more grabbed more, depriving the less developed regions. The regional disparities between well-endowed states, between urban and rural areas became too apparent, again leading to conflicts between the 'haves' and 'have nots.'

The gender issue runs through all these factors. Within the castes, within the religions, within the regions, the status of women is significantly low. Though there is legislative protection against barbaric practices like child marriage, prohibition of widow remarriage, atrocities on women, sexual harassment, dowry demand, and denial of property rights, these all exist in different degrees in some part of the country or the other. Women are now more aware of their rights and privileges; they demand equality including 30 per cent reservation in legislatures and Parliament so that they can participate in the decision-making processes. The traditional patriarchal society that has existed for centuries finds it difficult to accept these claims and serious efforts are made to maintain the status quo. This is yet another issue that has resulted in conflicts and confrontations.

In addition to all this, the political system stands splintered today. More than a dozen political parties have combined to run a fragile coalition government. The euphoria and the commitment that existed fifty years ago with the common objective of building a free country is no longer there. Everybody wants to grab power at any cost. There seems to be a collapse of ethical and moral values in politics.

Thus, Indian society today is fragmented and fractured on many counts. Long ago, whether in religion, caste, language, or region, there was greater acceptance and tolerance. Everybody had an identified role to play in the society. For example, in a temple procession, the *kshtriya* (royalty) led the procession, the *Brahmin* (priest) performed the rituals, the *Vysya* (businessman) contributed materially, and the *shudra* (artisans) beat the drums. Thus, everybody from the highest to the lowest caste had an assigned role to play.

Figure 2 pictorially depicts the causes and consequences of diversity. Diversity by itself is not an issue. It not only provides a certain identity but is also linked to an ascribed status. Mostly this ascribed status is hierarchical in nature, making certain identities superior and the others relatively inferior. In the name of egalitarianism that believes that all people are equal and should be treated equally in society, people have started questioning the assigned and accepted roles in society. While this is a commendable value, the transition has not been smooth. This leads to an unending challenge resulting in either harmony or disharmony. Valuing differences or appreciating different identities is a rare feature, especially because of vested interests. The ways and means of achieving harmony without the trauma of transition is a challenge to any democratic society and more so to a large democracy like India which is besieged by enormous problems.

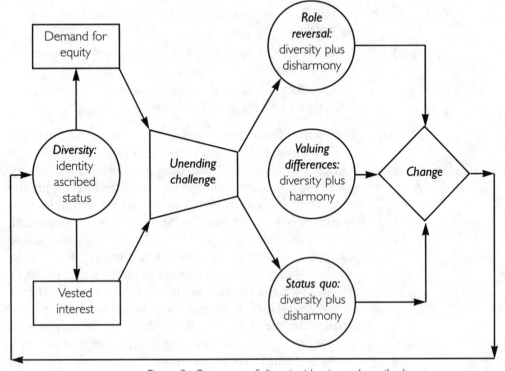

Figure 2: Outcomes of diversity, identity and ascribed status

Democracy and diversity

One of the fundamental principles of democratic society is equality and liberty. A democratic society believes that all people are of equal worth and should be treated equally in society. The passion for equality is at the heart of democracy. It encompasses the struggle against inequalities in social, political, and economic conditions. In liberal democracies, equality of rights tends to mean equality of opportunity and equal protection under the law. This implies that there shall be no discrimination based on race, religion, caste, descent, place of birth, residence, or gender.

The diverse nature of Indian society poses several challenges in terms of equity and social justice. Accepting this situation, the founding fathers of India have made several constitutional legal provisions. The preamble to the Indian Constitution reads:

> We the people of India, having solemnly resolved to constitute India into a Sovereign Democratic Republic and to Secure to all its citizens:
>
> JUSTICE social, economic and political;
>
> LIBERTY of thought, expression, belief, faith and worship;
>
> EQUALITY of status and of opportunity; and to promote among them all;
>
> FRATERNITY assuring the dignity of the individual and the unity and integrity of the nation.

The Indian Constitution has very clearly articulated the Right to Equality. Article 14 referring to equality before law states: 'The State shall not deny to any person equality before the law or the equal protection of the laws within the territory of India.' Article 15 delineates the prohibition of discrimination. It states: 'The State shall not discriminate against any citizen on grounds only of religion, race, caste, sex, place of birth or any of them.' Article 16 refers to equality of opportunity in matters of public employment. It states: 'There shall be equality of opportunity for all citizens in matters relating to employment or appointment to any office under the State. No citizen shall, on grounds only of religion, race, caste, sex, descent, place of birth, residence, or any of them be ineligible for or discriminated against in respect of any employment or office under the State.' At the same time Article 16(4) states: 'Nothing in this article shall prevent the State from making provision for the reservation of appointments or posts in favour of any backward class or citizens which, in the opinion of the State, is not adequately represented in the service under the State.' Article 14(4A) brought forth by the 77th Amendment of 1995, added that: 'Nothing in this article shall prevent the State from making any provision for reservation in matters of promotion to any class or classes or posts in the services under the State in favour of the scheduled castes and the scheduled tribes which in the opinion of the States, are not adequately represented in the services under the State.'

Thus, it can be seen that constitutional and legal provisions have been made in the interests of the socially and educationally backward people who constitute a significant proportion of the Indian population.

Preferential policies

India has two types of preferential policies. The first type is analogous to American affirmative action as regards to target groups and rationale for the preferences. The beneficiary groups and historically oppressed or excluded endogamous groups are at the bottom of, or outside, the stratified system in which their status is determined by birth. Even though barriers to upward mobility in economic and professional status have been overcome to some extent in respect of members of oppressed groups, there is a feeling that the social stigma attaching to that individual has been only marginally erased. Similarly, while migration from rural areas to towns in the case of protected minorities in India has lightened the burden of disabilities, the group's lowly and oppressed social status tends to be perpetuated from generation to generation.

The second type of preferential policy, permitted by the Constitution but formulated and operated at state or regional level, relates to schemes of preference for local ethnic groups, frequently the majority in that locality, irrespective of caste or tribal affiliation. Typically the policies are designed by and for the politically dominant group of that locality against certain minorities who are often regarded as more advanced or privileged in some respect but essentially of more recent domicile. Thus, these groups are perceived to have less claim to certain social and economic benefits and privileges, than the residents who belong to that locality. For example, in Tamil Nadu, the Brahmans who constitute only about three per cent of the population have historically enjoyed a higher social and economic status compared to the large percentage of the backward and most backward communities there.

The tensions related to the first type of policy are mostly inter-caste or inter-tribal. Those related to the second type may be between central government and state government, between two neighbouring states, between two regions of the same state, or between one region and the state government as a whole. The underlying principle here is very different from that governing protective measures for scheduled caste, scheduled tribes and Other Backward Classes. There is no presumption of backwardness. The sole operative principle is that those who are natives of a state or region are entitled to preference over those from outside.

This type of preferential policy leads to several problems and tensions. For example, a student belonging to one state is denied admission to a college or university in another state. This is also true about employment opportunities. At one stage, this policy of the sons-of-the-soil was carried to such an extent creating inter-regional tensions that Prime Minister Indira Gandhi made a statement in 1972:

> This is a matter on which one has to have a certain balance. While we stand for the principle that any Indian should be able to work in any part of India, at the same time it is true that if a large number of people come from outside to seek employment ... that is bound to create tension in the area ... [One] has to have some balance and see that local people are not deprived of employment.

Sivaramaya (1984) points out that Indian preferential policies are based on four principles: compensation for past injustices, protection of the weak, proportional equality, and social justice incorporating distributive justice and social welfare. The major thrusts of India's preferential policy in relation to Dalits[2] are in the fields of education in terms of admission, economic activity including land settlement, job reservations, and political elections with reservation of seats.

Inequality and discrimination

India has clearly articulated nation-wide preferential policies backed by appropriate legislation. While laws against untouchability, segregation, and discrimination are essential, they cannot possibly eliminate the impact of prejudice. Laws cannot compensate for group disabilities caused by environmental or historical circumstances. Mere laws cannot ensure the achievement of equal opportunity between individuals. The structural obstacles to mobility are most formidable where there has been a long history of prejudice, discrimination, and exclusion sanctioned by law or religion. Even if the legal and ideological basis of discrimination and exclusion can be overcome, prejudice and psychological conditioning continue to hinder progress for a long period.

The critical question is how one can break the vicious circle of prejudice, low expectations and aspiration, and wide disparity in achievement. Even if prejudice can be suppressed, there is a long time-lag before the other components of the cycle can be eliminated. Continued disparity in performance causes prejudice to resurface with a new legitimacy. For example, the scheduled caste/scheduled tribe students are admitted under the reservation policy to elite institutions like the IITs where only the cream of student population is admitted. There is enormous disparity in the academic performance of the under- and unprepared reserved category[3] students and the well endowed non-reserved category students. This does reinforce the prejudice and feelings of discrimination among the disadvantaged students.

If a group which has experienced extensive prejudice and discrimination has high levels of economic, educational, and professional expectations, the prospect of narrowing, eventually eliminating, or even reversing disparity is much higher. Mobility does help to undermine prejudice and such discrimination that is based on prejudice. For example, caste prejudices are rampant in rural areas where everybody knows everybody else's caste affiliation. One principal of a college located in a rural area narrated a very touching incident. An scheduled caste student came and sat next to upper-caste student in the same bench in a crowded classroom. The upper-caste student pushed this scheduled caste student out saying,

'How dare you come and sit next to me?' This would not happen in a crowded bus in a city where there is total anonymity of one's caste affiliation.

Indian protective discrimination has been designed not only to combat current prejudice and current discrimination against certain groups but also to overcome the cumulative impact of past discrimination and historical circumstances which are currently manifest in institutional, cultural, and environmental obstacles to mobility.

In a large democracy like India, which is also a very heterogeneous and diverse society, citizenship is based on a bundle of rights and duties, which every citizen has by virtue of their being a citizen and a human being. The quality of citizenship makes or unmakes a civic society. In this context, citizenship development becomes a crucial issue. The relevant question here is: What is the role of formal and higher education in this citizenship development? Is formal education a good means of conveying an understanding of the fundamental principles of equality and liberty as it applies in the historical and cultural context of a given society?

The quality of citizenship makes or unmakes a civic society.

Campuses and workplaces are becoming increasingly diverse. Participation in a campus community drawn from multiple cultures and experiences calls for an inclination to engage and learn across differences. This requires skills that have not been practised or valued. Here lie the challenges for higher education. Schneider (1995: xvi) puts it very eloquently:

> In its commitment to diversity, higher education assumes, therefore, both a distinctive responsibility and a precedent setting challenge. While other institutions in the society are also fostering diversity, higher education is uniquely positioned by its mission, values, and dedication to learning, to foster and nourish the habits of heart and mind to make diversity work in daily life.

How successful has been the Indian higher education in fulfilling this role and facing up to the challenges is a crucial question that deserves to be examined. To answer this question, it is necessary to understand the evolution of the higher education system itself in the Indian socio-cultural and historical context.

A portrait of higher education

It was pointed out that education and society are closely inter-linked. To examine, how the prevalent societal structure had a tremendous influence on the system of education and to understand the current context of higher education in India, it would be worthwhile taking a brief peep into the historical growth of the system. It is claimed that in ancient India, the Vedic period was marked by a stratified, though essentially non-class society (Jha 1991) and that education was not monopolised by any particular social group. However, from the later Vedic period which saw the crystallisation of the caste system, education gradually came to be monopolised by the upper castes, especially the Brahmans. Although women still managed to have some influence in the sphere of education, they were increasingly relegated to the background. Thus, while the names of 72 women rishis are found in Rigveda, there are only few names in the later Vedic period, e.g. Gargi and Maitreyi.

The medieval centuries (12th to 18th) in the history of India signified a major phase of social and cultural synthesis, resulting from an interaction between the widely diverse life style of the new settlers from central and western Asia and of the early inhabitants of the subcontinent. The totality of medieval Indian life came to be identified with an unmistakable unity in its fabric without annihilating the diversity in it. Alam (1991), analysing the history of higher education in medieval India, points out that it was marked by both continuity and change, signifying the medieval experience of co-existence of the diverse traditions of Islam and Brahmanical order. Both the existing Brahmanical institutions and the newly emerged *madrasas* (Islamic schools) contributed in shaping the medieval values and culture all over the subcontinent. The courses of study included both religious and secular sciences. The medieval education system promoted conditions wherein the people learnt to live together, notwithstanding their differences, but which sometimes also led to conflicts.

Basu (1991), tracing the history of higher education in colonial India, brings out how the education was spread unevenly and led to several inequalities. Higher education in colonial India remained concentrated in and around the metropolitan port towns of Calcutta, Bombay, and Madras,

141

where the first high schools, colleges, and universities were established. This enclavisation of higher education was in conformity with the nature of colonial underdevelopment. Though English education was in theory available to all, its spread was extremely uneven. Some regions were much more advanced than others. There were differences even within a region between one district or one group and another. Everywhere higher education was more widespread among men than women, in cities than in villages, and amongst the higher castes. The first groups to respond to Western education among the Hindus were the traditionally literate castes such as the Brahmans. It would have been almost impossible to find a rural scheduled caste or scheduled tribe woman studying in a college. Thus during the colonial period, serious inequality came to be in higher education.

One outstanding feature of the Indian higher education system in the past five decades since independence is its phenomenal growth and expansion. There were just 30 universities, 750 colleges enrolling 0,26 million students in 1950–51. By 1995–96, there were 207 universities, 9 278 colleges enrolling 6,4 million students. It was expected that this phenomenal growth in educational facilities would automatically lead to the levelling of the inequities in access to the socially, educationally, and regionally backward communities. The actual experience turned out to be very different.

Challenges of diversity in higher education

To recap, constitutional and legal provisions have been made for the reservation policy. A quota system, positive discrimination in terms of access, and financial support on the basis of caste already exist. These have to some extent brought down the gross inequalities in participation that existed a few decades back. Coupled with a social demand for higher education and regional mobility, the demographic profile of the campus has shown some significant changes.

According to data available for 1988–89, a total of 279 720 scheduled caste and 69 189 scheduled tribe students had enrolled in higher education constituting 7,3 and 1,8 per cent of total enrolment respectively. Though these are the national figures, there is a wide variation among the states and there is also an inter-institute variation depending upon the policy of the particular institution. For example, in Christian missionary institutions, there is distinct positive bias towards the admission of Dalit students.

As a result of the reservation policy and the financial support provided, there has been an increase in the number of Dalit students enrolled in higher education. However they are mainly in the liberal arts courses and their participation in professional courses like engineering and medicine is still very insignificant. In spite of the sons-of-the-soil policy operating in some states, the geographical mobility and the policy of providing admission to out-of-state students, especially in some centrally administered universities and professional institutions, has also contributed to the change in the demographic profile of students in higher education. There are hardly any exclusive men's institutions left in the country, though there are over 1 000 exclusive women's colleges and five exclusive women's universities in the country. With women's participation in higher education touching over one third of the total enrolment, gender is another significant factor adding to the diversity of student profile.

This diverse composition of students in higher education poses several challenges both academically and socially. The under-prepared and unprepared students from educationally disadvantaged families, with poor schooling and lacking communication skills, pose challenges to the maintenance of certain academic standards. The debate between equality and excellence has been going on ever since the reservation policies have been put into operation. In the requirement of fulfilling the quota under the reservation policy, the reserved category students are given admission even when they do not fulfil the minimum academic standards required. For instance, in the admission to the prestigious IITs, a reserved category student scoring zero marks in all the four papers of the Joint Entrance Examination (JEE)[4] had to be admitted as the quota was not filled! These students admitted under the quota could not cope with the high academic standards and the highly competitive climate prevailing in these elite institutions, resulting in severe psychological problems of adjustment. Subsequently, a separate lower percentage as minimum requirement was introduced below which the reserved category students could not claim admission, even if the quota was not filled.

The social challenges relate to preparing the students to integrate meaningfully with the 'rest' of the student population. For the reserved category, students who come from socially, educationally, and economically disadvantaged families, most probably from a backward region, their very entry into these institutions of higher learning can be a strange and traumatic experience. Facilitating these students is a problem, a challenge, and an opportunity.

Smith (1995) identified four distinct challenges of diversity in the context of higher education. Utilising this framework, Table 1 depicts the problems and opportunities associated with each one of these challenges. The first one, Representation, focuses on the presence or absence of particular groups in the college campus and seeks ways to increase their number. This challenge is the outcome of the accumulated distortions of the past. The reservation policy by and large addresses this problem of access to higher education to those sections that have been so far kept out of it for various socio-historical-cultural-political-economic reasons.

Problems	Challenges	Opportunities
Accumulated distortions of the past	Representation	Reservation Positive discrimination Quota
Prejudice and stereotype	Campus climate	Diversity positive initiatives Warm and supportive Empowerment
Disparity in performance	Educational mission	Reform curriculum Remedial education Provide life skills
Inequality and discrimination	Transformation	Social sensitivity Involvement of community Integration

Table 1: A framework for management of diversity

The second dimension, Campus climate, recognises the integral connections between institutional environment and educational attainment, and seeks to change those aspects of campus climate that prove chilly for a particular group of students, whether members of designated groups or women. The problem here is mainly due to the prevalent prejudices and stereotypes. This implies that it is not enough just making provisions for the access of the disadvantaged students. Specific diversity-positive initiatives are required for making the institutional climate warm and supportive, to enable the disadvantaged to feel empowered so that the access provided is meaningful and not just symbolic.

The third dimension, Educational mission, relates to the disparity in the performances of under- or unprepared students who come from disadvantaged background especially with poor schooling. The challenge is the realisation that all students benefit from an education that fosters knowledge and competence for a multiracial, multi-ethnic, multi-perspective and gendered world. In the Indian context, this translates into multi-caste, multi-religious, multi-regional, multi-language and, of course, gendered society. This calls for reform in the curriculum, opportunities for remedial education, and provision of life skills.

The fourth dimension, Transformation, connects all the other dimensions of diversity in a fundamental reconsideration of the educational institutions organising assumptions – societal, intellectual, educational, and institutional. The problem of prevalent inequality and discrimination needs to be corrected with social sensitivity and involvement of the community for better integration.

Objectives, roles and responsibility of higher education

The current scenario and challenges of the dynamism of diversity both within the campus and the society around it raise several questions. How can we maintain harmony in the face of growing dysfunction inside and outside the campuses? How can we reform the curriculum and assessment procedures while at the same time raising academic standards and still provide equal opportunity for the disadvantaged? How can we improve the management and efficiency of education through parental and community involvement? How can the campuses develop a mature set of values from which the society can benefit? Do the campuses have a social obligation to society beyond imparting knowledge and information? What are these social functions of the campus? How do they go about fulfilling these obligations? In brief, how do the campuses foster capacities and commitments to pluralism? These are not simple questions but very relevant issues that need to be addressed, about which strategies formulated, and actions initiated.

It is interesting to note that diverse perspectives have been articulated on the objectives of higher education. All along, the basic function has been recognised as generation and dissemination of knowledge. However, in recent times, the dimension of extension, that is, application of knowledge for the benefit of the society has also been recognised. Thus teachers are expected to invest some of their time in extension work in addition to teaching and research.

Higher education is also perceived as an important means whereby young people joining adult society sort themselves out and are sorted out for different employment positions and in a large measure for life opportunities. In the context of diversity, higher education is expected to be concerned with social equity focusing on the inaccessibility of higher education, especially to the prestigious institutions for the socially disadvantaged. Moving beyond this access, higher education is supposed to be concerned with socialisation and ascription of social identities and roles to young people through education and learning experiences. While there could be several objectives, one comprehensive objective cited is *that higher education is concerned with enhancing the quality of life through the development of personal survival skills essential for successfully negotiating an increasingly complex world.*

the characteristics of both the campuses and societies are undergoing rapid changes

While every word in this definition is full of significance, the key words are *successfully negotiating an increasingly complex world.* This is particularly appropriate in a dynamically diverse society like India. It was pointed out that the characteristics of both the campuses and societies are undergoing rapid changes. The strength of the identity of the students with the myriad communities that coexist within and outside the campus changes from time to time. This depends on the priorities and satisfactions derived from the participation in any of the activities and ideals shared. The intersecting and overlapping characteristic of the belongingness to the various communities simultaneously is one aspect which contributes to the complexity of interaction with the different communities. Further, the values and ideals of the various communities of which a student is a member simultaneously may or may not be in harmony. For example, a student belonging to a particular region but studying in another region, because of spatial displacement or replacement becomes a member of a minority community, at least for the time being, and this may lead to clash of values and result in conflict and even confrontation. This is not an uncommon feature in Indian campuses where students belonging to different regions or languages form their own close inner circles to protect their identity and interest. At times, when one group tries to dominate or marginalise the other groups, conflicts do erupt.

Similarly, there are several contributing factors resulting in the increasing complexity of the society around the campuses. The dynamism of the changing social equations due to changing political scenario in a liberal democracy like India is a major factor. The hitherto oppressed groups now feel empowered to raise their voices; now question the so far established and accepted norms; and are becoming more aggressive and militant. Some of these are due to genuine consciousness-raising efforts by socially committed people in the interest of social justice. However, a significant portion is due to vested interests of opportunistic politicians who would like to cash in on the vulnerability of the importance of identity of different communities.

Another significant reality in the context of higher education in India is that campuses differ widely in their sensitivity to social issues of the society around them. While students of the liberal arts are sensitive and at times over-sensitive, students from elite institutions and professional institutions of engineering and management do not exhibit much concern. These students are by and large the cream of student population, come from upper-class and upper-caste family backgrounds mainly from urban areas. Often they are concerned only about their own personal achievement and advancement, and are not concerned about giving back to the society from which they have benefited so mch. In fact, a large number of these students educated in elite professional institutes even migrate from the country in search of greener pastures.

Recently an eminent educationist wrote about the social concerns of students of the elite Indian Institute of Management (IIM). He pointed out that the students admitted that compassion for society is none of their concern and their main objective is to maximise the opportunity cost. We must ask whether there is something wrong with our education system, that it trains only the head without touching the heart.

It is significant to point out here that some prominent educationists themselves have no sensitivity to social issues and reality. Recently, the Ford Foundation came forward to support the spread of Campus Diversity Initiative by sensitisation, orientation, and skill development of teachers of undergraduate colleges through the existing set-up available at the Academic Staff Colleges. But some members of the Standing Committee of the Academic Staff College even refused to recognise that diversity is a challenge in the campus and that students need to be sensitised. They were in fact against any initiative in this direction. In the face of our society's diversity, the challenge is what strategies to put in place to prepare our students to learn to live effectively amidst diversity.

First and foremost, our campus leaders have a unique opportunity to be pro-active in creating a climate in which people belonging to and identifying themselves with different communities can engage with one another in a shared commitment to the common goal of an Indian nationhood. As already pointed out, it is not enough just to provide access to students from different communities. The leaders should move beyond access and provide a diversity-positive climate in which each student with a different identity should not only feel safe and comfortable with himself or herself, but is ready to cross the boundaries and venture into an understanding and appreciation of the values and ideals which are very different from his or her own.

New structures need to be set up to facilitate the students in building skills and capacities to interact with those who differ from themselves. They should be gently guided to venture out of the comfort zone of their own community to the adventure of appreciating the unknown experiences being offered by other communities.

A dysfunctional group leads to destructiveness; inequality and injustice result in disequilibirum. On the other hand, positive relationships with other communities brings variety, respect, mutuality, obligation, and justice.

Initiatives in Indian campuses: some experiences[5]

It was pointed out earlier that extension has been recognised as a distinct function of higher education institutions. With this objective, several schemes such as National Social Service, National Cadet Corps, and Adult Education Units have been introduced over the years. However, the levels of concern, commitment, and initiatives have varied extensively from campus to campus. Apart from these formal programmes for which financial support is available from the state and central government or from the University Grants Commission, several campuses have been actively participating in community outreach programmes on their own initiatives. The efforts of Christian Missionary institutions in this direction are noteworthy. While these programmes do address the diversity issues directly or indirectly, there has been no specific thrust in this direction. Of course, there are institutions which have taken specific initiatives for promoting communal harmony especially when there have been crisis situations like the agitations during the Mandal Commission Report implementation or the destruction of the Babri Masjid in Ayodhya.

The Ford Foundation-supported Campus Diversity Initiative (CDI) has been operative in 23 selected colleges from all over India for the past couple of years. This project-based initiative in just 23 colleges is too small for the enormous higher education system in India. However, this small effort has demonstrated that, provided a climate and an opportunity, the students' minds and horizons have been widened to value, appreciate, and celebrate diversity. Students have confessed how their blind spots have been removed and they have been sensitised to the way of life of people who belong to other communities whether based on caste, religion, region, or gender.

Some selected anecdotes from these CDI-participating colleges are recounted here to illustrate that diversity-positive initiatives do have the desired impact on students, teachers, and the community around.

A discussion of the objectives of the CDI, as perceived by the students and teachers, very clearly brought out the focus on bringing greater harmony between different groups based on caste, religion, gender, etc. Some salient objectives articulated by the students and teachers include:

- Bring better quality relationships among students from different backgrounds.
- Understand the customs of other people for mutual understanding and co-operation.
- Develop social awareness about social situations.
- Improve interaction with surrounding society to provide opportunity for social service to one's neighbours.
- Enhance the relationship of the college with the neighbouring community.

Different campuses have adopted diverse strategies in implementing the CDI efforts. Most of them had a component of involvement with the neighbouring society. Several of the colleges have carried out extensive socio-economic surveys using the student volunteers in the nearby and not so nearby rural areas or city slums. These surveys have focused on identifying the problems, needs, and priorities of people living in these disadvantaged settings. The very act of going to the villages, talking to them, and listening to them has sensitised the students to the totally different life conditions in which rural/slum people live without proper sanitary arrangements, protected water supply, lack of medical and educational facilities, no electricity, and sometimes not even a connecting road. Walking down to these villages and seeing their living conditions has been a humbling experience for many city-bred students coming from affluent socio-economic backgrounds. This has made students sympathetic to the problems of the economically disadvantaged. One student said, 'Before, we were living in our own world, unaware of what other people's lives are like.'

Another significant anecdote was reported with regard to the campus-community interaction in one of the CDI colleges. During the socio-economic survey of the neighbouring village, it was observed that children from these villages were not being admitted to the college. The community was unhappy about this but the college could not admit the students, as they did not come up to the minimum standards set by the college for admission. The survey also revealed that the schooling facility in the village was very poor. The students of the college volunteered and provided remedial coaching to the school children. This improved their performance and made them eligible for admission in the college. This is a significant experiment of how campus and community can forge links to overcome disparities.

Participation in the various national integration camps and interacting with students from the different regions of the country with varying languages, dress, and food habits have helped students to throw out several myths that they had about communities. For example, students used to seeing *glamourised, artificial, and exaggerated portrayal of tribals in the media*, especially on TV, could not believe that students from tribal backgrounds look like any other student in the campus. Joint celebration of festivals of different communities has opened up an entirely new arena of understanding and appreciation of other ways of life and culture.

These are just a few illustrations of the CDI efforts in the various campuses. These activities have had a significant impact on the students and teachers. It was heartening to listen to the impact and the benefits recounted by the students after their participation in CDI activities. Some of the comments about CDI include:

- Has broadened our outlook.
- Has transformed our personality.
- Has helped in better understanding.
- Has given us knowledge about each other.
- Has helped in positive thinking.
- Has improved interpersonal relations and interactions.
- Has changed our views and behaviour.

These are a few selective impacts reported by students and teachers. Some incidents reported illustrate the impact in behavioural terms. It was reported that inter-dining,

151

especially in rural areas, is taboo among people belonging to different caste or religious groups. One student reported, 'I never used to visit my classmate who belongs to another religion but now I even accept coffee in his house.' This is real transformation. How much of this will be internalised is a moot question!

Epilogue: campus, community and social transformation

The dynamics of diversity and the unequal development resulting in wide disparities even after 50 years of independence is indeed a matter of concern. There is an urgent need to create conditions of social justice for strengthening the foundations of democracy. Divisive forces that are fracturing and fragmenting the society need to be contained. Creating a cohesive and vibrant nation out of people speaking different languages, professing different religions, belonging to different castes, and possessing a variety of cultures is a great challenge. Fear, suspicion, and hatred are the fuel that feeds the flame of communal disharmony and conflict. People want harmony between various communities but this cannot be accomplished through the accommodation of the 'separate but equal' principle and not through submergence of minority culture into majority culture. Lasting harmony between heterogeneous communities can only come through recognition of the oneness of humankind, a realisation that differences that divide us along caste, religion, region, or language basis have no foundation. The education system will have to adopt an orientation and approach fundamentally different from the methods generated by the failed assumptions of secularism and materialism.

Fortunately, the National Policy of Education (1986) does recognise the inequities and disparities that exist in our society. It states that '[education] will be used as an instrument of social change to undo the accumulated distortion of the past'. Higher education has special importance for it can create a climate in the campuses to withstand the external forces that are disruptive and are rendering the society dysfunctional. Higher education should adopt strategies that would ensure wider awareness and breadth of vision on the part of the student. It should also cultivate a sense of values and purposes conducive to national integration and effective citizenship of our great democracy. The student also must be helped to develop a rational outlook, openness to change, commitment to truth and social justice, and a desire to value differences. Secularism and national integration are crucial for the survival of democracy and for peace and harmony in the country.

Our campuses cannot remain insensitive to the happenings in society around them. The campus cannot be just reactive, and must start becoming proactive. Students need to be sensitised to the past so that they can understand the present and plan to create the desired future. Cultural differences will continue to persist for they have deep-rooted functions. Students should be helped to balance values rooted in personal belief that do not clash with values held by others. The sense of superiority inherent in any culture lies at the bottom of all unhappy relationships, especially in a multicultural pluralistic society. For a country of India's cultural heterogeneity, social complexity, economic inequalities, and ideological differentiation, unanimity in respect of all values is not possible. Campuses can create a space for dialogue by developing an inclusive educational environment in which people can connect diversity and democracy. Campuses can also facilitate unlearning previous ways of thinking and living by creating opportunities for new and more effective ways of interacting across cultures.

The sense of superiority inherent in any culture lies at the bottom of all unhappy relationships

The future of the nation is in the hands of the youth. We need a totally new generation of leadership which is sensitive to the harm caused by divisive forces in the society and which is committed to the creation of a society with equity and social justice. Differences cannot be wished away. But higher education can take up the challenge of providing a campus climate in which the youth imbibe the quality of good citizens to live effectively amidst diversity in a pluralistic democracy like India.

NOTES

1 The Janata government when it came to power in 1977 appointed BP Mandal to head a commission to identify backward classes and make recommendations for their advancement. To gain political advantage, the report which was on hold was revived in 1990 after more than a decade. The then prime minister, VP Singh, announced

that his government had decided to implement the Mandal Commission's recommendations reserving 27 per cent of jobs in the government for the backward classes. This caused a big stir with some young men from the upper castes committing suicide by setting themselves on fire. Ultimately this agitation resulted in the fall of the VP Singh government.

2   The more self-conscious scheduled class prefer to call themselves Dalits, meaning the depressed class.

3   The scheduled caste/scheduled tribe students who are admitted under the reservation policy are referred to as reserved category and the others as non-reserved or general category.

4   Out of the nearly 90 000–100 000 students who take this highly competitive JEE, after intensive preparation, only 1 500 of the top students get admission.

5   The incidents reported here are based on the data obtained during the monitoring visits to the CDI colleges.

REFERENCES

Alam, Muzaffar (1991) 'Higher education in medieval India'. In Moonis Raza (ed.) *Higher Education in India: Retrospect and Prospect.* New Delhi: Association of Indian Universities.

Basu, Aparna (1991) 'Higher education in colonial India'. In Moonis Raza (ed.) *Higher Education in India: Retrospect and Prospect.* New Delhi: Association of Indian Universities.

Galanter, Marc (1984) *Competing Equalities.* Delhi: Oxford University Press.

Jha, DN (1991) 'Higher education in ancient India'. In Moonis Raza (ed.) *Higher Education in India: Retrospect and Prospect.* New Delhi: Association of Indian Universities.

Sivaramaya, B (1984) 'Affirmative action: the scheduled castes and the scheduled tribes'. In *International Perspectives on Affirmative Action*, USA Rockefeller Foundation.

Schneider, Carol (1995) *The Drama of Diversity and Democracy.* Washington DC: Association of American Colleges and Universities.

Smith, Daryl G (1995) 'Organisational implications of diversity in higher education'. In M Chemers, S Oskamp, and M Costanza (eds) *Diversity in Organizations.* Newbury Park, California: Sage Publication.

Strategic evaluation: an imperative for the future of campus diversity

Daryl G Smith

Centre for Educational Studies, Claremont Graduate University

In the last three decades, many colleges and universities in the United States have attempted to engage and educate the most diverse population of students in the history of higher education. Entered as a commitment to democracy and social justice, the efforts continue as the society becomes increasingly diverse and as the links between national and global issues converge. For the last ten years, the intensity, scale, and scope of the 'diversity movement' has increased and has expanded (Musil et al 1995). While still attending to student access and success for those African Americans, Latinos, and Native Americans who have been under-represented, efforts now also include engaging diversity at a number of different levels including the campus climate for marginalised groups based on ethnicity, gender, sexual orientation, and religion. Educational goals must include educating all students to live and work in a pluralistic society and a global environment. Finally, as a result of the increasing diversity of United States society, questions are being addressed that are directed to institutional viability and vitality. These explore hiring practices throughout the institution, the climate for a diverse work force, the capacity to educate in a diverse society, relationships with surrounding communities, and other aspects of institutional effectiveness in the context of a changing society. Indeed, perhaps the most profound shift has been the expansion of our understanding of diversity from institutions serving 'new' populations to including questions of institutional viability and vitality as the population, educational values, social context, and the economics of the country require fundamental shifts in thinking.

As we approach a new millennium, these changes and many others have challenged higher education to think through who it educates, how that education takes place, and what role higher education plays in the larger society. Creating a truly pluralistic society only begins with significant diversity; from that point, the challenge of creating communities that function well remains. At the same time, the field of evaluation itself is in transition. Indeed, as has happened with regard to many issues in higher education, diversity has uncovered another vulnerable area in education – the need to develop a new, more sophisticated understanding of evaluation appropriate to our current shifting situation. This paper attempts to outline some of the issues and progress being made. Increasingly, educators in all parts of our institutions are being asked to participate in developing the new knowledge necessary for higher education and the society in this time of great change.

The need

Campus efforts, some of them funded by major foundations, prompted early attention to questions of evaluation. They often began rather routinely with a notion of good practice – that both funders and campuses, alike, ought to be able to document the benefits and values of programmatic efforts. The questions were relatively simple. What has been the impact of these efforts and have foundation funds been well invested? The method was often equally basic – hire some outside 'experts' to visit campuses and evaluate the initiatives and the impact of the initiatives on the institution. The conclusions were not so simple. In the evaluation of Ford Foundation-funded projects, the evaluators reported, 'One of the most stunning surprises for the Ford Evaluation Team was how little assessment was done. Anywhere. Except in the most perfunctory ways, it was largely ignored as the valuable resource it can be for illuminating issues and improving learning' (Musil et al

1995: 45). The absence of ongoing institutional evaluation limited the degree to which outside evaluators could come to understand programmes or institutional progress. This concern has been echoed elsewhere in the literature (Smith et al 1997).

Effective evaluation, however, has never been a strong element of United States education, particularly in higher education. The system is extremely decentralised, not only among campuses, but on campuses. Except for the requirements of regional and specialised accreditation and occasional (though often perfunctory) programme reviews, systemic evaluation is not part of the ongoing efforts of most campuses or programmes. Many view evaluation as something done by experts. Others view it as either a luxury or a burden. Moreover, few studies have, until recently, paid attention to a broad range of constituencies – trustees, families, policy-makers, lawyers, the public. The urgency of the calls for evaluation have increased dramatically in the last few years and, it would appear, can no longer be avoided.

On the assumption that no societies have achieved the kind of cultural democracy envisioned in the current diversity initiatives and that few, if any, individuals have ever fully participated in such diverse cultural environments, research and evaluation are emerging as necessary to study the evolution and effectiveness of particular approaches and strategies. Good will and lists of programmatic efforts will not be sufficient if they do not result in building institutional capacities for diversity throughout higher education as well as the capacity to communicate to broader publics. Indeed, early evaluation reports suggest that campuses in their efforts 'to respond' to increasing pressures, may simply be adding programme upon programme, initiative on initiative, resulting in burn-out for individuals without cumulative benefits (Musil et al 1995; Smith 1997). Indeed, the impact of these efforts is rarely understood even within the institution. Most typically the data are not available for informed conversation.

The urgency of the need, however, can be seen in the context of three other pressures looming large in the United States. First, higher education is under enormous pressure to contain the growth of expenses. Second, there has been

157

pressure to demonstrate accountability and higher standards in all that is done. The calls for accountability have resulted from public concern about educational effectiveness, the increasing cost of education, and from a broader understanding that higher education will be better served by paying more attention to educational results than simply resource allocation and programmatic efforts (Astin 1991). Finally, the urgency emerges from fundamental legal and voter challenges to the use of race and gender in the process of admissions and hiring in education, and, in government programmes. Recent court cases and state ballot initiatives have placed affirmative action and the use of race and gender categories in jeopardy. There are many interpretations as to why non-supportive public opinion and policy initiatives appear to be emerging. It is apparent that insufficient information, lack of understanding, and poor timing have put supporters of diversity on the defensive, which has played right into opponents' hands. Moreover, many well meaning people perceive that attending to diversity causes problems – that it is essentially divisive, counterproductive, unfair, and undemocratic. Until recently, little evidence was available for a response, and few efforts were made to effectively communicate both the purposes and results of campus-based efforts. How frustrating to be seen as fostering divisiveness when so many efforts on campuses go to the heart of developing an effective society (Association of American Colleges and Universities 1995).

Evolution of the concept of diversity

One of the elementary challenges to responding to calls for evaluation is that the concept of diversity has also been evolving. Today, without a reasonable conceptual framework, its meaning and purpose can be so vague or so all encompassing as to be difficult to evaluate. Moreover, the deeper understanding of diversity has necessitated continuing focus on issues of language, how issues are framed, and on the development of a conceptual framework critical to evaluation that is strategic.

Language

The use of the term 'minority' or 'disadvantaged minority' and the names given to groups are rooted in assumptions about language and the relationship between language and power. Thus, no paper on this topic can be written without attentiveness to language and its use. Today, it is most widely understood that 'self naming' is a statement about power with enormous political implications. How a group is named, by whom, and for what purpose has become central rather than trivial. The evolution of the terms African American and Black, lesbian and gay, has mirrored and shaped societal discussions about race. The terms Asian American and Latino, despite the enormous variety among Latino and Asian American groups, have come to embody a political reality to highlight and strengthen, through aggregated numbers, the perspective of groups that had been largely invisible in the traditional discourse about race in education. More and more attention is now being focused on these issues by scholars who believe that not to do so limits the understanding of race and ethnicity in America (e.g. Hune and Chan 1997). For the purposes of this paper, 'persons of colour' and Latino, African American, Native American, and Asian American have been used as terms for the major ethnic groups under discussion. Newly emerging issues include the growth in the number of 'multiracial' persons and how they should be 'counted', and the use of the term 'racialised' instead of race (Darder and Torres 1998; Mukhopadhyay and Moses 1997).

Framing

How issues are framed influences the problems identified for evaluation and the solutions developed. Framing also influences the design and implications of any research, but especially evaluation research. These often mirror the larger societal and educational discussions as well as the predilections of different evaluation disciplines. As United States higher education focused on issues of access to higher education and opened its doors to those who had been excluded, it became apparent that simply opening doors was not sufficient to achieve equity in access. Because the concern was framed in terms of why certain groups were not well represented or succeeding, years of research have focused on the characteristics (often in psychological terms) of individuals that could explain lack of qualifications, merit, or success. The response has been to develop initiatives and programmes for deficits. This was reflected in a literature that described 'the problem of diversity' (Smith 1989). For example, many studied the characteristics of women – brains, hormones, socialisation styles to explain their absence in science. Others have studied the characteristics of culture and family that might explain the absence of certain ethnic groups in higher education. Diversity was understood to be vested in solving the problems of those groups. In this context, one can see why issues related to Asian American students who were labelled 'model minorities' were ignored for years. Only when issues of the climate of the campus and the adequacy of the curriculum were addressed, did other racial groups appear to be important.

Today's discussions about competitive admissions based on standardised tests focus, often, on improving the academic preparation of students, not on the adequacy of the tests as indicators of merit. Framing issues of preparation and excellence in terms of scores on standardised tests narrows and limits the evidence which can be used in discussions of success and access. That limited framing of the issue is central to the legal and public policy challenges which are occurring in the United States during the late 1990s. Tests are being used as evidence for lack of merit, thus allowing legal and public policy debates to infer that certain underrepresented groups should not be allowed entrance into competitive public institutions because they lack merit (Sedlacek 1997).

A focus on the institution, its approaches, and its role have emerged only recently. With that has come more inquiry into the ways in which institutional approaches, traditions, and certain values can alienate and exclude those that have no history in higher education. Further, by focusing on the viability of institutions in a pluralistic society, diversity becomes important not only to serve new populations, but to maintain the health and well-being of the institution. Indeed, the focus on the problems students bring with them means that the efforts to transform the curriculum have too often been based on rather weak arguments about self-esteem rather than on issues concerning the educational viability, adequacy, and scholarly integrity of the material being presented. Research on the success of special purpose institutions, such as women's colleges or Historically Black Colleges and Universities, illuminates the factors related to success in

diversity becomes important to maintain the health and well-being of the institution

these institutions and also frames the issues primarily in terms of the institution itself (Smith 1989).

How an issue is framed takes on great importance in the recent policy and public debates on affirmative action. These have been almost entirely framed in terms of the legacy of racism and sexism on the preparation of individuals to 'play on a level playing field'. Almost none of the discussion has been framed in terms of the capacity of institutions and individuals to diversify admissions, hiring, and selection procedures; yet we know that part of the imperative of affirmative action was to encourage institutions and processes to be more accountable in criteria and evaluation of merit and potential. Similarly, campuses have been on the defensive with regard to whether ethnic group activities on campus promote divisiveness rather than attempts to address both support and intergroup activities (e.g. Duster 1995, Tatum 1997).

The history of engagement with racial diversity in the United States has historically emphasised relations between African Americans and whites. That emphasis continues to some degree today. However, in the current scholarship of diversity in the United States, intersecting differences that cut across race, class, gender, sexual orientation, religion, and other marked categories dominate the discourse. There is a greater understanding of how race, for example, is gendered, or how gender is divided by class, or how religion influences attitudes towards sexuality. Moreover, in parts of the United States where there are increasing numbers of Latinos/as, Asian Americans, Native Americans, and strong white ethnic communities, campuses and communities struggle to conceptualise issues in ways that honour the histories of current communities, recognise the tension between and within ethnic groups, and engage power and economic issues within the larger society. These need not be framed in ways that divide groups; but they too often are. Attaining a new sense of multiple and overlapping identities and the complexities of such a reality is an issue on campuses throughout the country.

What is clearly emerging today is the necessity to develop greater clarity and complexity in terms of language, framing of issues, and in terms of the focus of attention in the discussion of diversity in higher education.

A multi-dimensional view of diversity

The evolution of campus diversity initiatives has prompted many to call for increasing clarity about what is meant by diversity. As the concept has broadened in its meaning, some have argued that this breadth will negate its significance. Conceptually, thinking of diversity as operating in a number of dimensions has become useful. By looking at multiple dimensions, the meaning of diversity and its relationship to specific groups, by race, ethnicity, gender, sexual orientation, and so on, and to specific efforts, such as curricular reform, can be articulated more clearly. Moreover, attending to each of the dimensions reveals both their distinctiveness and the connections among them. Indeed, this framework suggests that each dimension, taken separately, is critical; all of the dimensions understood collectively is imperative.

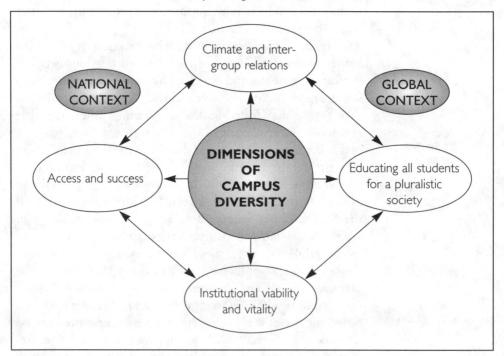

Figure 1

Figure 1 depicts four interrelated dimensions of campus diversity. These dimensions can be seen through the lens of specific groups involved, campus activities, or initiatives focused in the area, through the lens of institutional efforts to enhance vitality and viability, and through the kinds of

162

evaluation questions one might ask. The first dimension, access and success, is concerned principally with the inclusion and success of historically underrepresented groups and concerns for social justice. Diversity efforts began here and have been focused on historically under-represented racial and ethnic groups, and on white women. Success here has largely been studied through numbers, representation on campus, representation in relation to some larger population, and graduation/completion rates for students.

The second dimension, campus climate and intergroup relations, focuses on the environment of the campus for groups traditionally marginalised. Here the focus has expanded to include not only issues of racism and acts of intolerance concerning race and ethnicity, but issues related to sexual orientation, and the climate for women and more marginalised religious groups. Because of the increasing recognition of the importance of diversity for civic democracy, the continuing focus on creating supportive climates on campus has expanded to include attention to intergroup relations and the ways that all student, faculty, staff, and individuals do (or don't) interact and work with one another. Evaluation efforts here often focus on percep-tions of the climate, patterns and levels of interaction, the conditions under which diverse individuals come together, the results of increased interactions, and the effectiveness of a wide variety of programmes to improve the climate and intergroup relations.

The third dimension characterises the concerns about diversity from the perspective of the educational and scholarly role of the institution. This is an issue of significance for all students and might be seen as parallel to recent efforts to transform our campuses so that students can function in a technological society. The educational dimension, then, focuses on educating all students to live and function in a very pluralistic society and increasingly linked global community. Evaluation efforts focus on questions of curricular content, scholarly activities, faculty diversity, teaching and learning, and faculty development. How adequate is the current curriculum and scholarship for educating all students for a pluralistic society and world? What teaching and learning strategies serve this purpose?

How effective are efforts to deepen faculty engagement with new scholarship and research related to diversity within and among the disciplines? What differences are the large number of curriculum transformation projects making in student learning? How prepared are students to participate in a diverse work force?

Finally, the last dimension steps back and asks about the role of diversity in ensuring institutional viability and vitality. What kind of institutions will best serve and be seen as appropriate for a diverse society? One might also ask the question as a negative. What does it mean for the success of institutions to lack diversity, to lack the capacity to engage pluralism in all its forms, and to ignore students' capacity to be part of a pluralistic society? What does it mean if the student body is diverse, but the rest of the institution is not? Significantly, this dimension focuses attention not just on students, but on the staff and faculty, relationships to important constituencies such as alumni and trustees, institutional mission and planning, and on relationships to communities outside the institution. In each of these domains issues of diversity emerge. The negative frame of this question underscores the centrality of diversity in this period of history. Evaluating diversity from this institutional perspective encompasses the prior dimensions but centres the questions in terms of institutional capacity and success. Institutional 'audits' can begin to capture the stories of institutional engagement, history, and development. Some have assembled portfolios as a means of assessment (Ingle 1994).

While each dimension can be seen discretely, they are deeply related. Issues of access and success, for example, have been directly related to such issues as campus climate, curriculum, and faculty hiring. Similarly, the focus on intergroup relations on campus has directly led to more intense study and scholarship in areas related to intergroup relations and the ways in which the curriculum and teaching and learning link students with one another on shared tasks. All of these questions fundamentally inform institutional success in terms of attributes like effective teaching, scholarship, vitality, or mentoring. Moreover, each is deeply linked to societal issues of economic, political, and social well being.

Evolution of evaluation in the context of diversity in the United States

Evaluations of diversity initiatives take place in the larger context of higher education policy and practice, and, of course, in the context of evaluation more generally. How questions are framed, the methodologies employed, and the use to which the evaluation is put all are critically important and cannot be ignored.

Evaluation methodologies have themselves undergone significant change: in early periods, the primary focus was on assessment of individuals through the use of emerging testing techniques. This was followed by efforts to describe and then evaluate the worth of programmes designed to ameliorate some condition (Mertens 1998). In general, evaluation is viewed as a kind of research, though generally targeted to some particular applied purpose within a limited time frame. Like research, much of the early work in evaluation was developed using scientific approaches in the service of scientific management. More recent critiques of the field of evaluation reflect, in part, developments in the field of research, paradigmatic shifts in knowledge, and increasing concern for the uses to which evaluations are put. In both cases, many authors suggest that traditional models with their emphasis on 'proof', 'objectivity', 'value-free' design, quantification, measurement, and neutrality hold assumptions that are open to serious critique, and do not reflect the growing need for evaluations that reflect the complexity and context for such areas as diversity. A value-free approach, so central to notions of science and often linked to evaluation, are questioned, in part, because it suggests that the results of the effort are not the responsibility of the scientist. It also suggests a single notion of 'truth'. The focus on technical expertise related to evaluation methodology and the emphasis solely on quantification can fail to capture on its own the complex context in which most evaluations are conducted. Perhaps among the most disturbing aspects of the scientific model of evaluation is that it vests in the hands of 'experts' the capacity to know and renders others as unqualified to pursue evaluation. The result is that little evaluation is conducted and even less is linked deeply and directly to the institution's capacity to learn and improve. Neglected, too, in much of the literature has been the significance of evaluation for broader public audiences.

A number of authors, including Guba and Lincoln (1989), Mertens (1998), Greene (1994), and Darder (1994), describe new approaches to evaluation that fundamentally alter its assumptions. Guba and Lincoln use the phrase 'Fourth Generation Evaluation' to capture the changes from a scientific model to what one might call an emergent and heuristic post-modern model. Similarly Mertens (1998) suggests an 'emancipatory' model of evaluation to capture the particularly distinctive features of evaluation that serve 'social justice'. Patton (1997) elaborates on the 'paradigm' wars suggesting a more utilitarian approach. For contemporary authors, what is as important as method and technique are the values and groups being served. While scientific evaluation remains an important part of evaluation methodology, it is clear that new approaches and new frameworks are being introduced (Greene 1994).

In Guba's and Lincoln's model, they suggest six important properties of a 'fourth generation' approach:

- Evaluation is not a description of 'some "true" state of affairs' but instead represents efforts by those affected to 'make sense' of the situation (1989: 8).
- In a pluralistic society, where multiple values must be negotiated, a key part of evaluation is to be conscious of the values involved, whose values are being represented, and how different values might be included.
- Constructions of knowledge and meaning are linked to the social, physical, and cultural contexts in which they are found. The continued evidence in the United States of widely divergent perspectives on any one of a number of issues based on race and gender underscores the need to see evaluation from multiple perspectives.
- Evaluation can be used to empower or disempower groups by the uses to which they are put, the questions framed, and the methodologies employed. It also broadens the range of informed participants substantially beyond 'evaluation experts'.
- Evaluators must take into account the decisions to follow and to commit to decisions that will reflect the multiple participants involved and to be involved in the negotiating process necessary to decide on appropriate outcomes.
- Fourth generation evaluation emphasises that those

involved in evaluations need to be treated with dignity and respect beyond the normal criteria used in evaluation to the point of involvement, knowledgeability, and participation.

Clearly such an approach is quite distant from a model of evaluation that is a numbers driven, technical process, that simply produces data and facts for others to use as they will. Importantly, this approach also recognises, consistent with the more advanced notions of physics today, that interventions are not stable but are affected by their context. Today, for example, as many are attempting to evaluate curricular changes, one is faced with the fact that the efforts themselves are changing and are very much affected by the institutional context in which the changes are taking place. Finally, newer approaches to evaluation encourage thoughtful participation by a wide range of people who can contribute to what is seen and known. Perhaps what is most needed is an experimental approach to evaluation that engages participants and encourages newer strategies and tools.

Strategic evaluation

In the evaluation of diversity initiatives, these approaches can form the basis for negotiating the complex relationships of groups, outcomes, and context. Moreover, they can provide the promise of an investment in evaluation for the purposes of improvement, learning, and judgement that can be embraced by the multiple constituencies inevitably involved. By empowering participants to think systematically about what one needs to know and to develop multiple means of ascertaining that knowledge, the potential is created for internalising evaluation to improve education and position evaluation to serve strategic institutional and national purposes. What appears to be developing is the need for evaluation to be both systematic and strategic. As the issue of diversity moves to the center of national policy, legal challenges, and educational debates, the need increases for strategic evaluation. While strategic approaches suggest a deep engagement with audiences and efforts outside the institution (or programme), the need for ongoing systematic evaluation remains. In the spirit of new forms of evaluation, the process will need to be contextual, collaborative,

167

instructive, continuous, developmental, and open. Central, however, is the articulation of the purpose of evaluation, the important decision-makers, key participants, and those who might be affected by the evaluation. Clearly, in the past, traditional evaluation approaches neglected many key groups both on and off campus. Understanding who these are will inevitably influence the kind of questions asked. Too many evaluations begin as either pro forma concerns about satisfaction or ask 'it would be interesting to know …'. Yet, the methods and the sources of information require knowing more about the effort, its purpose, how results will be used, and by whom.

Evaluation, whether of an individual, a programme, an approach, or an institution, can be conducted for a broad range of societal, institutional, and programmatic reasons. Today, it must serve a number of important systematic and strategic purposes within and beyond a programme or campus:

- to build on the knowledge base that exists through systematic and ongoing information;
- to address questions and interests of those connected in some way to the programme or approach;
- to meet institutional needs – impact, developing priorities, strategic planning questions, accreditation;
- to enhance public learning and understanding;
- to respond to questions raised through the media, public dialogue, national issues and international policy interests;
- to answer legal questions and concerns;
- to serve as a methodological approach to programme reviews, self studies, and accreditation;
- to contribute to the larger field of evaluation as new approaches are developed.

Foundational to this participatory process is that expertise is vested in the participants and audiences who bring multiple perspectives and insights to the effort. Interestingly, these qualities are quite consistent with lessons that appear to be emerging across the United States from those who are engaged in a wide variety of efforts to evaluate diversity. Emerging from the literature, from studies on the evaluation of diversity, and from practitioners, these lessons help illuminate both the practice, context, and framework for strategic and systematic evaluation.

Lessons and observations from the field

Evaluation is inevitably part of the change process. In contrast to more traditional understandings of research that attempted to develop 'neutral' forms of truth, often applying to broad theories of human development, diversity evaluation can rarely avoid the reality of the perspectives and values that inform the questions asked, the methods employed, and the interpretations given to the data. Inevitably then, evaluation is part of the process of change – whether policy, human development, or theory. Evaluation research matters. Generating a study of graduation rates by race/ethnicity and by gender matters. How it is interpreted matters. The consequences for different groups matters. The degree to which results legitimate or challenge stereotypes matters. Thus, it requires a commitment to a more complex and thoughtful process – one that takes into account the implications as well as the design. Simply 'crunching' numbers will rarely be adequate.

The context for evaluation and key questions and issues must be understood. Evaluation – its design and its interpretation – is a human process. Results can be used in multiple ways. It is important therefore to be conscious of the context in which a given study is being done, its purpose, the intended audiences, and the multiple interpretations that can be offered. Indeed, it is apparent that the audiences today for evaluation research are much broader than ever before. The public must now be part of the circle of key participants as must others in the institution.

Understanding the purpose and framing the questions are important evaluation issues. Deficit models of research framed the research questions in terms of deficits to be found. Accountability in the institution and individual strengths could not be explored or discovered in such models. To conduct an evaluation in terms of institutional as well as individual or group roles in education requires a broader frame and a broader design. Legal needs, prompted by court challenges to affirmative action, are different than public policy needs directed to legislative bodies. How one

169

defines success must also be developed to serve the needs of different kinds of institutions.

There is power in voice and multiple methods. Many evaluation studies reflect an increasing use of multiple methodologies. Rather than relying simply on statistical analysis derived from empirical approaches such a demographic or survey data, campuses are combining these approaches with a wide variety of qualitative approaches. It is important to recognise that systematic qualitative research is not 'merely' anecdotal. Not everything should be studied via surveys, and not all questions can be quantified. Focus groups (e.g. Duster 1995), interviews (e.g. Musil 1992), institutional data (e.g. Nettles and Hudgins 1995), and case studies (e.g. Musil et al 1995) can all be used productively for particular needs. Hearing the voices of individuals attending to their experiences has a validity not represented by group means. Combined with aggregated data that reflect patterns within the institution, these 'voices' add power and substance to the evaluation. Moreover, in promoting change, campuses and policy makers find that these voices may be harder to dismiss and ignore than tables and statistics concerning, for example, the campus climate. Indeed, while it is often thought that only numbers hold sway with policy advocates, it is often the story accompanying the data is most influential.

Hearing the voices of individuals attending to their experiences has a validity not represented by group means.

The use of qualitative data also helps address one of the significant problems in evaluation research: how to or whether to aggregate diverse groups. While quantitative studies require a certain number to perform a statistical analysis, qualitative methods do not. It is common to read reports indicating that there was not enough of some group to report their data. The analysis for that group is commonly eliminated. Alternatively, aggregating across groups is commonly done to create larger groups or to simplify the analysis. Women as a group, for instance, are often not disaggregated by race which obscures differentials within various kinds of women. Latinos are commonly grouped regardless of the diversity of experience among Chicanos, Cubans, or Puerto Ricans. Similarly the experience of Asian Americans can be vastly different and typically requires delineation among Asian ethnic groups, especially between new immigrant groups and, say, fourth generation Asian Americans. Qualitative complimented by quantitative approaches can provide powerful insights.

There is a need for multiple participants. It is extraordinarily difficult for any one person to see all the dimensions of an evaluation question – developing a team that brings a number of diverse perspectives to the table seems more likely to uncover hidden assumptions, frame appropriate questions, and to create a study that will address issues appropriately. Recent discussions among lawyers and researchers about court challenges to affirmative action, for example, have revealed the very different questions that each professional group tends to raise. Evaluations designed to address legal questions may require quite a different focus than those designed to address educational questions. The same would be true about research designed to address media inquiries. By participating together, more people are empowered to think about what is needed while still bringing relevant expertise to the table.

The evaluation should be informed by related research and theory. Well meaning questions that can inform evaluation studies might, in fact, be framed in ways that are not constructive. Being aware of the larger critical literature on issues of diversity can assist in framing questions most likely to lead to useful results. Moreover, existing theories in the field can serve to deepen the knowledge. For example, work in intergroup relations – all theoretically driven – has been very important in deepening the understanding of some behavioral dynamics. In a similar fashion, there is relevant and important basic and applied research occurring in a surprisingly wide variety of fields, from population demographics, to biology, to history, to philosophy that can contribute significantly to research questions, methods, and conceptual issues.

Similarly, much of higher education research in the United States is centered in domestic issues and rarely explores an international context or the lessons emerging outside of our national borders. There are, however, several diversity efforts that warrant systematic study in their own right and for their implications for research and practice in the United States. The Ford Foundation's trinational diversity initiative involving India, South Africa, and the United States provides opportunities to study the dynamics of institutional change in diverse national contexts. In addition, the Kettering Foundation's work in eastern Europe might also have implications for building diverse communities that have histories of tension and conflict. These other locations of theory, culture, and history can provide a framework that explains and contextualises results.

Evaluation research must be placed in an institutional, and even a national, context. An intergroup relations project, a course transformation, faculty development efforts, student retention – all exist in an institutional context that can deeply influence effectiveness, volatility, and resource needs. Indeed, newly emerging work suggests that a student's experience of particular diversity efforts is directly influenced by their perceptions of an institutional commitment to diversity (Hurtado et al 1996). In the same way, institutional commitment, mission, history, geographical location, served populations, resources, and stage of development have an impact on perceptions about programmes and initiatives. Community colleges will often see student success, for example, as having multiple definitions. Colleges dedicated to a particular mission or group may frame issues and evaluation in ways appropriate for the group, including defining an approach to education that is 'value-added' rather than selective. Evaluation studies are probably best understood from at least three perspectives of the individual involved, the programme, and the institution.

Multiple tiers help to keep evaluation manageable. No matter where an evaluation begins, whether analysing graduation rates, the campus climate, or faculty hiring, the process of discussion and analysis inevitably leads to almost every other dimension. The end result is that evaluating the campus or even a programme can be difficult to manage. Numerous strategies for keeping evaluations manageable and yet appropriately broad must be emphasized. One strategy involves determining the fundamental issues and questions that need to be evaluated either on an ongoing basis or for special purposes. Qualitative and open-ended techniques permit important issues to emerge without an evaluation team prejudging what they are. At the same time, campus climate studies and institutional satisfaction studies allow ongoing evaluations of a wide variety of campus experiences and activities within a very manageable campus survey approach. Where needed, linking campus strategies to ongoing public opinion and public policy issues fosters an institutional capacity to frame public conversations and influence decision-making.

Communication and process are essential. In the world of evaluation, it is common for an evaluator to be chosen who will remain distant from the issues at hand, will collect data, and then will issue a report from afar. More than on most topics, issues of communication and design are fundamental to diversity evaluation. In areas of diversity, evaluations are often politically and emotionally charged. These days researchers, programmers, and institutions are on the defensive. This reality is both an opportunity and a challenge. From the beginning, decisions about language, framing, process, and important groups to be consulted or included must be thought through. In addition, campuses rarely have identified locations (committees, public forums, cabinet meetings) where the results can be discussed and the implications developed. Thus, many are left to deal with contradictory interpretations that feed divisions rather than facilitating communication. This occurs in national conversations as well. Recent public opinion polls in the state of Washington, sponsored by The Ford Foundation Public Information Campaign, revealed greater support for campus diversity initiatives than many on campus assumed and suggested ways in which people understood these issues.

diversity evaluations are sensitive, prone to undetected bias, and open to multiple interpretations

The challenge is that diversity evaluations are sensitive, prone to undetected bias, and open to multiple interpretations from multiple perspectives. Indeed, any evaluation will need to recognise and deal with the deep underlying issues of racism, power, and marginality. It is not lost on many people that while some insist that the educational value of diversity be proven, few are calling for similar efforts related to technology on campus.

173

Nevertheless, evaluation of diversity efforts and deep discussion and communication of the results provide opportunities to study and learn about strategies for improving campus approaches, involving a broader range of the community in thinking of diversity, and creating forums in which systematic study can inform policy and practice. Moreover, communication about efforts and results need to be developed in partnership with public relations, media, and others so that appropriate publics are more informed about diversity commitments and consequences.

Synthesis of existing studies is needed. Rarely is a single study complete in and of itself. Moreover, there is a tendency to ask for 'proof' of some policy approach in ways that any single study cannot provide. Indeed, even dozens of studies are rarely definitive. Rather, social science research relies on patterns that emerge across a wide variety of studies. For that reason, in the absence of research that can, for example, 'prove' the positive impact of diversity initiatives in a politically charged policy context, there is an urgent and continuing need for synthesis and critiques in the form of reviews of the literature. It is especially important to look at these results through a variety of research methodologies. There are a number of challenges, of course, including the need for coherent frameworks for presentation of a multidimensional set of questions, and the difficulty of keeping track of campus based and often unpublished research. Nonetheless, this kind of research can be very important both for establishing research needs in the field and for suggesting trends or conclusions.

Campuses struggle to become organisational learners; a role for foundations and funders. In addition to the complex issues already described, more work is needed on the development of effective models of evaluation and tools. Some of the recent attempts to study student learning have been hampered by the need to develop approaches and questions sufficiently sensitive to the diversity of student and faculty perspectives. Leadership support and a culture focused on organisational learning are also key. Evaluation of diversity initiatives is directly tied to the issues of assessment more generally. It would appear, however, that the requirement to do evaluation prompted by outside agencies and foundations is a powerful incentive that could be strengthened by greater attention to resources and design.

Conclusion

The evaluation studies of diversity in higher education must maintain a multifocal perspective that includes the success of underrepresented students, the dynamics of institutional climate and change, the educational and research needs that educating all students for a diverse society requires, and finally the question of institutional health and viability. At its core we must begin to study with greater depth and clarity what it is that a focus on diversity contributes and how diversity evolves. At the same time, we must underscore what the absence of diversity and attention to diversity might mean educationally and societally. The communication of these efforts in clear, concise, and compelling language will increase in its urgency.

The issues surrounding evaluation deal both with the particulars of diversity initiatives and evaluation methodology. The vulnerability of most diversity initiatives and the marginality of its participants and programmes require both strategic and systematic designs and process. Current approaches tend to disempower even the brightest and most creative academics by claiming a technical and 'expert' knowledge. Developing a more robust and creative approach to evaluation and positioning the evaluation to function as a part of the development of an institution's capacity to learn and to progress is now well within the range of possibility.

REFERENCES

Association of American Colleges and Universities (1995) *The Drama of Diversity and Democracy*. Washington, DC.

Astin, AW (1991) *Assessment for Excellence*. Washington, DC: American Council on Education.

Darder, A (1994) 'Institutional research as a tool for cultural democracy'. In DG Smith, LE Wolf, T Levitan (eds) *Studying Diversity in Higher Education. New Directions for Institutional Research*, 81. San Francisco: Jossey Bass.

Darder, A and Torres, R (1998) 'Latinos and society: culture, class and politics'. In A Darder and R Torres (eds) *The Latino Studies Reader: Culture, Economy, and Society*. London: Blackwell.

Duster, T (1995) 'They're taking over! And other myths about race on campus'. In M Bérubé and C Nelson (eds) *Higher Education Under Fire*. New York: Routledge.

Greene, JC (1994) 'Qualitative programme evaluation: practice and promise'. In NK Denzin and YS Lincoln (eds) *The Handbook of Qualitative Research*. Thousand Oaks, Ca.: Sage.

Guba, EG and Lincoln, TY (1989) *Fourth Generation Evaluation*. Thousand Oaks, Ca.: Sage.

Hurtado, S, JF Milam, WR Allen and AR Clayton-Pedersen (1996) Improving the *Climate for Racial/ethnic Diversity in Higher Education*. Report to the Common Destiny Alliance, College Park, Maryland.

Hune, S and Chan, KS (1997) 'Special focus: Asian Pacific American demographic and educational trends', *Fifteenth Annual Status Report on Minorities in Higher Education*. Washington, DC: American Council on Education.

Ingle, HT (1994) 'Charting campus progress in promoting ethnic diversity and cultural pluralism'. In DG Smith, LE Wolf, T Levitan (eds) *Studying Diversity in Higher Education. New Directions for Institutional Research*, 81. San Francisco: Jossey Bass.

Mertens, DM (1998) *Research Methods in Education and Psychology: Integrating Diversity with Quantitative and Qualitative Approaches*. Thousand Oaks, Ca.: Sage Publications.

Mukhopadhyay, CC and YT Moses (1997) 'Reestablishing race in anthropological discourse', *American Anthropologist*, 99(3): 517-533.

Musil, CM (ed.) (1992) *The Courage to Question: Women's Studies and Student Learning*. Washington, DC: Association of American Colleges and Universities.

Musil, CM (ed.) (1992) *Students at the Center: Feminist Assessment*. Washington, DC: Association of American Colleges and Universities.

Musil, CM, M García, Y Moses, and DG Smith (1995) *Diversity in Higher Education: A Work in Progress*. Washington, DC: Association of American Colleges and Universities.

Nettles, MT and C Hudgins (1995) *Tolerance on Campus: Establishing Common Ground Initiatives*. An evaluation of the Philip Morris Companies, Inc.

Patton, MQ (1997) *Utilisation-focused Evaluation: The New Century Text*. Thousand Oaks, Ca.: Sage Publications.

Sedlacek, W (1997) 'Strategies for social change research'. Unpublished paper, University of Maryland.

Smith, DG (1989) *The Challenge of Diversity: Involvement or Alienation in the Academy?* ASHE-ERIC Report No. 5, Washington, DC: George Washington University Press.

Smith, DG (1997) *The Progress of a Decade: An Imperative for the Future*. A report to the James Irvine Foundation. San Francisco, Ca.

Smith, DG and associates (1997) *Diversity Works: The Emerging Picture of How Students Benefit*. Washington, DC: Association of American Colleges and Universities.

Tatum, BD (1997) *Why Are All The Black Kids Sitting Together In The Cafeteria And Other Conversations About Racial Identity*. New York: Basic Books.

176

College outreach and the college curriculum

Sharada Nayak

Educational Resources Centre, New Delhi

'*Democracy must, in essence, mean the art and science of mobilising the entire physical, economic and spiritual resources of all the various sections of the people in the service of the common good of all.*'

—Mahatma Gandhi

The challenge of the Diversity Initiative is to transform society by engaging the many divisions, differences, and disparities in our midst through the educational process. To educate young people in a situation that is not linked with the human condition of the people around is not the goal of an educational institution. Diversity is an inclusive term that embraces all the differences we see around us. In this context, we would redefine community to encompass the unassimilated different groups that touch the college, its place in the area, and its space where all these differences converge. The college has a commitment to the pluralistic community, but most often its role does not extend beyond the scholarship and course offerings to the students. Its interaction with diversity remains passive and rarely does it engage with the contentious issues that frequently arise from this pluralism.

The word 'community' in India has a definition that is peculiarly Indian. Most often it refers to a specific religious or caste group. When a conflict develops between two religious groups we call it a communal problem; when a person refers to his or her own community it invariably means a caste or social group with which that person

177

identifies, ethnically and socially. Here we are looking at a community that is neither of these two: we rather refer to a population of a town or city that lives within the proximity of the college and from which the college draws its students. Therefore, the social and economic diversity issues that arise have a direct impact on the college. One of the most important elements of the Campus Diversity Initiative is its linkage and interaction with the community. In Community Outreach, we would list our goals as:

- increasing student consciousness of the social concerns and problems that are created by the differences in the community;
- involving the students in nation-building by engaging them in diversity issues, and attempting to reduce the tensions that arise from social and economic disparities by bridging them;
- establishing contacts and involving the community in campus activities and concerns, through parents of students, social organisations and professional clubs, and non-governmental organisations engaged in developmental work;
- making the campus a focal point of community discussion thereby widening the educational parameters beyond the academe.

The Campus Diversity Initiative in India has involved the participating colleges in community outreach in many ways. Firstly, it has built on existing programmes that have been in place through the nation-wide government policies. Secondly, it has identified individual projects for effectively linking the college with its own immediate community.

Since the 1960s we have talked about the increasing irrelevance of our higher education, a consequent alienation of academics and deterioration in the campus environment. Gandhi had clearly foreseen such a situation for he used to plead for students being given constructive responsibility in community development programmes. In 1969, the year of Gandhi's birth centenary, the Government launched a scheme called the National Service Scheme (NSS) linking higher education with the needs of the community. The NSS added a new dimension to the process of education, bringing students in touch with community development and in the process sensitising them and helping to build them into self-confident citizens.

NSS is a selective and voluntary scheme – a fixed number of students are selected from applicants in colleges. The emphasis is on learning through community service, combining study with service, and thus developing own character and identity. These volunteer student groups have been involved in national issues and problem-solving endeavours: drought, environmental degradation, eradication of malaria – these are some of the areas in which students have engaged in community service. The slogan is 'Personality Development through Community Service'. Today the NSS has over 1,35 million student volunteers spread over 158 universities and junior colleges. (Due to the popularity of the system, the scheme was extended to the last two years of high school/junior college years). The expenditure is shared between the Central Government and the States. The programmes are of two kinds: regular activities, where students are expected to work as volunteers for a continuous period of two years rendering community service for a minimum of 120 hours per year, and camping programmes, where youth camps are held for ten days duration to work on a project. The government spends RS 120 per volunteer for the Regular programme and RS 120 for the Special Camps.

Although the work of the NSS is laudable, it has lost its momentum and effectiveness through the years. At the commemoration of 25 years of NSS, a stock-taking was done. The main criticisms were directed towards a lack of leadership at the university level, due to lack of interest of the faculty. The faculty member in charge of NSS activities on a campus is given this project as an additional extra-curricular activity, i.e. in addition to teaching duties. The effectiveness of the programme depends on his or her enthusiasm for, and dedication to the scheme. The university continues to emphasise teaching and research and the dimension of extension is still short-changed. Other criticisms include no proper monitoring of the NSS programmes, and a lack of integration with the academic curriculum. The university system is so conservative that to change the decision-making bodies in universities and to bring faculty involvement into such programmes remains a stumbling block. There have been recommendations by Commissions appointed by the Government that the NSS should be integrated into the curriculum and made mandatory for all students, not merely for a group of volunteers. But these recommendations have not been accepted so far.

The Campus Diversity Initiative (CDI) colleges have linked their Diversity projects with the existing NSS programmes on their campuses. Their work has gone beyond the NSS dimension, however, by involving the whole campus and bringing faculty into the scheme with renewed emphasis. The system of giving the students credit for their work in the community has been instituted in some colleges. In other campuses, the sensitisation of students to social issues in CDI programmes has made the NSS group better motivated. One college faculty member told me that after an NSS camp to which he took a group of students, the National Service Scheme organiser and leader asked him why his students were different and better motivated than the representatives from other college groups. The faculty member opined that the CDI efforts had started in the freshman year with a programme that impacted on their personality development and commitment to service. This, he felt, had made all the difference to the students' attitude to community problems.

Community outreach, extension programmes and the curriculum

India has one of the largest higher education systems in the world. It has grown rapidly since independence; colleges and universities have multiplied more than ten times since 1950. At the time of Independence in 1947, there were only 20 universities and 500 colleges in the country. In 1997, there are 171 central and state universities, 38 deemed universities and 9 278 colleges.

Several reforms have been attempted but the size and the structure of the university system is a major constraint. Under the system of affiliating colleges that we have inherited from colonial days, the curriculum is approved by the university and must be adopted by the colleges. The affiliating colleges do not have the freedom to introduce courses and formulate curricula. Examinations are conducted and degrees offered by the university. Some universities have more than 250 affiliating colleges, with a wide variety in the quality of education offered, and in the social composition of the students enrolled. Frequently the academic courses offered have little relevance to the economic and social needs of the students.

However, among the more than 9 000 colleges in the country, there are 113 colleges (spread over 8 states) that have opted for and sought autonomous status. This implies that the college can formulate its own curriculum and evaluation, although the university awards the degree.

The Education Commission (1964–66) proposed initially to grant autonomy to selected colleges in the country. The affiliating university's role would be to grant autonomy (if a college meets specified criteria), to ensure through general supervision that the college lives up to expectations, and to confer degrees on students recommended by the college. The University Grants Commission (UGC) began the process of implementing the scheme in 1973 with the aim of giving an opportunity to teachers and students to make innovations, utilise their creative talents, improve the standards of teaching, examination and research, and quickly respond to social needs.

Of the 23 institutions participating in the Campus Diversity Initiative (see Annexure), there are four autonomous colleges and two universities which have the freedom to introduce curriculum changes. Six colleges are minority institutions managed by religious bodies, Christian and Muslim, who have special privileges and autonomy granted to them legally. The curriculum designed by these institutions has been either directly introduced as part of the Campus Diversity Initiative, or existing programmes have been strengthened and given a wider application as a result of the CDI grant. A few of these community outreach programmes are described here.

Many of the grantee colleges in the Campus Diversity Initiative have established rural extension projects where students have contributed their time and labour towards development of poorer communities. Some of the outreach programmes are limited to surveys done by students that relate to their course work – the study of rural employment, cottage industries, employment generation, and farming activities. For the urban students from upper income families, this exposure to rural problems has been a

181

memorable and a humbling experience. Despite the lack of amenities and proper educational facilities in rural areas they have seen how students of their age are bright and motivated, and have the same aspirations as their urban counterparts. All the students we have talked to in these colleges express an understanding of developmental problems and empathy for the people.

Other colleges have an ongoing programme of extension work in which all students are involved during their three-year undergraduate study. St Joseph's College, Tiruchirapalli, has a programme of rural outreach called SHEPHERD which had been introduced by the college to establish close links with rural communities and thus to foster change and empowerment through mutual exchange.

The strength of the programme lies in its ability to engage the entire student community.

The strength of the programme lies in its ability to engage the entire student community, so that every learning activity is a two-way process, a collective activity of the faculty, students and the villagers. The college has outreach programmes in 60 neighbourhood village communities. The Campus Diversity Initiative has strengthened this activity which in turn has improved inter-student and student-faculty relationships. The changes in the curriculum are effected through an inter-disciplinary approach where all the departments of the college, both in the sciences and the humanities, are involved in the rural programme. The science courses include rural technology and science projects with rural schools. Every student is required to put in 70 hours of work in this extension programme.

St Xavier's College, Palayamkottai, has a similar programme of rural outreach where students give 100 hours of their time per year, staying weekends in villages, to work with the villages in various extension projects. Being an autonomous college, St Xavier's is also engaged in curriculum reform, incorporating the concepts of diversity in a multi-disciplinary approach.

St Mary's College, Tuticorin, has a project in slum areas of this port city where the college is located. The students work in the areas of literacy and health, particularly with the women, encouraging them to take up income generation activities and helping them start small savings in banks. The women from these poorer sections of society are invited to visit the college so that there is an attempt to bring them in contact with students other than those who work with them, through cultural programmes which the students and the slum dwellers present. Although this minority women's college does not have autonomous status, they have sought and received the recognition of the university of this extension course as a part of their undergraduate degree syllabus.

Farook College, Calicut, involves its students in two major outreach activities: one in a village near the college where the students helped build a road, and the other in a slum area where they have cleared drains and built sanitation facilities leading to a marked improvement in the surroundings. The rapport built up by the students with the population in these areas is an important link for the college with the community, even though they do not receive academic credit for their work. The students comment on how this activity has sensitised them to the needs of the marginal population in the city.

Several other colleges have started programmes with rural or low income groups in the vicinity of the campus and linked these activities to the curriculum. For example, women's studies courses have been strengthened in two women's colleges, Isabella Thoburn College, Lucknow, and Savitri Girls College, Ajmer, through the students' work with women's groups in the poorer sections of society. Departments of Sociology are incorporating studies conducted by students in tribal areas in Madhya Pradesh (Narmada College, Hoshangabad), the hill areas of Uttar Pradesh (DAV College, Dehra Dun), and the Himalayan region of West Bengal (Kalimpong College, Darjeeling district). And the botany syllabus is related to the medicinal plants that are used by the indigenous people in these areas. At the last National Conference of the Campus Diversity Initiative, we discussed how the colleges could work out collaborative research projects that could be a valuable outcome of the diversity programmes.

SNDT Women's University has introduced two courses for freshmen entering the colleges affiliated to the University: History as Heritage and Current Concerns. These have been very well received by the students, and after some orientation this multidisciplinary approach to teaching subjects through Foundation courses has been accepted by the faculty. Still in its initial stages of evaluation, this attempt by the University is however a major step towards offering an integrated approach towards an understanding of the diversity of India in many dimensions.

These are all early beginnings in attempts by some of colleges to widen the educational experience of undergraduates, but the impact on students was evident in their discussions with CDI consultants in the campus visits.

The question we asked the college faculty and students is whether the impact on the students remains a campus issue or whether there is a wider social transformation through the campus-community interaction. Indian students generally learn their values from a close-knit traditional family structure in our society. Caste and religion are the strong underpinnings of traditional Indian society. When conflicts arise between social groups, students are drawn into them through the neighbourhood factions. Two of the CDI colleges have had to tackle explosive issues in the community by counselling the students and inculcating a spirit of harmony and acceptance of caste differences. When a riot broke out in the port town of Tuticorin between two groups of people living on the fringes of society, some of the girls in St Mary's College lost members of their family in the violence. On the campus efforts were made to talk to the students, discuss the issues, and bring about understanding and a sense of mutual tolerance among girls who were directly affected by the riot. The college principal and faculty feel that they had brought a feeling of fellowship among their girls. However, the students returning to their homes in the smouldering neighbourhoods may not be effective peace-makers. But the college holds out the hope that they have effected a change in the thinking of the younger generation and the campus climate is calm.

Another college, this time a men's college, is equally affected by the violent confrontation between two social groups who have – through the better part of the century – carried on a feud that has its genesis in land ownership and rural inequalities. The principal and faculty of St Xavier's College have successfully kept the conflict away from the campus but continue to fight the pressures from the caste groups in the neighbourhood. The boys from these communities now have the opportunity to study in college – an education to which their fathers had no access. The conviction that education and economic betterment of the Alesser communities would bring about a change in the outlook of the younger generation keeps alive the courage of conviction when the going gets tough.

Involving the students in rural projects implies not only fighting the social prejudices in the villages, but also the thinking of the students who have had such discriminating practices inculcated in them in their family upbringing. As one of them stated, 'I live and work with girls of all caste groups in my college without any discrimination. But it would be difficult to take my friends home if my parents and grandparents object – though I do argue with my family on this matter.'

One of the goals of the Campus Diversity Initiative is to work to counter the forces of caste and religious differences. These are so varied in different parts of the country that when representatives of the colleges meet at seminars and conferences they are often surprised to hear about the experiences of faculty from different regions of the country. At a recent meeting, principals and teachers from colleges managed by traditional Hindu groups were surprised to hear about the depth of social differences among Christian groups in some parts of the country which were for centuries divided along caste lines.

In this sharing of experiences one often hears others say, 'We never knew that ...'. While projects and programmes like the Campus Diversity Initiative attempt to inculcate the spirit of humanism and social equity, it is important to study more closely whether the programme has affected the minds of a generation that is struggling to reconcile tradition with the global impact of technology and economic interdependence. The time is undoubtedly right for launching the Initiative and the next phase must involve a closer research into the qualitative changes that have taken place as a result of the Campus Diversity Initiative.

Partnerships in the second phase of the Diversity Initiative

After an initial evaluation of the Diversity Initiative we felt encouraged to extend CDI activities to a second phase through the award of partnership grants. After inviting proposals from all the 23 grantee colleges currently participating in the Initiative, ten colleges have been selected, each of whom will network with four or five colleges in their region and thus widen the scope of the diversity programme. These partner institutions are diverse, some serving a rural or tribal population, some technical or vocational colleges, and some minority institutions. The interaction within each group of colleges, with the CDI grantee college as the nucleus, will allow for joint projects, as well as for programmes on individual campuses where students from other colleges will come together in shared activities. The grants are modest and the colleges are expected to cost-share in campus activities, but the enthusiasm of the smaller colleges in this group participation will hopefully extend the message of the diversity initiative to groups of students hitherto not touched by such programmes.

There is some effective networking among CDI colleges in the different regions of the country through activities in clusters of colleges. The host colleges informs all the other CDI grantees of their plans, inviting their participation. Where funds are available, groups of students travel long distances to join in these events and the feedback we receive from these students is very heartening.

I started by mentioning the lack of relevance of our education and academic offerings to a large section of our youth. This is particularly true of students from rural backgrounds. Making education relevant to their needs by introducing courses that are skill-orientated and linked to employment sources in the district is an important dimension that needs to be emphasised. This will lessen urban migration that is a consequence of the frustration of students who find that a bachelor's degree leaves them unemployable in their home districts. There is a great need for universities, local government, agro-businesses, and non-governmental agencies engaged in developmental work to work in co-operation, so that education for youth, both rural and urban, will involve them in the social and economic development of the area. The University Grants

Commission recommended the re-structuring of courses to make them vocational but many colleges have not been able to relate this effectively to their individual college and local community needs. To give two contrasting examples: a rural college in Andhra introduced courses in fisheries, forestry, dairy farming, and electronics. These were not popular either with the students or the faculty: they were seen as limited, for no post-graduate course in these subjects was envisaged. There were not enough funds allocated by the University Grants Commission for field-based training. It is evident that a programme of faculty in-service training, discussions with the community organisations and leaders, and a survey of the development needs of the region, are all pre-requisites to curriculum changes to strengthen diversity programmes.

A second example is that of a college which introduced re-structured courses with great success. After discussions with the community about the need for vocational skill training, the principal had the co-operation of the faculty in developing extension courses. The level of participation and student interest has transformed the campus. It is evident that integrating new courses and diversity issues into the curriculum requires a committed leadership both at the college and the university level. With a commitment from the college principal and a supportive vice-chancellor, there could be similar success stories.

integrating new courses and diversity issues into the curriculum requires a committed leadership

As stated earlier, one of the important goals of the Initiative is to overcome disparities. This can tackled by developing the potential of rural and disadvantaged youth, through programmes that will give them skills and confidence.

There are several possible important spin-offs from the Diversity Initiative but much thoughtful planning still needs to be done, and hopefully by the end of Phase II we will have drawn some important conclusions. The CDI colleges could then be models for future plans in curriculum innovations that reflect diversity concerns.

List of institutions that have received grants from the Ford Foundation for Campus Diversity Initiative in the first phase 1995–1998.

ANNEXURE

Sl. No.	Name and location	Management	Type of institution
1.	Ashutosh College, Calcutta, West Bengal	Private trust	Affiliated
2.	College of Arts & Commerce, Zuarinagar, Goa	Private trust	Affiliated
3.	DAV (PG) College, Dehra Dun, UP	State government	Affiliated
4.	Farook College, Calicut, Kerala	Minority religion Muslim trust	Affiliated
5.	Government Art and Science College, Durg, Madhya Pradesh	State government	Affiliated
6.	Government Narmada Mahavidyala, Hoshangabad, MP	State government	Autonomous
7.*	Isabella Thoburn College, Lucknow, Uttar Pradesh	Minority religion Christian missionary	Affiliated
8.	Jai Hind College of Arts, Science and Commerce, Dhule, Maharashtra	Private trust	Affiliated
9.	Kalimpong College, Darjeeling, West Bengal	State government	Affiliated
10.	MPC College, Baripada, Orissa	State government	Affiliated
11.	Nowrosjee Wadia College, Pune, Maharashtra	Private trust	Affiliated

Sl. No.	Name and location	Management	Type of institution
12.	Parvathibai Chowgule College of Arts and Science, Margao, Goa	Private trust	Affiliated
13.	Presidency College, Calcutta, West Bengal	State government	Affiliated
14.*	SNDT Women's University, Mumbai, Maharashtra	State government	Affiliating women's university
15.	Sahyadri College of Science, Shimoga, Karnataka	State government	Affiliated
16.*	Seethalakshmi Ramaswami College, Tiruchirapalli, Tamil Nadu	Private trust	Autonomous
17.	Sardar Patel University, Vallabh Vidyanagar, Gujarat	State government	Unitary university
18.*	Savithri Girls' College, Ajmer, Rajasthan	State government	Affiliated
19.*	St Bede's College, Shimla, Himachal Pradesh	Minority religion Christian missionary	Affiliated
20.	St Joseph's College, Tiruchirapalli, Tamil Nadu	Minority religion Christian missionary	Autonomous
21.*	St Mary's College, Tuticorin, Tamil Nadu	Minority religion Christian missionary	Autonomous
22.	St Xavier's College, Palayam Kottai, Tamil Nadu	Minority religion Christian missionary	Autonomous
23.	Yashwant Rao Chavan Open University, Nashik, Maharashtra	State government	Open university

* Exclusive women's colleges

Section IV

Concluding issues

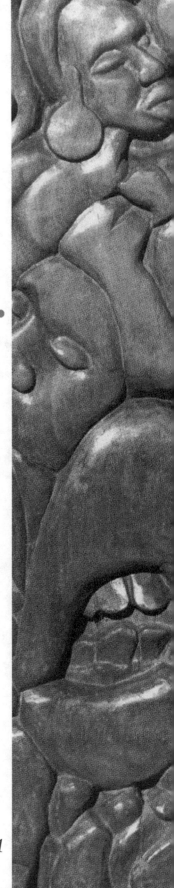

Avoiding closure and challenging frameworks

Michael Cross
*Department of Education,
University of the
Witwatersrand*

Nico Cloete
*Centre for Higher Education
Transformation*

The time has come for critics and artists of the new cultural politics of difference to cast their nets widely, flex their muscles broadly, and thereby refuse to limit their visions, analyses, and praxis to their particular terrains. The aim is to dare to recast, redefine and revise the very notions of 'modenity', 'mainstream', 'margins', 'difference', 'otherness'. We have now reached a new stage in the perennial struggle for freedom and dignity. And while much of the First World intelligentsia adopts retrospective and conservative outlooks that defend the crisis-ridden present, we promote a prospective and prophetic vision with a sense of possibility and potential, especially for those who bear the social costs of the present. We look to the past for strength, not solace; we look at the present and see people perishing, not profits mounting; we look toward the future and vow to make it different and better. (West 1995a: 171)

In this chapter we synthesise and explore key themes and ideas discussed during the ten-day Seminar. It is not our aim to provide a comprehensive account of all issues covered by the delegates. We have selected only those issues which we consider the knots of our intellectual networks with colleagues in other countries, i.e. the issues that may be the focus of our conversations, theoretical and practical engagements, with other diversity practitioners in the future. The task of moulding it into some comprehensible shape has not been easy. It would never have been accomplished without the preliminary thoughts distilled by the team of 'Wise Women', who received the task of facilitating continuity of conversation with previous meetings in India and the United States, of shaping questions and discussion over the ten-day period, and identifying crosscutting or recurring themes that could open opportunities for lively engagement and the possibility of future international collaborative projects. Their report provided a basis for some of the arguments outlined here.

The Seminar was designed in such a way as to provide suitable context for a critical examination of prevailing constructions surrounding Campus Diversity Initiatives (CDI), and jolt pre-conceived notions and mental sets that have been the starting point for many of these initiatives in the participating countries. This was to be achieved through a programme which immersed participants in various facets of South African life, opened a window on the many divergent and converging South African voices, and mapped out local and regional histories and particularities. Site visits in KwaZulu-Natal, Eastern Cape and Western Cape were chosen precisely with the primary purpose of locating the Seminar within the complex matrix of South African society and, as such, avoid enclosure and open new opportunities and possibilities, theoretical and practical, to the theme of the Seminar. As the group progressed down the eastern coast, public campus forums were held at the Universities of Natal and Fort Hare, and Peninsula Technikon. These were followed by campus-based interest group discussions facilitated by local staff at the host institutions. This multifaceted experience which presented the organisers with some interesting logistical challenges was to ensure that the

the Seminar had a catalytic effect on local campus diversity initiatives

Seminar had a catalytic effect on local campus diversity initiatives by making the knowledge and experiences of the visiting delegates accessible to as wide an audience as possible.

The three-day formal seminar in Durban focused on conceptual papers which set the scene for the rest of the Conference. These spoke to the emergent 'Diversity' theory, and practitioners' papers, which outlined some ways in which these theories have been translated into campus programmes, did not compromise academic rigour. The programme served to underscore a frequently raised contention about the fluidity and vexing nature of conversations that deal with difference and diversity.

An important feature of these emergent conversations is that participants were given an opportunity to step back, backtrack, and interrogate their particular discourses around diversity initiatives – and more specifically, their assumptions behind the issues such as 'what we are doing', 'how are we doing it', 'why we are doing it', and 'why we are doing it in a particular way'. As such the Seminar emerged as an attempt to introduce some movement into the concepts at work in CDI – concepts such as 'diversity', 'unity', 'identity', 'multiculturalism', and 'citizenship'. This posed a challenge which required asking these sorts of questions: Will current conceptualisations of CDI in America survive the challenge of an increasingly complex American society? Can these conceptualisations provide an adequate basis for current or similar initiatives in other participating countries, particularly in South Africa? Is there a principled way of closing the gap between American practitioners and Indian and South African practitioners who see themselves as profoundly involved in transformative projects taking place in their countries – and may as such feel sceptical about some concepts and practices that came to be accepted in the American context (starting with the name of the initiative itself – Campus Diversity Initiative)? Are we prepared to move beyond a universalising model that is mainly concerned with improving how others practise our precepts? Is there something for us to learn from colleagues in other national and cultural settings? Asking such questions with an open mind was not just a matter of ecumenism of goodwill. It was a way of enriching the answers to questions, which increasingly affect our understanding of, or engagement with, issues of diversity. To this end, Deputy President of the Ford Foundation Bernstein set the tone at the outset by reminding the Seminar that unless 'we couple what we are learning from each other, with constructive, bold, innovative action when we return to our respective locales, then this will be nothing more than a great academic exercise in which participants flex their intellectual and ideological muscles – but nothing more'.

194

Globalisation, diversity, and identity

This theme emerged most clearly in discussions about concepts and constructs associated with globalisation, the cornerstone of so many policies and debates at present. In the context of campus diversity, globalisation can be conceptualised as a process of emission and reception of 'common places' at a global level, which increasingly is becoming institutionalised particularly within discourses of major international cultural organisations. As a cultural endeavour, globalisation has its own conceptual problematic, particularly in the manner in which questions are framed. Should, for example, globalisation as a form of 'global communication' be understood as an encounter between different cultures? Or as an encounter between individuals of different cultures? Or both? What are the theoretical and practical implications of these questions?

There are two basic approaches to globalisation and all of them have relative strengths and weaknesses. The first approach is the market-place approach, i.e. the acceptance of globalisation as the determination of a 'common place' by market forces. This is tied up with the assumption that it is unrealistic for the people on the margins to think that they can sidestep the patronage system of the global village driven by world's hegemonic forces. Future identities will be determined by competitive flow of ideas, knowledge, technology, values, symbols, and all cultural imaginary that can be channelled throughout the world though improved means of mass communication. Explicitly or implicitly, concerns were voiced about this view. The pushes for globalisation, it was argued, may institutionalise or disguise the embedded hierarchisation of cultures and the reality of privileged access to this global culture and identity. The question of unequal access to the benefits, which purportedly flow from global citizenship, should not be dismissed. As was argued by one participant, globalisation and global citizenship posit a convergence in which developing countries will 'lose the race', as many types of 'defeated knowledge' are not part of globalisation, as 'our diversity is taken away from us'.

The second approach is a move towards what West (1995a: 167) refers to as the 'Go-it-Alone' attitude, which very often assumes the form of an 'arrogant group insularity'. Not only would this reproduce and encourage parochialism and narrow chauvinism but, if it becomes permanent, 'it is self-defeating, in that it usually reinforces the very inferior complexes promoted by the subtly racist mainstream' (West 1995a: 167). It would certainly risk nations to self-ghettoisation, as some dialogue and the forging of alliances and coalitions (CDI for example) are inevitable and necessary at the international level for almost any creative practice. If all these options entail sailing in troubled waters, what are then the challenges?

Certainly, globalisation as a market-place where a 'common personality' of groups and nations is forged regardless of their identities, differences, and unequal access to resources, an arrest into an 'arrogant group insularity', or the disempowering 'Go-it-Alone' attitude offer no or limited opportunities. As Cloete and Muller (1998: 4) have argued elsewhere, 'the distance and tension between cosmopolitan and local traditions has eased' with the changing forms of production of knowledge and concomitant epistemological bases. With them, we endorse insight from Scott (1997: 20):

> So long as the intellectual and scientific culture of the West persisted in its universalising claims, other cultures were marginalised, obliged to choose between imminent (and irreversible) redundancy and angry ideological opposition. But these claims have been eroded from 'within', in the cognitive sphere, by the radical scepticism that has always been part of the Western tradition and the epistemological doubts that have emerged recently; and from 'without', in the wider social and economic environment, by new patterns of knowledge production. As a result, the tension between Western and 'other', elite and democratic knowledge traditions has eased. Perhaps we no longer have to choose because perhaps we can no longer clearly differentiate them.

A critical 'coming-together' type of strategy should be found which will ensure a just balance between (global) universality and (local) singularities through suitable dialogue and conversations. Choices should be made about what forms of communication are appropriate to achieve this ideal. Balibar (1997: 175) tentatively considers the following options:

It is what allows a discussion of the 'good' and 'bad' forms of communication: those that tend to institute the universal in respect for singularities or that find a 'balanced' way of combining them, as opposed to those that crush singularity under uniformity (currently such an effect is often feared to result from the contemporary evolution of 'mass communications' and the world-wide diffusion of certain hegemonic models) or that, going to the opposite extreme, exacerbate singularity to the point of isolationism. The median, desirable path would put communication in the service of the reproduction of differences, that is, it would affirm singularity by the mediation of the universal. And, reciprocally, it would affirm the reality of the universal by the mediation of singularities.

Promoting an 'intellectual hospitality of ideas'

The words 'unity', 'diversity', 'identity', 'democracy', and 'citizenship' dominated our conversations. Not only are these words in constant use throughout the world but they have also become central to our everyday discourses. We made use of them as if we had common understanding of the meaning(s) attached to them. Yet as conversations unfolded we came to realise that they are highly contested words and no single definition of them remains undisputed. We persistently tended to look at them through the tainted lenses of our own particular histories, cultural and intellectual settings, with innocent reluctance to move beyond the narrow frontiers they impose on us and to embody the views and knowledges of the other. No country was immune from the tendency to push for closure by preaching the ascendancy of their reading of diversity. This was best summed up by a participant who talked about the need for the group to develop an intellectual hospitality of ideas. As Visvanathan put it, 'Local knowledges, tribal knowledges, gendered knowledges, civilisational know-ledges, dying knowledges, all need a site, a theatre of encounter which is not patronising, not preservationist, not fundamentalist, but open and playful.' Certainly 'without this mix of theory, the communities of knowledge one is searching for might be stillborn' (Visvanathan, Chapter 4) and the diversity project may be doomed to failure. This idea came to the fore most forcefully at the University of Fort Hare in discussions about the difficulty, if not impossibility, of bringing local or indigenous knowledges into the formal, professionally accredited curriculum.

In a world of richly diverse histories and traditions as represented by the delegates, detailed prescription of universal applications of concepts entailed in the diversity initiative is neither helpful nor desirable. Of central importance is an understanding of their complexity to appreciate that much needs to be learned about the parameters, constraints, or resources, within which ideals of democratic practices are to be performed and a life of democratic virtue to be pursued. To this end, the Seminar was indeed successful – particularly in highlighting through South African history that those who make use of, or instrumentalise, diversity concepts in the pursuit of democracy should be aware of the long history and great wealth of meaning which lie behind them, and the need to problematise them in the changing historical contexts.

Against this background, the Seminar brought to the forefront the importance of contextualisation of research and concepts on diversity. Research on diversity cannot be disconnected from history and context (Smith 1997: 4). As Bernstein has noted, the South African past highlights the fact that unless discussions of diversity are informed by, linked to, or focus on an analysis of disadvantage and social-justice values (reaffirmation of identity, redistribution of power, privileges and opportunities), we are not likely 'to fulfil our best aspirations'; for arguments for simple affirmation of diversity 'fail to challenge relations of dominance and subordination'. In this perspective, a plea was repeatedly made for the reworking of diversity concepts and an awareness of the danger in closing the debate too early. This approach opened up opportunities for lively debate and created a range of possibilities for future engagements. These will receive our particular attention in the following sections.

'Cultural diversity' or identity diversity?

The way in which culture has become a prescriptive rather than an analytical category was a concern shared by the South African and Indian delegates. What is striking today is the generalisation of the discourse of culture to characterise both identity and non-identity. Neither are the connections between culture and identity clear, nor have they been thoroughly interrogated. This important theme dominated part of the proceedings of the Seminar. The issue raised was whether the answers to the haunting questions 'Who am I?', 'Who are we?' or 'Who are they?' can be adequately addressed with reference to culture. Put differently, how sustainable is the argument for identification in the field of culture under present socio-cultural circumstances?

Cloete *et al* (see Chapter 3) left the orthodoxy puzzled by drawing attention to the limited possibilities offered by culture in the modern world as a key domain of identification as a consequence of the increasing 'thinning of culture'. This refers to the blurring of cultural frontiers as group's or people's cultures in society converge; people are increasingly finding a 'common place' and becoming 'cultural partners' – in the South African case, more South African than they have come to realise. This is not to fall into an essentialising or homogenising trap which regards all South Africans as really alike, and which obliterates class, gender, ethnic, regional differences, or differences in sexual orientation. These differences challenge the very possibility of constituting culture as the field of experience in which identities can be recognised. In this regard, the 'crisis of cultural diversity' as the field of identification is imminent.

Alternatively, Cloete *et al* see diversity as a plurality of identities, which are not necessarily the effect of an enunciation of difference, determined by cultural representation. This would certainly naturalise identity by making it a matter of culture, an inescapable trait of one's being by virtue of belonging to a particular cultural constellation. For them it makes more sense to talk about 'identity diversity' than 'cultural diversity', particularly within the South African context where 'apartheid's leaders celebrated diversity in their own venal, perverse way, and this led to greater injustices and a denial of rights to the majority'. Identity diversity is *primarily* determined by current struggles over control or access to resources. This re-conceptualisation of difference has two important dimensions. On the one hand, it provides for the agency, capacity, and ability of people who have been culturally degraded, politically oppressed, and economically deprived by apartheid to come to grips with the constraints on their

199

life chances. On the other, it shines away narrow and divisive fundamentalist particularisms, parochialisms, separatisms, false universalisms, and homogenous totalisms or cultural essentialisms – and all other pathological '-isms'.

In his recent evaluation of the role that cultural identity plays today, Balibar pursues a similar argument but tackles the issue from a different angle which brings to bear other conceptual and theoretical complications of the traditional 'cultural diversity' paradigm. He proposes the following double thesis: (a) there is identity only by and for subjects; (b) there is culture only by and for institutions (Balibar 1995: 183).

Within the framework of cultural diversity, identity is more precisely a 'discourse of tradition'. As Balibar (1995: 187) argues, in this domain there are no identities but identifications ('either with the institution itself [culture or tradition] or with other subjects by the intermediary of the institution'); identities are only the ideal goal of processes of identification. In this process, some identifications succeed in a contradictory way; others fail and even become unliveable. Nothing tells us that in all cultural contexts, cultural representations, and the images individuals develop about themselves or others culminate in the distinctions 'I' and 'we', key manifestations of inclusion and exclusion, and as such of identity.

The idea that cultural diversity culminates in diverse cultural identities can only be relative or accidental. The processes that would allow for translation of individual subjectivities into an objective cultural identity or for the perfect realisation of the norms of collective culture in the identity of subjects may be contradictory or conflicting. This is particularly because individuals are increasingly moving from 'unique' (or singular) cultural spaces into cultural intersections with the prominence of globalising and converging movements in culture. Or as Balibar (1995: 176) himself puts it,

> One might doubt this merely by observing the repetition of negative observations of the type: 'culture', 'cultural identity' cannot be grasped except by articulating objective and subjective dimensions, universal and singular, not sacrificing popular (or mass) culture to the high culture of the elite or vice-versa, and so on.

In this regard, Cloete *et al* allude to possible choices that individuals make about cultures on ethical grounds – e.g. good or bad – based on the assumption that the identity of each culture would have to be recognised as containing a universal value. This for Balibar (1995: 174-75) has tremendous implications: 'It is what permits, for example, a distinction to be proposed between a "good" and a "bad" concept of cultural diversity, from an ethical and political standpoint (to put it schematically, an egalitarian concept and a hierarchical one).' Related to this is the fact that 'the same discourse that makes the very culture into a "whole" poses as an impossibility belonging to several cultures', which means that no nation or community could be multicultural (Balibar 1995: 187).

Similarly West sees identity as a matter of desire and death. For him understanding identity construction requires that we look at the various ways in which human beings have constructed their desire for recognition, association, and protection over time and in space, for access to resources, always under circumstances not of their own choosing, and the role of material resources and the various systems that generate their distribution and consumption (West 1995b: 16). Rancière (1995: 70) holds that identity is first about fear: the fear of the other, the fear of nothing. The two definitions are complementary and relevant to our discussion. This explains for example the problems of narrow nationalism and xenophobic identity politics in Europe, United States, India, South Africa, and the rest of the continent.

Re-thinking multiculturalism

What bedevils discussion of multiculturalism and the interaction between culture and identity is often the way in which the terms are used, progressively, dynamically, interactively, or restrictively. The three 'Wise Women' were often hard pushed to ensure that this dissent did not fragment or close off discussion by attempting to refocus group anger to ensure that dissent opened up questions and became a generative creative force. It came without surprise that *reflectionist* arguments were posed by some delegates which hold that the fight against marginalisation for positive representation and recognition must reflect or mirror the real communities of the marginalised, not simply the negative and depressing representations of them; or social engineering arguments claiming that since any form of representation is constructed and selective in light of broader aims, the marginalised – particularly blacks – should offer positive images of themselves in order to inspire achievement among young people and counter stereotypes (borrowing conceptualisation from West 1995a:160). Both arguments reflected the reminiscence of multiculturalist ideologies. These arguments were met with strong criticism from those delegates who not only have lost hope on the multiculturalist project but also consider it profoundly mistaken; for 'it is a diversity of identities, not of cultures, that lies ahead'. With the thinning of the cultural content of identities, identity politics is about respect and recognition, not about cultural content.

By developing an argument for identity rather than culture, a number of delegates coming from all three continents were challenged in their assumption that multiculturalism is part of a progressive politics. Some South African and Indian delegates were also challenged to re-interrogate their experience of certain forms of multiculturalism as a reactionary politics. To both groups, the politics of identity provided a temporary compromise and a promising alternative route for exploration as a more empowering basis for diversity.

Universities as sites or spaces for diversity and democracy practices

Campus diversity initiatives have gained credit by notably authorising higher education institutions and activities to be considered as the pre-eminent site in which to seek a resolution to social tensions to which democratic citizenship has become a response. This theme arose when the debate focused upon the role of higher education in developing citizens for a new democratic order and on the continuing importance of institutional programmes of redress. The theme poses three main difficulties. First, the question remains as to whether the development of democratic citizens by lecturers is a possibility, given that they themselves have not experienced a true democracy: they are located within a higher education system with continuing historical disparities and divergences and a society with entrenched inequalities.

Second, diversity, citizenship, and democracy intersect

in such a way as to make it impossible to plan campus programmes or diversity initiatives without engaging with the underpinning discourses or ideologies. As has been the case with diversity, citizenship is a highly contested concept. Conversations around citizenship highlighted the difficulty confronting any attempt to achieve widespread agreement on a generous, holistic and all-embracing definition of citizenship. As Heater (1990: 282) puts it:

> The evidence of history provides little cause to believe that any search for an agreed, all-embracing, and permanent definition of citizenship might be successful. Both its theory and practice have constantly changed in response to particular economic, social, and political circumstances. The justification for the concept and institution, it can well be argued, lies precisely in its pragmatic flexibility.

In 1995, Schneider made the following observation:

> Our nation's campuses have become a highly visible stage on which the most fundamental questions about difference, equality, and community are being enacted. To this effort, filled with promise and fraught with difficulty, the academy brings indispensable resources: its commitments to the advancement of knowledge and its traditions of dialogue and deliberation across difference as keys to the increase of insight and understanding.

These ideas were reiterated at the Seminar as participants explored the possibilities that universities offered as laboratories for democratic citizenship and a testing ground for relevant practices.

CDI grew out of the realisation that campuses or higher education institutions could play an important role as sites where issues of tolerance, inclusion, access, and structural inequities in society could be addressed effectively. Different and competing approaches to CDI emerged, particularly in the United States. Some saw CDI as a way of dealing with earlier homogeneity both at a particular institution or in higher education. Some saw CDI as promoting access and participation to previously excluded groups. Others saw it as setting a climate conducive to greater heterogeneity. Others approached it as establishing an environment for the development of learners to their full potential or as doing all these things simultaneously. In the United States, Smith classifies the whole range of activities taking place under CDI into four dimensions:

- representation embracing all activities designed to foster inclusion and success of previously underrepresented groups;
- campus climate and intergroup relations including programmes aimed at addressing the impact of institutional environment on institutional and student success;
- education and scholarship for programmes focusing on the inclusion of diverse traditions in the curriculum, the impact of issues of diversity on teaching methods, and the influence of societal diversity on scholarly inquiry; and
- institutional transformation which refers to the restructuring processes to meet the needs of a diverse student body and to prepare students to live and work in a pluralistic society (Smith 1997: 8–14).

Details on the actual programmes and activities fall beyond the scope of this chapter.

It seems however that in the South African context, irrespective of the divisive past, conceptions that stress commonality at the expense of plurality and respect of differences are doomed to failure. In the same way, conceptions that deny any form of commonality in the name of plurality and difference will not succeed. Current trends in the South African debate seem to favour a form of commonality that accommodates or respects diversity and makes room for different forms of identities or indivi-dualities within a democratic setting.

Future plans

In the concluding session of the Seminar, each country reported on possible activities for the future. Not surprisingly, the United States delegation concluded that the Seminar had reinvigorated participants to pursue their individual programmes and activities. For the Brazilians, the Seminar led to a much greater awareness of diversity issues in their own country and they decided that they are going to explore ways of developing diversity programmes. The Indian delegation decided on a dual strategy. Some will pursue their existing campus diversity programmes with new insights and vigour while others intend to engage in critical reflection on CDI in India. Surprisingly, the South Africans agreed that the primary issue was transformation and not diversity, but that diversity is an important component of any transformation project. They also agreed that campus diversity programmes will be developed in two broad areas: students' services (with a new focus on promoting citizenship and tolerance), and curriculum restructuring (in relation to different kinds of knowledges and its forms of organisation).

While the Seminar provided an impetus for renewed interest in country-specific programmes, some participants were disappointed by the fact that, despite the promises of globalisation, the group did not manage to suggest a single transnational project.

The next Tri-National Seminar will be take place in the United States in October 1999.

REFERENCES

Balibar, Etienne (1997) 'Culture and identity' (working notes). In John Rajchman (ed.) *The Identity Question*. New York and London: Routledge.

Cloete, N and Muller J (1998) 'South African higher education reform: what comes after post-colonialism?' Paper prepared for European Review. Pretoria: CHET.

Heater, Derek (1990) *Citizenship: The Civic Ideal In World History, Politics And Education*. London and New York: Longman.

Rancière, Jacques (1995) 'Politics, identification and subjectivization'. In John Rajchman (ed.) *The Identity Question*. New York and London: Routledge.

Schneider, Carol (1995) 'Higher education and the contradictions of American pluralism'. In *The Drama of Diversity and Democracy – Higher Education and American Commitments*. Washington DC: Association of American Colleges and Universities.

Scott, P (1997) 'Changes in knowledge production and dissemination in the context of globification'. In N Cloete, J Muller, M Makgoba & D Ekong (eds) *Knowledge, Identity and Curriculum Transformation in Africa*. Cape Town: Maskew Miller Longman.

Smith, Daryl G (1997) *Diversity Works – The Emerging Picture Of How Students Benefit*. Washington D C: Association of American Colleges and Universities.

West, Cornell (1995a) 'A matter of life and death'. In John Rajchman (ed.) *The Identity Question*. New York and London: Routledge.

West, Cornell (1995b) 'New cultural politics of difference'. In John Rajchman (ed.) *The Identity Question*. New York and London: Routledge.

APPENDIX A

Agenda:
Tri-national seminar on campus diversity
South Africa
March 1998

THURSDAY, 12 MARCH 1998

Arrive in Durban

You will be met by an Edward Hotel representative, and transported to the hotel by bus.

If you have any problems call the Edward Hotel (tel: 031-337-3681) and ask for Linda Benwell

Book into the Edward Hotel

(If you have any problems/queries, contact the CHET Office in the Edward Hotel)

Evening at leisure

FRIDAY, 13 MARCH 1998

9:00–11:00 Collect "per diem" from the CHET Office (Edward Hotel)

11:00–12:00 **Welcome**
- Richard Fehnel (Programme Officer, Ford Foundation)
- Nico Cloete (Director, CHET)

Introductions

Announcements
- Judith Hawarden (Project Consultant, CHET)
- Ann Harper (Project Consultant, CHET)

Venue: Thekweni Room. Edward Hotel

12:00–12:30 Light lunch

Venue: Thekweni Room, Edward Hotel

12:45 Depart for the Social History Tour

This tour will provide a window into the lives of those people and communities who were "consigned by decades of urban segregation and apartheid, to occupy the marginal, peripheral, undesirable spaces of Durban", one of sub-Saharan Africa's most important port cities.

Starting at the Kwa Muhle Museum, dedicated to this history, we will go through Cato Manor, one of the areas most affected by the group areas proclamations which devastated the lives of thousands of Indian and African residents from the 1950s. Continue to the Bambayi Development Project and Gandhi Settlement, where we'll visit some of the residents and project leaders. Return to the Edward Hotel via Ohlange Institute, where President Mandela chose to cast his vote in the 1994 elections, with a stop for tea and refreshments at the Killie Campbell Museum and Archives.

(Recommended reading: Paul Maylam and Iain Edwards (ed) *The People's City*. University of Natal Press. 1996)

Meet in front of the Edward Hotel

17:30 Return to the Edward Hotel

17:30–19:00 Leisure time

19:00 Formal Dinner & Opening

Welcome
- Brenda Gourley (Vice-Chancellor, University of Natal)
- Nasima Badsha (Deputy Director General for Higher Education, Department of Education)
- Alison Bernstein (Vice President, The Ford Foundation)

Venue: Prince of Wales Foyer, Edward Hotel

SATURDAY, 14 MARCH 1998

9:00–10:30 **Seminar**

Diversity & Unity: The Role of Higher Education in Building Democracy

(South African Perspective)

Presenters
- Sury Pillay (Legal Consultant)
- Michael Cross (Professor, University of Witwatersrand)
- Nico Cloete (Director, CHET)

Chair
- Njabulo Ndebele (Vice-Chancellor, University of the North)

Venue: Victoria Room, Edward Hotel

10:30–11:00 Tea

11:00–11:30 Group Photographs

Entrance to the Edward Hotel

11:30–1 3:00 **Seminar**

Diversity & Unity: The Role of Higher Education in Building Democracy

(Indian Perspective)

Presenter
- Shiv Vishvanathan (Senior Fellow at the Centre for the Study of Developing Societies, New Delhi)

Chair
- Mushirul Hasan (Professor of History and Director, Academy of Third World Studies, Jamia Millia Islamia University, New Delhi)

Venue: Victoria Room, Edward Hotel

13:00–14:30 Lunch

Venue: Smorgasbord, Edward Hotel

14:30–16:00 Seminar

Diversity & Unity: The Role of Higher Education in Building Democracy
(American Perspective)

Presenter
- William Kirwan (President, University of Maryland)

Chair
- Mildred Garcia (Associate Vice Provost, Arizona State University)

Venue: Victoria Room, Edward Hotel

16:00–19:30 Tea and leisure time

19:30 Supper

Venue: Chinese Restaurant, Edward Hotel

SUNDAY, 15 MARCH 1998

9.00–11.00 Discussion

Introduced by Synthesising Group, "Three Wise Women"
- Ann Harper (Project Consultant, CHET)
- Jasbir Jain (Former Professor of English, University of Rajasthan)
- Caryn McTighe Musil (Senior Research Assistant & Director, Curriculum and Faculty Development Network Association of American Colleges and Universities)

Venue: Victoria Room, Edward Hotel

11.00–12.00 Tea and leisure time

12.00–13.00 Lunch

13:00–14:15 "Diversity and Unity in the South African Constitution"

- Guest Speaker – Albie Sachs (Constitutional Court Judge)

Venue: Causarie, Edward Hotel

14:30–15:45 **Practical Paper 1 – South Africa**

"Gender, Democracy and Citizenship"

Presenters
- Amanda Gouws (Acting Director, African Gender Institute, UCT)
- Shireen Hassim (Research Specialist, Human Sciences Research Council)

Chair
- Padma Ramachandran (Vice-Chancellor, The Maharaja Sayajirao University of Baroda)

Venue: Victoria Room. Edward Hotel

16:00 Tea and leisure time

17:45 **Depart for Supper at the BAT Centre** *(Dress: Casual)*

Visit to the BAT Centre (Bartel Arts Trust) on the Victoria Embankment and Esplanade, which was established "to support the development of a vibrant artistic practice which celebrates our rich cultural diversity, and builds respect for artists and their role in society." This is an opportunity to visit the artists in residence, enjoy KwaZulu's traditional performing and visual arts and our local foods. There will also be an opportunity to purchase local arts and crafts and enjoy the bay at sunset.

Meet in the front of the Edward Hotel

22:00 Bus returns to the Edward Hotel

MONDAY, 16 MARCH 1998

9:00–10:15 **Practical Paper 2 – India**

"Campus-Community Interaction"
- Jayalukshmi Indiresan (Consultant, Asian Centre for Organisational Research & Development)

"Community Outreach & Curriculum"
- Sharada Nayak (Director, Educational Resources Centre Trust)

Chair
- Constance Rice (Executive Vice President, Seattle Community College)

Venue: Victoria Room, Edward Hotel

10:15–10:45 Tea

10:45–12:00 **Practical Paper 3 – United States**

"Strategic Evaluation: An Imperative for Campus Diversity Initiatives"

Presenter
- Daryl Smith (Professor of Education and Psychology, The Claremont Graduate University)

Chair
- Cecil Bodibe (Dean of Students, Technikon SA)

Venue: Victoria Room, Edward Hotel

12:15 **Bus departs for the University of Natal**

Depart from the Edward Hotel lobby

12:30 Lunch at the University of Natal

Host
- Brenda Gourley (Vice-Chancellor, University of Natal)

14:30–16:15 **Public Forum**

"Bringing Diversity into Conversation"

Panel
- Caryn McTighe Musil (Senior Research Assistant & Director, Curriculum & Faculty Development Network Association of American Colleges & Universities)
- Daniel Herwitz (Professor & Head of Department of Philosophy, University of Natal)
- Mushirul Hasan (Professor of History & Director, Academy of Third World Studies, Jamia Millia Islamia University)
- Mapule Ramashala (Vice-Chancellor & Rector, University of Durban-Westville)

Chair
- Brenda Gourley (Vice-Chancellor, University of Natal)

Venue: L4. T.B. Davies Building

16:30–18:30 **Campus Interest Groups**

Detailed information in seminar folders

18:30 Depart for Edward Hotel

Meet at the main University entrance

Evening Leisure time (for own account – private arrangements)
PLEASE SETTLE YOUR ACCOUNT WITH THE EDWARD HOTEL

TUESDAY, 17 MARCH 1998

4:15 Please have luggage ready by 04:15

4:45 Depart for Durban Airport for travel to the Eastern Cape

Depart from the Edward Hotel lobby

7:30 Arrival at East London Airport

8:00 Depart by bus from the East London Airport for the University of Fort Hare

Commentary on Local History:
- Dr. R.G.S. Makalima

9:30 Arrival at Fort Hare

10:00 Tea

10:30–12:30 Tour of the University Campus, Centre for Cultural Studies & Art Gallery (this gallery has an important collection of South African Art)

13:00–14:00 **Lunch**

14:30 Travel to Kings Lodge and the Arminel Mountain Lodge, The Hogsback

Depart from the University of Fort Hare

15:00–17:00 Leisure time (rest and/or walk)

17:00–19:00 Introduced by Synthesising Group

Venue: Lounge, Kings Lodge

19:30 Supper

Welcome
- Mbulelo Mzamane (Vice-Chancellor, University of Fort Hare)

Venue: Kings Lodge

WEDNESDAY, 18 MARCH 1998

8:00 Depart for the University of Fort Hare

Meet in front of the Kings Lodge

9:00–11:30 Public Forum

"Diversity & Challenges to the Traditional Curriculum"

Panel
- Moyisi Majeke (Comparative Law, University of Fort Hare)
- Deon Pretorius (Director, Institute for Development, Planning and Research, University of Port Elizabeth)
- Khaya Matiso (Director, Student Services, University of Port Elizabeth)
- Justice Noruwana (Deputy Vice-Chancellor, University of Transkei)
- Mike Davidson (Rhodes University) (pending)

Chair
- Jan Kirsten (Vice-Chancellor, University of Port Elizabeth)

Venue: Sports Auditorium

12:00–14:00 VIP Lunch

14:30–16:00 **Campus Interest Groups**

Curriculum/Course Restructuring – Challenges to the Traditional Curriculum:
- Mbulelo Mzamane
- Moyisi Majeke

Diversity & Gender Issues:
- G.N. Moshoeu

Science & Technology (including Indigenous Technology):
- Mike Magwa

Local History – Research and Development:
- Themba Sirayi

Curriculum - National Development, Reconstruction, Work Place & Job Market:
- Sipho Buthelezi

Bringing Human Rights Issues into the Curriculum:
- Willy Kgositsile

Venue: To be announced

16:30 Depart for East London Airport

Depart from University of Fort Hare

18:55 Fly to Cape Town

Evening Book into the President Hotel, Bantry Bay

THURSDAY, 19 MARCH 1998

8:30 Depart for Social History Tour

Meet in the lobby of the President Hotel

9:30 Arrive at Mayibuye Centre – Bellville

The Mayibuye Centre is a pioneering project helping to recover areas of South African history that have been neglected in the past. It also provides for cultural creativity and expression in a way that promotes the process of change and reconstruction in a democratic South Africa.

11:00 Depart for District Six, Cape Town

11:30 Arrive at District Six Museum

The District Six Museum is a project of the District Six Foundation, an organisation that aims to keep alive the rich cultural history of District Six, a racially mixed, residential area in Cape Town. This area was destroyed under Apartheid in terms of the Group Areas Act, and Forced Removals. Blacks who lived here were forced to relocate to sub-economic housing schemes on the windy, gangster controlled Cape Flats.

13:00 Depart District Six Museum for Biesmiellah Restaurant in "Bo-Kaap"

13:30 Lunch at Biesmiellah

Local historian will give an outline of the history of the area and talk about Malay Culture

Venue: Biesmiellah Restaurant

14:30–16:00 Discussion

Introduced by Synthesising Group

Venue: Biesmiellah Restaurant

16:00 Return to hotel & leisure time

19:00 VIP Dinner

Host:
• Brian Figaii (Rector, Peninsula Technikon)

Venue: President Hotel

FRIDAY, 20 MARCH 1998

8.00 Depart for Peninsula Technikon

Meet in the lobby of the President Hotel

9:00–11.30 **Public Forum**

"Contestations around Affirmative Action"

Panel
- Arjun Dangle (President of the State Unit of the Bharatiya Republica Party, India)
- Yolanda Moses (President, City College, New York)
- Naledi Pandor (Member of Parliament and Deputy Chief Whip, ANC)
- Barney Pityana (Chairperson, Human Rights Commission)

Chair
- Brian Figaji (Vice-Chancellor, Peninsula Technikon)

Venue: Auditorium, Peninsula Technikon

12:00–13:30 **Lunch**

Venue: 2nd Floor, Administration Building, Peninsula Technikon

14:00–16:30 **Campus Interest Groups**

Environmental Unit:
- Kenneth Salo

Research and Development:
- Tahir Wood

Curriculum Development:
- Hilton Fransman

Science and Technology:
- Dhiro Gihwala

Student Affairs:
- Vuyisa Tanga

217

Gender Issues:
- Peninsula Technikon Equity Committee

Venue: Auditorium, Peninsula Technikon

17:00 Depart for Spier Wine Estate

Depart from Peninsula Technikon

18:30 Informal Closing Dinner and Entertainment

Venue: Spier Wine Estate

SATURDAY, 21 MARCH 1998

(Human Rights Day – originally Sharpeville Day)

8:00–9:30 Breakfast
and
Presentation on the Historical Importance of the Day

Venue: President Hotel

9:30–11:45 **Discussion**
Introduced by the Synthesising Group

Venue: President Hotel

11:45 **Closure:**
- Edgar Beckham (Program Officer, The Ford Foundation)

12:00–14:00 **Lunch**

Venue: President Hotel

Afternoon Own plans/Departure
(Optional tour of Robben Island or Wine Route)

APPENDIX B	# Participants

SONYA ANDERSON

PRESENT POSITION: Program Assistant in the Education, Media, Arts and Culture programme at the Ford Foundation.

PREVIOUS POSITION: Secondary school teacher in Mississippi.

She works with the Ford Foundation co-ordinator of the Campus Diversity Initiative and with programme officers in the field of community and national service.

Sonya Anderson   Program Assistant
Education, Media, Arts and Culture Program
The Ford Foundation
320 E 43rd Street
New York, NY 10017
Tel: (212) 573-5061
Fax: (212) 351-3650
E-mail: S.Anderson@fordfound.org

DAVID ARNOLD

PRESENT POSITION: Executive Vice President and currently Acting President of the Institute of International Education (IIE), the largest international educational and cultural exchange organisation in the United States.

219

PREVIOUS POSITIONS: Prior to joining IIE, he served as the Ford Foundation Representative for India, Nepal and Sri Lanka, overseeing the Foundation's programmes in the areas of governance, reproductive health, rural poverty, education and culture, and international affairs. During his thirteen year tenure with the Foundation, he held several other positions including Deputy Director of the Governance and Public Policy Program in New York.

Member of the Asia Society and formerly served on the Board of Trustees and Executive Committee of the US Educational Foundation in India. His research has focused on local and state economic development and improving democratic governance practices both in the US and developing countries.

David Arnold Executive Vice President
Institute of International Education
809 United Nations Plaza
New York, NY 10017
Tel: (212) 984-5377
Fax: (212) 984-5563
E-mail: darnold@iie.org

EDGAR F BECKHAM

PRESENT POSITION: Program Officer in the Education and Culture Program, The Ford Foundation. Oversees the Foundation's Campus Diversity Initiative. Also serves as Chairman of the Board of the Donna Wood Foundation.

PREVIOUS POSITIONS: Dean of the College Emeritus of Wesleyan University in Middletown, Connecticut. Also served as Chairman of the Connecticut State Board of Education.

Widely involved in field of education policy and curriculum transformation.

LECTURES/PAPERS: Lectured in English and German in both the United States and Europe on US race relations and African-American history; also presented papers on AIDS and education, cultural transactions and educational quality, and diversity and higher education.

Edgar Beckham Co-ordinator – Campus Diversity Initiative
Education, Media, Arts and Culture Program
The Ford Foundation
320 E 43rd Street
New York, NY 10017
Tel: (212) 573-4947
Fax: (212) 351-3650
E-mail: E.Beckham@fordfound.org

ALISON BERNSTEIN

PRESENT POSITION: Vice President of the Education, Media Arts and Culture Program at the Ford Foundation.

PREVIOUS POSITION: Associate Dean of Faculty at Princeton University.

PUBLICATIONS/PAPERS: She has published numerous articles on community college transfer issues, access for women and minorities into higher education, and the impact of women's studies.

Alison Bernstein Vice President
Education, Media, Arts and Culture Program
The Ford Foundation
320 E 43rd Street
New York, NY 10017
Tel: (212) 573-4730
Fax: (212) 351-3670
E-mail: A.Bernstein@fordfound.org

CECIL BODIBE

PRESENT POSITION: Dean of Student Affairs at Technikon SA.

PREVIOUS POSITIONS: He served as Deputy Director and Acting Director of Student Development Services at Vista University where he was responsible for overseeing the Counselling Division.

His major research interests are multicultural counselling, Afrocentric psychology, indigenous healing, and change and diversity management.

221

RECENT PUBLICATIONS Include a focus on the role of the psychologist in a culturally diverse Southern Africa, traditional healing as an indigenous approach to mental health in the Southern African context as well as a comparison between traditional healing and Western therapeutic approaches. He has contributed to the development of a multicultural counselling curriculum and multicultural teaching to combat racism in school and community.

He serves on the Steering Committee of Technikon SA, which addresses issues of racism, affirmative action and diversity management and heads the Transformation Task Team at Vista University.

Cecil Bodibe Dean of Students
Technikon SA
Private Bag X6
Florida 1710
Tel: (11) 471-2634
Fax: (11) 471-2849
E-mail: treynold@tsamail.trsa.ac.za

NIGEL BROOKE

PRESENT POSITION: Representative of the Ford Foundation in Brazil.

PREVIOUS POSITIONS: Senior Researcher at the João Pinheiro Foundation and advisor to the State Government of Minas Gerais, Brazil, Program Officer for Education at the Brazil Office of the Ford Foundation.

Educational Sociologist with a PhD from the Institute of Development Studies, University of Sussex, England, with 24 years' educational research and planning experience in Brazil and Mexico.

Nigel Brooke Representative
The Ford Foundation
Caixa Postal 49
Rio de Janeiro, RJ
CEP 20001-970 Brazil
Tel: (5521) 556-1586
Fax: (5521) 285-1250
E-mail: N.Brooke@fordfound.org

NICO CLOETE

PRESENT POSITION: Director of CHET.

PREVIOUS POSITIONS: Research Director for the National Commission on Higher Education, Co-ordinator of the Post-Secondary Education report of the National Education Policy Investigation (NEPI) and the Policy Forum of the Union of Democratic University Staff Associations (UDUSA). Worked at numerous South African universities, including the University of the North, Transkei and Witwatersrand where his teaching and research was mainly concerned with psychology and student services.

RESEARCH INTERESTS Are primarily in education policy and the role of intellectuals in politics and knowledge production.

Serves on the Advisory Council for Universities and Technikons and prepared reports for government and NGOs on education policy. Has published widely in psychology, sociology and education.

Nico Cloete Director
Centre for Higher Education Transformation
134 Pretorius Street
Pretoria 0001
Tel: (12) 324-1024
Fax: (12) 324-1044
E-mail: nc@tirelo.hsrc.ac.za

MICHAEL CROSS

PRESENT POSITION: Associate Professor at the Department of Education, University of the Witwatersrand.

His interest on Campus Diversity initiative is directly related to his research interests, extension or outreach work. He has been running a training programme for the last three years aimed at enabling faculty members from a historically disadvantaged background to participate in the mainstream research and publication activities – the Authorship Development Project (Audepro). In this regard, he has introduced book series on Critical Issues on South African Education, of which the first volume focuses on institutional transformation in higher education.

PUBLICATIONS/PAPERS: Has published several books and articles on issues of identity and diversity, including *Resistance and Transformation* (Johannesburg: Skotaville Publishers), *Dealing with Diversity: The Politics of National Curriculum in South Africa* (Cape Town: Juta Press, 1998) and *Images of Identity in South African Education* (Carolina Academic Publishers, forthcoming).

Michael Cross   Associate Professor
Department of Education
University of Witwatersrand
Private Bag 3
Wits 2050
Tel: (11) 716-5293
Cell: 082-883-5464
Fax: (11) 339-3956
E-mail: 022cross@mentor.edcm.wits.ac.za

ARJUN DANGLE

Poet and writer in Marathi.

Important name in the politics and literature of Maharahstra. Founder member of militant Dalit youth organisation and Dalit Panthers. President of the State Unit of the Bharatiya Republican party. Arjun Dangle is a writer in Marathi. His only English book is *Poisoned Bread*. His diversity work has been with his people, the Dalits in the State of Maharashtra.

Arjun Dangle   Writer in Marathi
7/134 Jai Vikrant
Sahaker Nagar #5
Chembur
Mumbai 400 071
Tel: (91-22) 522-6701
Fax: through Sharada Nayak
E-mail: through Sharada Nayak

NEDOALDO PONTES DE AZEVEDO

PRESENT POSITION: President of the Union of Municipal Heads of Education and Municipal Secretary of Education for the city of Jo Pessoa, Brazil.

PREVIOUS POSITION: Rector of the Federal University of Paraiba, Jo Pessoa, Brazil.

Has taught Brazilian literature both at the Federal University of Paraiba and the University of Toulouse, France. His particular research interests are the works of authors from the Northeast region of Brazil on which he has published widely. As Rector, he gave great importance to the social role of the University in one of the poorest, and most racially mixed states of the Federation. He is a defender of Public State-funded higher education and a firm believer in the importance of international exchange within higher education. As Rector he also gave particular support to student exchange programmes involving African and Latin American students.

Neodoaldo Pontes De Azevedo Secretaria Municipal de Educa
Rua Santo Dumont
80 Centro
58000-000Jo Pessoa, PB
Cell: 083-241-5941 / 083-9815003
Fax: 083-241-4766
E-mail: sedec-jp@terra.npd.ufpb.br

EUNICE RIBEIRO DURHAM

PRESENT POSITION: Member of the National Council of Education.

PREVIOUS POSITIONS: Professor of social anthropology at the University of S Paulo, President of the Brazilian agency for the development of graduate studies, National Secretary for Higher Education and National Secretary for Educational Policy.

Has been engaged in educational research for the past 10 years. At present is working on a project to promote the entrance of African American students in Brazilian Universities.

Eunice Ribeiro Durham NUPES-N3cleo de Pesquisas sobre Ensino Superior
Universidade de S Paulo
Rua do Anfiteatro, 181
Colm, Favo 9
Cidade Univesita
05508-900 S Paulo, SP
Tel: (5511) 815-4134/818-3272/818-3353
Fax: (5511) 818-3157/815-4134
E-mail: nupes@org.usp.br or erdurham@usp.br

TROY DUSTER

PRESENT POSITION: Professor of Sociology and Director of the Institute for the Study of Social Change at the University of California, Berkeley.

PREVIOUS POSITIONS: Member of the Assembly of Behavioural and Social Sciences of the National Academy of Sciences, Special Commission of the Association of American Law Schools, and Commission on Meeting the Challenges of Diversity in an Academic Democracy. Held appointments as Visiting Professor or Visiting Scholar at the London School of Economics, the University of Melbourne, and Columbia University.

Has studied, taught, and published widely on diversity in higher education in the United States.

PUBLICATIONS/PAPERS: Include *Aims and Control of the Universities, Cultural Perspectives on Biological Knowledge* (co-edited with Karen Garrett), and *Backdoor to Eugenics.* Senior author of *The Diversity Project*, a report of how students on the Berkeley campus of the University of California adjusted to the sharp demographic changes in ethnic and racial composition during the last decade.

Troy Duster Professor of Sociology & Director
Institute for the Study of Social Change
University of California, Berkeley
2420 Bowditch
Berkeley, CA 94720-5670
Tel: (510) 642-0813
Fax: (510) 642-8674
E-mail: Nitrogn@socrates.Berkeley.edu

RICHARD FEHNEL

PRESENT POSITION: Ford Foundation Programme Officer, with responsibility for education in southern Africa.

He has been working on higher education issues in South Africa since 1991. Prior to that he was an independent consultant specialising in human resources and institutional development in the fields of education and government, and worked primarily in developing countries during 1983-1991. From 1970 to 1978, Dr. Fehnel held academic positions at The American University in Washington, DC and the University of

Oregon. From 1978-1983, he was Dean of Continuing Education and Off-Campus Programs at Linfield College in Oregon.

Has special interests in higher education policy and institutional transformation, particularly with regard to serving the needs of adults and disadvantaged communities, and in the use of technology for improving access, quality and efficiency of education. His most recent publications concern the role of donor agencies in human resource development.

Richard Fehnel Program Officer
The Ford Foundation
PO Box 30953
Braamfontein 2197
Tel: (11) 403-5912
Fax: (11) 403-1575
E-mail: R.Fehnel@fordfound.org

BARBARA S FRANKLE

PRESENT POSITION: Associate Dean for Academic Affairs and Professor of History at LeMoyne-Owen College, a historically Black institution in Memphis, Tennessee. Directs general education, with Afrocentric core.

PREVIOUS POSITIONS: Has taught at The Evergreen State College, Olympia, Washington; Siena College, Memphis, Tennessee; and Morehouse College, Atlanta, Georgia. Also directed the Eight College Consortium on interdisciplinary general studies. Involved in service-learning projects embracing diversity in LeMoyne-Owen College community.

PUBLICATIONS/PAPERS: Has written on Afrocentric, multicultural education; international perspectives in education; and the core curriculum and the canon in United States higher education.

Barbara Frankle Associate Dean of Academic Affairs
LeMoyne Owen College,
807 Walker Avenue
Memphis, TN 38126-6595
Tel: (901) 92-7363
Fax: (901) 942-7809
E-mail: barbara_frankle@qm.lemoyne-owen.edu

MILDRED GARCIA

PRESENT POSITION: Associate Vice Provost for Academic Affairs and Associate Professor in the Social and Behavioural Sciences Department, Arizona State University West, Phoenix, Arizona; also Associate Director of the Hispanic Research Centre, Arizona State University.

PREVIOUS POSITION: Assistant Vice President for Academic Affairs, Montclair State University, New Jersey; previously executive assistant to the president at Hostos Community College, City University of New York.

Has researched at-risk students and underrepresented faculty, staff, and administrators, as well as implications for policy and practice

PUBLICATIONS/PAPERS: Has published on diversity in United States higher education, affirmative action, and is writing on faculty of colour and strategies for survival in academia.

Mildred Garcia Associate Vice Provost,
Arizona State University – West
4701 W Thunderbird Road
Phoenix, AZ 85069
Tel: (602) 543-4513
Fax: (602) 543-7012
E-mail: millieg@asu.edu

AMANDA GOUWS

PRESENT POSITION: Senior lecturer in Political Science at the University of Stellenbosch and Acting Director of the African Gender Institute at UCT in a seconded position.

She specialises in feminist theory and has done research on women and citizenship, which includes issues of identity and diversity. She served as a member of the Gender Equity Task Team in the Department of Education from October 1996 to December 1997. During this time she investigated sexual harassment and abuse in tertiary and secondary education. She has served as a member of a Commission of Inquiry into Gender Discrimination and Sexual Harassment at the University of Stellenbosch. She is interested in the role of civic education in building democracy.

Amanda Gouws Acting Director
African Gender Institute
University of Cape Town
Private Bag
Rondebosch 7701
Tel: (21) 650-2970
Fax: (21) 685-2142
E-mail: agouws@agi.uct.ac.za

ANN HARPER

PRESENT POSITION: Private practice and project consultant.

PREVIOUS POSITIONS: Dean of Student Services at the University of Natal. Registered psychologist with 20 years experience in higher education as a lecturer in teacher training and psychology, student counsellor and senior administrator.

She has a particular interest in gender issues, chaired the Durban City Council Gender Advisory committee and has an on-going interest in leadership training for women and community projects. Many years of organisational and practical experience in the areas of mental health, primary health care, community development and leadership.

She was a member of the National Commission for Higher Education Technical Committee on Student Access, Selection and Development and represented the Committee of University Principals on the TEFSA Board and the National Advisory Committee on the National Student Financial Aid Scheme.

She serves on the Campus Diversity and Student Services steering committees of the Centre for Higher Education Transformation (CHET) and presented papers at the Campus Diversity conferences at Philapheldia, Goa, Seattle, New Delhi and Miami.

Ann Harper Project Consultant
71 Florida Rd.
Morningside
Durban 4001
Tel: (31)23-6987
Fax: (31)23-6987
E-mail: aharper@iafrica.com

229

MUSHIRUL HASAN

PRESENT POSITION: Professor of History and Director, Academy of Third World Studies, Jamia Millia Islamia University, New Delhi.

PREVIOUS POSITION: Pro-Vice Chancellor of the Jamia Millia Islamia University.

Mushirul is a widely published historian who has a strong interest in pluralism, campus conflict resolution and minority/identity issues in higher education. Research areas include modern and contemporary Indian history with a special interest in the Indian Nationalist Movement, the rise and fall of 'communalism', and the legacy of India's partition in August 1947. Represented the government of India at the UNESCO conference on Management of Social Transformation (MOST) in Paris, March 1994. Has held fellowships at Oxford and Cambridge and is currently Fellow in Residence at Wissenschaftskolleg zu Berlin.

Mushirul Hasan former Vice-Chancellor
Professor of History
Jamia Millia Islamia University
presently at:
Wissenschaftskolleg zu Berlin
Wallotstrasse 19
D-14193
Berlin, Germany
E-mail: hasan@wiko-berlin.de

SHIREEN HASSIM

PRESENT POSITION: Research Specialist at the Human Sciences Research Council. She will be joining the Department of Political Studies at the University of the Witwatersrand.

PREVIOUS POSITIONS: Lectured at the Universities of Natal in Durban and Durban-Westville. She has done extensive work on issues of gender policy and state. She was guest editor of a special issue on gender and state for *Politikon*, Journal of the South African Political Science Association.

Shireen Hassim Research Specialist
Human Sciences Research Council
Tel: (12) 302-2873
E-mail: shassim@silwane.hsrc.ac.za

JUDITH HAWARDEN

PRESENT POSITION: Project Consultant, Counsellor.

PREVIOUS POSITIONS: University of the Witwatersrand, Johannesburg. Worked for twelve years in the Academic Development programme of the University. Eight of those years were spent as a student counsellor, working particularly on the non-academic problems of previously disadvantaged and excluded students. The following four years were spent as Acting Director of the Programme, focusing chiefly on issues of access, curriculum and student and staff development. Served on various Senate Committees, including those with special focus on admissions and academic development, and on the Sexual Harassment Panel.

Awarded the Benjamin Progrund medal for promoting non-racialism on campus.

SPECIAL INTERESTS: Mediation and conflict resolution, gender issues and human rights.

PRESENTED PAPERS On issues of higher education at academic conferences and on apartheid education at various human rights conferences.

Judith Hawarden Project Consultant
11A Jack Road
Norwood
Johannesburg 2192
Tel: (11) 728-0800
Fax: (11) 483-1455
E-mail: heyjude@cis.co.za

JAYALAKSHMI INDIRESAN

PRESENT POSITION: Consultant to Ford Foundation Campus Diversity Initiative in India and has been involved with the project since its inception.

PREVIOUS POSITIONS: Senior research fellow in the Higher Education Unit at the National Institute of Educational Planning and Administration, New Delhi, and senior consultant at the Asian Centre for Organisational Research and Development

RESEARCH INTERESTS include faculty development, institution building, renewal and evaluation. Jaya has participated in a number of cross-cultural studies with colleagues from Japan, UK, Malaysia, Sri Lanka, Nigeria and India and Canada. Jaya has published widely in these fields. She has also been a consultant in designing, developing, organising and conducting executive development programmes for educational administrators with a special interest in training for women at the grass-roots level, students, teachers and administrators in higher education.

Jaya Indiresan Asian Centre for Organisational Research and Development
B-57, Hill View Apartments
Vasant Vihar
New Delhi 110 057
Tel: (91-11) 687-5091
E-mail: indires@doe.ernet.in

JASBIR JAIN

PRESENT POSITION: Working on a project entitled 'Contextualising Modernism: The Novel in India 1880-1940' on a KK Birla Foundation Fellowship for Comparative Literature.

PREVIOUS POSITIONS: Professor of English, senior administrator and Director of the Academic Staff College at the University of Rajasthan (Jaipur). President Rajasthan University Women's Association and Vice President of the Fullbright Alumni

Jasbir has 34 years of teaching and research experience and has lectured and presented seminars in both the USA and UK. Author of numerous books and research papers in the broad field of literature with a strong focus on drama, ideology, feminist and post-colonial literatures. She is a life member of several literary associations.

Her other interests include gender studies, women's movements, Gandhian Ideology, pedagogy and informal education.

Jasbir Jain Former Professor of English
P-3 University Campus
University of Rajasthan
Jaipur 302004
Tel: (91-141) 516-290
Fax: (91-141) 510-586
E-mail: colrjain@jpl.vsnl.net.in

ZIN JIYA

PRESENT POSITION: Director, Academic Development Programmes at the University of Fort Hare.

PREVIOUS POSITIONS: Senior Lecturer in Physics at the University of Fort Hare and school headmaster.

RESEARCH INTERESTS Include alternative conceptual frameworks and misconceptions in relation to the learning of physics at tertiary level, language and learning for second language speakers in a discipline-related context, and issues of meaningful conceptual access to higher education for the majority of students entering the higher education system.

At a national level, he is concerned with science and technology as these relate to national development and the transformation of the higher education sector. This includes curriculum restructuring with special focus on the affirmation of non-traditional forms of knowledge acquisition.

Zin Jiya Director
Academic Development Centre
University of Fort Hare
Private Bag X 1314
Alice 5700
Tel: (4060) 22-143
Fax: (4060) 22-143
E-mail: jiya@ufhcc.ufh.ac.za

WILLIAM E KIRWAN

PRESENT POSITION: President, University of Maryland, College Park, Maryland.

PREVIOUS POSITIONS: Has taught mathematics, and also served as vice chancellor for academic affairs at the University of Maryland.

Played a pivotal role in university initiatives including increased emphasis on undergraduate education and achievement of diversity goals for underrepresented minorities.

PUBLICATIONS/PAPERS: Co-edited book, *Advances in Complex Analysis*; has published numerous articles on mathematical research. Has also served as an editor of Proceedings of the American Mathematical Society.

William Kirwan President
University of Maryland
1101 Main Administration Building
College Park, MD 20742
Tel: (301) 405-5804
Fax: (301) 314-9560
E-mail: Wkirwan@deans.umd.edu

NOZIPHO KWENAITE

PRESENT POSITION: Executive Director – Student Development and Support Services (Dean of Students), University of the North.

PREVIOUS POSITIONS: Director of Residence Life – University of Western Cape; Senior Warden (University of Natal).

Nozipho's current job is to provide the support and services necessary to facilitate the overall physical, psychological, educational, and vocational development and well being of all students within the University of the North environment which is conducive to learning and teaching. The four main thrusts of the position are namely: management and supervision of the whole division of Student Development and Support Services (formerly Student Affairs); policy implementation; trouble-shooting; advocacy role.

Nozipho Kwenaite Executive Director
Student Affairs
University of the North
Private Bag X1106
Sovenga 0727
Tel: (15) 268-4102
Fax: (15) 267-0154

YOLANDA MOSES

PRESENT POSITION: President, The City College of New York.

PREVIOUS POSITION: Vice President for Academic Affairs and Professor of Anthropology, California State University.

President of the American Anthropological Association, chairs the ACE Commission on the Status of Women and the United Negro College Fund Advisory Board for Service

Learning, and serves on the Executive Board of the Association of American Colleges and Universities (AACU). Yolanda has many years of experience in higher education administration, faculty development and curriculum reform.

PUBLICATIONS/PAPERS: Author of numerous articles, monographs and papers on issues related to cultural change in the United States and the Caribbean, cultural change in higher education, cultural diversity and public policy issues. She was a consultant and researcher for the AACU that resulted in the ground breaking monograph 'Black Women in Academe'.

Yolanda Moses President
The City College of New York – CUNY
Convent Avenue and 138th Street
New York, NY 10031
Tel: (212) 650-7285
Fax: (212) 650-7680
E-mail: ytmcc@cuny.vm.cuny.edu

JOHAN MULLER

PRESENT POSITION: Professor of Education and Head of the School of Education, University of Cape Town.

PREVIOUS POSITIONS: Has taught at the Universities of the North and the Witwatersrand. Formerly Director of the Education Policy Unit at the University of the Witwatersrand.

Widely involved in the field of education policy development.

PUBLICATIONS/PAPERS: Has published extensively on the impact of globalisation on the production of knowledge and on the organisation of the higher education curriculum, higher education governance, and conceptual and theoretical issues in the sociology of knowledge.

Johan Muller School of Education,
University of Cape Town
Private Bag
Rondebosch 7700
Tel: (21) 650-2760
Fax: (21) 650-3489
E-mail: jpm@education.uct.ca.za

CARYN McTIGHE MUSIL

PRESENT POSITION: Senior Research Associate and Co-Director of American Commitments: Diversity, Democracy, and Liberal Learning, at the Association of American Colleges and Universities, Washington, DC.

PREVIOUS POSITIONS: Executive Director, National Women's Studies Association; Associate Professor of English and Women's Studies, LaSalle University, Philadelphia, Pennsylvania.

Focuses on women's issues and diversity in higher education; her expertise centres on curriculum and faculty development and institutional change.

PUBLICATIONS/PAPERS: Has published on diversity and educational integrity in higher education and the development of diversity initiatives on American campuses. Among many other publications in women's studies, edited *The Courage to Question: Women's Studies and Student Learning, and Students at the Centre: Feminist Assessment.*

Caryn McTighe Musil Senior Research Associate
Director, Curriculum and Faculty Development Network
Association of American Colleges and Universities (AACU)
1818 R Street, NW
Washington, DC 20009
Tel: (202) 387-3760
Fax: (202) 265-9532
E-mail: musil@aacu.nw.dc.us

SHARADA NAYAK

PRESENT POSITION: Director, Educational Resources Centre Trust.

PREVIOUS POSITIONS: Executive Director, United States Educational Foundation in India.

Sharada is a consultant to a number of international agencies in India including the Ford Foundation, New York State Consortium of Independent Colleges Program, Columbia Teachers' College seminar, as well as the Indian

236

University Grants Commission initiative on community colleges.

Recipient of the distinguished achievement award in the field of international education from the Dr TMA Pai Foundation.(1997) and the distinguished service award of the J William Fullbright Foreign Scholarships Board.

As a member of the Centre for Women's Development Studies and the editorial board of the *Indian Journal of Gender Studies* she has a strong interest and experience in international multicultural exchanges, diversity in higher education, social justice and affirmative action and gender issues.

Sharada Nayak Director
Educational Resources Centre Trust
12A Shopping Centre
SFS Apartments, Hauzkhas
New Delhi 110 016
Tel: (91-11) 685-3117
Fax: (91-11) 652-6387
E-mail: eduresou@nda.vsnl.net.in

S-41 Sujan Singh Park
New Delhi 110 003
Tel: (91-11) 469-4582
Fax: (91-11) 461-0520
E-mail: terct@nda.vsnl.net.in

FR ANTHONY A PAPPURAI

PRESENT POSITION: Principal, St. Xavier's College, Palayaamkottai, Tamil Nadu.

PREVIOUS POSITIONS: Lecturer at St. Xaviers College and Loyola College, Madras.

Research interests: India's Foreign Investment Policy, An Appraisal through American Corporations.

Father Anthony Pappurai Principal
St. Xavier's College
Palayamkottai
Tel: (91-11) 462-579-744
Fax: (91-11) 462-579-744

JANICE PETROVICH

PRESENT POSITION: Director, Education, Knowledge and Religion at the Ford Foundation.

PREVIOUS POSITIONS: National Executive Director of ASIPRA , a national Latino youth organisation , Director of Research Studies at the American Council on Education (ACE), Director of the Research Institute of the Inter-American University of Puerto Rico.

Janice has a background in teaching, chemistry and educational policy research. She has published work on Hispanic women in higher education and the expansion of post-secondary schooling in Porto Rico. She founded the Centre for Research and Documentation of Women at the Inter-American University of Puerto Rico.

Janice Petrovich Director
Education, Knowledge and Religion
Education, Media, Arts and Culture Program
The Ford Foundation
320 E 43rd Street
New York, NY 10017
Tel: (212) 573-4872
Fax: (212) 351-3650
E-mail: J.Petrovich@fordfound.org

SURYKUMARIE PILLAY

PRESENT POSITION: Attorney and independent consultant to several organisations. She has worked closely with the National Institute for Public Interest Law and Research (NIPILAR) and the Centre for Higher Education Transformation (CHET). She is currently a consultant to the Support for Economic Growth and Mandela Scholars Project (SEGA/MEST Project).

PREVIOUS POSITIONS: Participated in the strategic planning task team of the Department of Labour and the Department of Trade and Industry. Her involvement in the private sector includes working on issues of diversity management and employment equity.

Sury K Pillay PO Box 1056
Boksburg 1460
Tel (11) 917 3423
E-mail: surypillay@yahoo.com

NATASHA PRIMO

PRESENT POSITION: Co-ordinator of the Women-in-Research Programme at the Centre for Science Development

From 1995 to January 1998, she was the co-ordinator of the postgraduate Women's and Gender Studies Programme at the University of the Western Cape. Her areas of interest are gender and development, race, gender, and subjectivities of (black) South African women, gender and curriculum, staff and student development, and research capacity development.

Natasha Primo Co-ordinator of the Women in Research Programme
Human Sciences Research Council
134 Pretorius Street
Pretoria 0001
Tel: (12) 302-2028
Fax: (12) 302-2421
E-mail: nprimo@silwanye.hsrc.ac.za

PADMA RAMACHANDRAN

PRESENT POSITION: Vice Chancellor, Maharaja Sayajirao University of Baroda, Gujarat.

PREVIOUS POSITIONS: Chief Secretary to the Government of Kerala as head of the Public Services in the State and Secretary to the State Cabinet.

Special interest in women's issues and educational management. Was instrumental in getting Women's Studies sanctioned as a unit at Kerala University and is a life member of the Indian Association for Women's Studies and the Centre for Women's Development Studies in New Delhi. Padma has also written extensively in the area of management and training, as well as development administration.

Padma Ramachandran Vice-Chancellor
Maharaja Sayajirao University
Vadodara
Gujarat 390 002
Tel: (91-265) 795-600 (w)
      (91-265) 795-499/792-175 (h)
Fax: (91-265) 793-693
E-mail: vc.@msub.ernet.in

SHARADA RAMANATHAN

PRESENT POSITION: Program Officer, Culture & Media, at the New Delhi office of The Ford Foundation.

PREVIOUS POSITIONS: Founder member of Society for Promotion of Indian Classical Music amongst Youth (SPIC-MACAY), a 20-year-old national voluntary movement in India. Main tasks were to co-ordinate programme growth and stabilisation of SPIC-MACAY in southern India. Has served as Branch Manager, Child Relief & You (CRY), a national philanthropy for child welfare and community development. Was also the Arts Consultant at the Ford Foundation and co-ordinated the setting-up of Indian Foundation for the Arts (IFA) with the participation of Indian/International donors. Worked in senior capacities in the advertising and communications industry and in journalism. Also worked with Indian Television on productions of cultural films and programmes.

Practitioner of South Indian classical music and non-professional composer of alternative film music.

Sharada Ramanathan Program Officer
The Ford Foundation
55 Lodi Estate
New Delhi 110 003 India
Tel: (9111) 461-9441
Fax: (9111) 462-7147
E-mail: S.Ramanathan@fordfound.org

CONSTANCE W RICE

PRESENT POSITION: Senior Vice Chancellor of the Seattle Community College District (SCCD).

PREVIOUS POSITIONS: Served previously as President of North Seattle Community College and Vice Chancellor for Institutional Advancement. Co-founded the CITIES project, which integrates technology into the classroom. Formerly taught in fields of ethnic studies, public administration, social work and political science.

Committed to providing students equitable access to opportunities in technical and scientific studies and careers.

PUBLICATIONS/PAPERS: Has published on displacement trends in the Seattle Central area; ethnic studies in the Pacific Northwest; and perceptional analysis of Black Studies.

Constance Rice Senior Vice Chancellor
Seattle Community College District
1500 Harvard Avenue
Seattle, WAS 98122
Tel: (206) 587-4104
E-mail: crice@sccd.ctc.edu

ALBIE SACHS

PRESENT POSITION: Member of the Constitutional Court of South Africa.

PREVIOUS POSITIONS: Lectured in the Law Faculty of the University of Southampton (1970-1977); first Nuffield Fellow of Socio-Legal Studies, at Bedford College, London, and Wolfson College, Cambridge; Professor of Law at the Eduardo Mondlane University in Maputo, Mozambique; Director of Research in the Ministry of Justice, Maputo, Mozambique (1983); Professor at the Law School and in the Department of International Affairs at Columbia University in New York; Director of the South African Constitution Studies Centre, based at the Institute of Commonwealth Studies at the University of London. In 1992, the Centre moved to the University of the Western Cape, where he was made Professor Extraordinary. He was also appointed Honorary Professor in the Law Faculty at the University of Cape Town. He took an active part in the negotiations for a new Constitution as a member of the Constitutional Committee and the National Executive of the ANC. He was awarded Honorary Doctorates of Law by the University of Southampton and the University of York, Toronto.

Author of many books on culture, gender, human rights and the environment. His book *The Jail Diary of Albie Sachs* was dramatised for the Royal Shakespeare Company and broadcast by the BBC. Another autobiographical book *The Soft Vengeance of a Freedom Fighter*, which deals with his recovery from the car bomb, is presently being dramatised for the BBC.

241

Albie Sachs Member of the Constitutional Court of South Africa
Private Bag X32
Braamfontein 2017
Tel: (11) 359 7429
Fax: (11) 403 8816
E-mail: sachs@concourt.org.za

DARYL G SMITH

PRESENT POSITION: Professor of Education and Psychology at The Claremont
Graduate University.

PREVIOUS POSITIONS: Vice President for Planning and Research, Scripps College;
also served as dean of students and associate professor of
psychology. Has extensive professional background in college
and university administration, planning, institutional research,
and student affairs.

Research, teaching, and publications in the area of
organisational implications of diversity.

PUBLICATIONS/PAPERS: Has published studies on diversity in higher education,
including an analysis of misconceptions about achieving faculty
diversity and a review of the impact of the outcomes of
diversity initiatives on students.

Daryl Smith Associate Professor
Education & Psychology
Centre for Educational Studies
The Claremont Graduate School
Harper Hall – Room 212
150E 10th Street
Claremont, CA 91711-6160
Tel: (909) 607-4002
Fax: (909) 621-8390
E-mail: Daryl.smith@cgu.edu

STEPHEN HIRO SUMIDA

PRESENT POSITION: Associate Professor, Department of English Language and
Literature; and Asian/Pacific American Studies Program, in the
Program in American Culture of The University of Michigan,
Ann Arbor. Director, Summer Institute (for incoming graduate
students of colour), Horace H Rackham School of Graduate
Studies, The University of Michigan.

PREVIOUS POSITION: Director of Undergraduate Studies, Department of English Language and Literature, The University of Michigan.

Specialises in interdisciplinary Asian/Pacific American studies; multicultural American Studies.

PUBLICATIONS/PAPERS: Has published on postcolonialism, nationalism, and the emergence of Asian/Pacific American literatures; Asian/Pacific American literature in the classroom; and Hawaiian literary traditions.

Stephen Sumida Professor of English
University of Michigan
400 Mark Hannah Place
Ann Arbor, MI 48103
Tel: (313) 663-9809
Fax: (313) 663-6129
E-mail: Shsumida@umich.edu

SHIV VISVANATHAN

PRESENT POSITION: Senior fellow at the Centre for the Study of Developing Societies, Delhi.

PREVIOUS POSITION: Lecturer at the Delhi School of Economics. His primary work is on science and technology with a focus on violence in science and the need for pluralistic knowledges. He has worked with NGOs on human rights issues and is presently co-ordinating projects on (1) Corruption and (2) Cross-cultural values and the Environment.

Shiv Visvanathan Centre for the Study of Developing Societies
29 Rajpur Road
Delhi 110 054
Tel: (91-22) 245-3703 (h)
Fax: (91-11) 294-3450
E-mail: sscsds@ren.nic.in
(or) csds@de12.vsnl.net.in